INSIDE/OUTSIDE

INSIDE/OUTSIDE

Adventures in Caribbean History and Anthropology

Richard Price

The University of Georgia Press · Athens

Published by the University of Georgia Press
Athens, Georgia 30602
www.ugapress.org
© 2022 by Richard Price
All rights reserved
Set in Warnock Pro by Melissa Buchanan
Printed and bound by Books International
The paper in this book meets the guidelines for
permanence and durability of the Committee on
Production Guidelines for Book Longevity of the
Council on Library Resources.

Most University of Georgia Press titles are
available from popular e-book vendors.

Printed in the United States of America
26 25 24 23 22 P 5 4 3 2 1

Library of Congress Cataloging-in-Publication Data
Names: Price, Richard, 1941– author.
Title: Inside/outside : adventures in Caribbean history
and anthropology / Richard Price.
Description: Athens : The University of Georgia Press, [2022]
Identifiers: LCCN 2022019872 | ISBN 9780820363059 (hardback) |
ISBN 9780820362656 (paperback) | ISBN 9780820362663 (ebook)
Subjects: LCSH: Price, Richard, 1941– | Anthropologists—United States—
Biography. | Historians—United States—Biography. | Caribbeanists—
United States—Biography. | College teachers—United States—Biography. |
Caribbean—History. | Saramacca (Surinamese people) | Lévi-Strauss,
Claude. | Mintz, Sidney W. (Sidney Wilfred), 1922–2015.
Classification: LCC GN21.P75 A3 2022 | DDC 301.092 [B]—dc23/eng/20220607
LC record available at https://lccn.loc.gov/2022019872

for Sally

CONTENTS

FIRST WORDS

Covid-19 and isolating with Sally in our new home in semitropical Florida. One canceled lecture after another—in Paris, Lund, Uppsala . . . writing prefaces, forewords, book reviews, articles . . . reading Caribbean novels and poetry . . . watching/listening to Wagner on Met Opera on Demand . . . worrying about U.S. politics. . . .

I've just read an interview given by our friend Maryse Condé, who remarks, "When you are an old writer, you tend to think all day about yourself."[1] Which prompts me to begin thinking about myself . . . and my trajectory as a historically minded anthropologist . . . and trying to write something about it.

But just a few pages in, I realize how imprecise is memory. And I recall the advice that the Bucharest-born cabaret singer who had recently married my grandfather gave to nineteen-year-old Sally on our wedding day in 1963: "Darlink, always leave a little bit to the imagination."

Coquina Key, Florida
July 3–September 30, 2020[2]

---

1   Anita Sethi, "Interview: Maryse Condé," *Guardian*, July 3, 2020.
2   Various bits and pieces were added later, as I remembered them.

INSIDE/OUTSIDE

Summer 1958. At sixteen, it seemed like a good time to venture west of the Hudson, time to explore the USA. How did I hear about the trip proposed by the Presbyterian ministry of Cornell University? I really don't know. But I do remember being excited by the idea of making a vast circle that included several-day stays on Indian reservations—the Navajo and Hopi in the Southwest and Nez Perce in Idaho. The group would travel in two 1951 Dodge flatbed trucks, with canvas-covered wooden enclosures built onto the back, boys sleeping in one and girls in the other.

From the very first days, my eyes were opened. . . . Racist lawn signs in the yards around Earlham College in Indiana, a night spent on a prosperous Black-owned family farm in Colorado, and other new experiences now obscured by the passage of time. But all this was building up to the planned visits to Indian reservations, where the organizers' missionary connections had secured permission to spend a total of ten days. Forget about the lawn signs and family farms. . . . The reservations opened my eyes to a break from the life I'd lived so far, a vision of a possible direction for the life to come. I was mesmerized by this brush with peoples whose lives seemed so fundamentally different from my own.

Leaving behind the high mesas of the Southwest, we headed through Death Valley at night to avoid the heat. As dawn broke, the trucks were descending from Towne's Pass on the western rim of the valley, heading toward Panamint Springs and Lone Pine, California (the scene of many Hollywood Westerns), with their teenage cargos fast asleep in the back. Suddenly the first Dodge lost its brakes and began accelerating. Descending through three thousand feet, it careened through a turn and flipped over onto the boulders by the side of the road.

Waking up in critical condition in Southern Inyo Hospital, with multiple contusions and a badly fractured spine, I was told that I'd been thrown a hundred feet onto a rock-strewn area and that the boy who'd been in the sleeping bag next to me was dead. After being flown home several days later on a stretcher, I lay immobile in a hospital bed in the family living room where doctors debated the best treatment. Most counseled large casts and prolonged traction in a hospital. A couple of younger ones said that I was in good enough shape that, with luck, I would heal with simple rest. After much discussion, my parents and I decided to forego the casts and take a chance, and in the end we won. Two months later, I was serving as cocaptain of my (1958 MAAPS champion) high school soccer team, and to this day, I have no ill effects. But as I lay on that hospital bed, I had plenty of time to revisit my early brush with death. And I began to think seriously, perhaps for the first time, about the future.

After high school graduation in 1959, a couple of friends and I drove a car out to Navajo and Hopi country, sometimes camping out, sometimes sleeping in schoolhouses. An eight-page handwritten letter that somehow survived the subsequent half-century in shoeboxes filled with family photos captures the excitement that I felt at our stop in New Oraibi, Arizona, around the beginning of July. Reading it now, I see that a fascination for cultures that I hadn't been brought up in was already teasing me toward a life in anthropology. It seems to me that the length of the letter, its ethnographic detail, its seriousness, and its reflexivity (telling how I felt about what I was witnessing) foreshadows the kind of anthropology—and writing—I came to engage in as a professional.

> Dear Mom + Dad,
> I am writing on a table in the Hopi High School. We drove through the Painted Desert this morning . . . and arrived at Oraibi around 3:30. The rather sudden change from the arid flatlands of the western part of the Navaho reservation to the mesa and butte country of the Hopis was a wonderful sight. [Details about the founding of New Oraibi and the split with more traditional Old Oraibi.] Went to visit Mrs. White, White Bear's aunt. [I'd met White Bear the previous summer and had been corresponding with him.] She spent about an hour talking with us. I believe she is the most intelligent and best educated of all living Hopi, somewhat past middle age but quite active. She was interested in us because we were students. . . . Mrs. White described to us her tremendously difficult situation being a part of two civilizations. She speaks perfect English and taught school for 30 years and knows white civilization very well. But of course her Hopi ties have not been lost. Many years ago, she decided to break with Hopi tradition. She also described how, gradually, she has come back to basic Hopi values, realizing their true worth. Her life has been very difficult but for the last twenty years she feels that she has lived in a well-balanced equilibrium. . . . She wishes to accept fully neither Hopi nor white standards but to take the best from each.
> I was amazed at how she spoke so similarly to Walter O'Kane's book.[1] . . . Her comments about the oldest generation and the sadness

---

1   I had read, in preparation for the trip, Walter Collins O'Kane, *The Hopis: Portrait of a Desert People* (Norman: University of Oklahoma Press, 1953).

of their passing were very much in step with O'Kane's. . . . She knew all the books that had been written about the Hopis and also knew the authors. Mrs. White is now working on three books which she feels she must write. No one has ever understood the Hopis, she feels, the way that a Hopi can. . . . She has pages and pages of notes taken throughout her life. Many contain conversations with people of her grandparents' generation. These are the people who have given her the real insight into the Hopis. She is much saddened by the westernization going on, even though she is as much western as Hopi. It is painful for her to see ceremonies watered down. But she herself cannot ever rationally believe anymore that a rain prayer causes rain. She thinks the belief is beautiful but she can't really believe it. This was a sad thing to see.

At about 5 o'clock she told us there was a Flute dance at Shungopavi. She said she had not seen a flute dance since she was very young. So we drove her to a village on a mesa top to watch the dance. This village was really old, the adobe and sandstone pueblos arranged around the ceremonial plaza. Mrs. White was recognized by nearly everyone + we were able to climb atop a pueblo bordering the plaza to view the dance, which took about an hour and was a complicated ritualistic rain dance. There was much chanting in a modal sort of music + a recorder-like instrument gave the whole thing an eerie sound. The scene looking down into the plaza will be a hard one for me to forget. I couldn't help thinking how many generations had asked for rain in the same way.

As the dancers filed out of the plaza. The large Hopi audience became jubilant. Smiles showed everywhere. Rain was beginning to fall. Soon, a torrential thunderstorm was upon the village. Kids played in the mud. Parents moved happily into their houses. Mrs. White took us into the house of a friend, Peter, an elderly man. We were really lucky to spend twenty minutes inside a Hopi home with kids running between our legs + giggling at us.

Mrs. White, on the way home, expounded on the beauty and simplicity of the Hopi belief in nature. If one is really in harmony with nature, one can influence such things as rain. Even she asked whether the rain had to be a coincidence. She obviously had her doubts. In her, I could see the beautiful Hopi teachings which were ingrained when she was a girl, living side by side with a university education and wide experience with the world outside the reservation. She was deeply interested in the problem of the old ways + how they are changing. While we were at Shungopavi she interviewed Old Peter about his feelings on the matter. Although they spoke mostly Hopi, I felt a real understanding of what they were feeling + the tragedy of it. Tomorrow

home with kids running between our (3)
legs & giggling at us.

Mrs. White, on the way home, expounded
on the beauty & simplicity of the Hopi
belief in nature. If one is really in harmony
with nature, one can influence such things
as rain. Even she asked whether the
rain had to be a coincidence. She
obviously had her doubts. In her, I
could see the beautiful Hopi teachings
which were ingrained when she was a girl,
living side by side with a university
education + wide experience with the world
outside the reservation. She was deeply
interested in the problem of the old ways
+ how they are changing. While we were at
Shungopavi she interviewed old Peter about his
feeling on the matter. Although they spoke
mostly Hopi, I felt a real understanding
of what they were feeling & the tragedy of it.
Tomorrow we will visit the other Hopi
villages, see Old Oraibi, senile chief etc.
Then we will probably head back through
Tuba City + up to Monument Valley. This country
has a real attraction to me + I will really
enjoy our time here. To Don + Steve it is just another
place, but for some reason it is a little enchanting to me.
Must get some sleep. Love Kirk

we will visit the other Hopi villages, see Old Oraibi's senile chief etc. Then we will probably head back through Old Tuba City + up to Monument Valley. This country has a real attraction to me and I will really enjoy our time here. To Don + Steve [my two high school classmates and traveling companions] it's just another place, but for some reason, it is a little enchanting to me. Must get some sleep. Love Rich

After leaving Hopi country, we briefly visited the site of my accident (I needed to see where I'd almost died), and I then went off on my own to spend the bulk of the summer high in the Rockies, keeping up the musical side of my life by playing viola in the Aspen Festival Youth Orchestra. Following years in a Manhattan youth ensemble, and years as well of piano lessons, it was largely a filial gesture to my mother, who was a pianist and had been trained as a music teacher (MA from NYU) and encouraged my musical efforts. Aspen was inspiring and fun—Darius Milhaud once conducted us—but it marked the end of my life as a middling musician. I never played again (the sole exception being that I continued to play Schubert four-hands with my mother until she was well into her nineties, whenever we visited her).[2]

At summer's end, before leaving for my freshman year at Harvard, I received a glossy booklet in the mail about a new initiative, the Freshman Seminar Program. For the first time, Harvard was offering incoming freshmen seminars taught by the university's most famous professors in a number of disciplines. Flipping through the pages, my eye was caught by the announcement of a "Navajo seminar" to be taught by the chair of the Anthropology Department, Clyde Kluckhohn. Without a moment's hesitation, I filled out the application.

---

2   Likewise, my father, a tennis champion, had always encouraged me in that game, but after I left the family fold for college, I never again picked up a racket. My sister, Joan, who played the cello, continued her musical life longer, graduating from the University of Michigan School of Music before marrying, then traveling to Lima to serve in the Peace Corps with her husband, and finally settling in western Massachusetts.

CHAPTER TWO

EARLY ENCOUNTERS WITH CULTURAL DIFFERENCE

My mother once told me that when she was still in the hospital on the Sunday after my birth, listening to a radio broadcast of the New York Philharmonic, a voice interrupted the Shostakovich symphony to announce, "The Japanese have attacked the American Naval Base at Pearl Harbor."

A very early memory. Nose pressed up against a frosty windowpane by my bed, looking down Broadway at a trolley car surrounded by gesticulating people, stranded in the swirling nighttime snow. The war was still on, it would have been 1944. Whenever my grandmother, who lived in that same 115th Street apartment house across from Columbia University, took me out with her, we'd walk hand in hand down that same stretch of Broadway to Shuck the butcher's, where thick sawdust formed little mountains on the floor; we'd go past Yee's Chinese Laundry, the flower shop, and Salter's bookstore and stop in at Saul the grocer's, who might give me a piece of candy, before we went next door to the fruit and vegetable (and cut flowers) man, whose name now escapes me but who had brass scales with clocklike hands hanging from the ceiling. Each time, it was, "Good morning, Mrs. Swee" (or if I was with my mother, "How are you today, Mrs. Price?"). It seems to me that in the apartment—whether ours or my grandparents' one flight downstairs—clothes were always drying on pull-up racks in the kitchen or, in good weather, on lines operated by pulleys, strung across to the next building. There was also the itinerant knife and scissors sharpener, who sang out his presence, voice echoing between the walls of apartment houses and who kept a monkey on a leash. And bottles of milk delivered at dawn by horse-drawn wagon.

When I was four, my parents enrolled me in New York's public school for gifted children, then called Hunter Model School. I remember the carpeted room where a man gave me the IQ test for admission—placing different sized blocks into holes, answering a series of questions.[1] Our blond kindergarten teacher, Miss Carney, taught us to read from *Dick*

---

1 Run by Hunter College, by the twenty-first century the elementary school had become more selective than Harvard, admitting only 2 percent of applicants. Abby Jackson, "New York's Hottest Public School Is Harder to Get Into Than Harvard," *Business Insider*, November 25, 2016.

and Jane, stories about a White suburban household—a boy, his two sisters, an office-going father, a homemaker mother, a dog named Spot. That year, my father took me to 110th Street, across from Central Park, where I picked out a red two-wheeler and soon was riding up and down the sidewalk along Riverside Drive.

Saturdays were special. My father, a dentist, took Fridays off, but worked on Saturdays. So, on Saturday mornings, my mother's father, an immigrant from Russia who sang in the chorus of the Metropolitan Opera, would take me for walks down Broadway all the way to 110th Street, then over to Riverside Drive, and finally, slowly, back along the park. As we walked, Pop would tell me the story of operas and tales of travel with his Met companions—by train (which he loved) to Chicago and "Saint Louie," by ocean liner to perform in front of kings and queens in Europe. He said Wagner was his favorite composer, *Die Meistersinger* the greatest opera, *Parsifal*, the most exquisite music. He told me the story of *The Ring of the Nibelungen*. When I was six or seven, he started taking me down to the old Met for Saturday matinees, where the costuming ladies would dress me up, and we would enter the crowd scene in the marketplace and wander around the stage hand in hand. Amply proportioned Russian and Italian women in the chorus would pinch my cheeks, call me endearing names, and envelop me in their bosoms, nearly suffocating me with their perfume. It was in the market scene of Carmen that I first became aware of illusion: seeing twisted shreds of crudely painted cloth hung from hooks and being told that from the audience, they looked like chickens, geese, and ducks.

Pop, born in 1887 in Vyazma, not far from Moscow, arrived in New York in 1905 and debuted at the Met as solo tenor in 1918 in an opera starring Enrico Caruso.[2] He'd begun singing in the chorus while still a teenager and continued till retirement. But he also had another job, selling wholesale buttons out of a little suitcase to Macy's, Gimbels, and other

---

2   He sang the role of Postman in the U.S. premier of Mascagni's *Lodoletta* and performed in it six times during the 1918 season. But his favorite small part was as an apprentice in *Meistersinger*. My mother described how, when she was five or six, her father accompanied his friend Caruso back to the ship carrying him home to Italy, stopping for lunch near the docks, eating spaghetti and drinking wine, with her not understanding a word of their conversation. People always said my grandfather could pass for Italian. Besides his native Russian and Yiddish, he also spoke fluent French, German, and of course English. In his nineties, he spent hours with a little blue grammar book, bent on learning Spanish.

department stores. His lifelong fear was that his boss, Mr. Blumenthal, would come to the opera and recognize him—he held two full-time jobs throughout his working life, with neither employer the wiser. When the Saturday matinee didn't involve children, my mother and I would listen to the broadcast, sponsored by Texaco and introduced by Milton Cross, on the wooden Philco console, taller than I was, in our living room.

Not long after the crowds celebrated V-J Day (my parents took me downtown to see the jubilation), a series of inventions began making their appearance. These harbingers of progress, these icons of modernity, periodically came into my consciousness, usually in someone else's apartment first, then after a while in our own. Each defined a moment, each caused a flurry of excitement and pride of possession—the washing machine, with a ringer on top (my grandmother's, around 1946); the Dumont television (nine-inch screen, our own, around 1947), on which I watched first *Howdy Doody*, then *Captain Video and His Video Rangers* (dramatically accompanied by the overture to *Der Fliegende Holländer*), and later *The Lone Ranger* (accompanied by the overture to *William Tell*); the hi-fi long-playing phonograph (which replaced our wind-up Victrola in the late forties). Then, after the move to our own house in the almost-suburbs (Riverdale, the Bronx) in 1948, yet more significant lifestyle changes—a basement washer-dryer, a "deep freeze" that made BirdsEye frozen vegetables a staple of dinnertime, and, for my sister and me, a dog (named Pepper, not Spot, but small difference). Shopping by car at the A&P (on Broadway, but miles north of the earlier stores), just across the city line from our new house, in Yonkers. Our neighbors were mostly Irish and Italian. The boys with whom I played cowboys and Indians or rode sleds on 263rd Street went to nearby St. Margaret's rather than the local PS 81.

My parents decided to enroll me in Riverdale Country, a coed private school. Each afternoon, after the yellow school bus dropped me a couple of blocks from my house, I had to get by a large, red-headed girl (she said her name was Betsy) who would lie in wait for me behind a bush. Every time she caught me, she pushed me down, sat on me, and pummeled me with her fists, laughing all the while. I learned to run very quickly by that spot. Once safely home, I comforted myself reading The Hardy Boys (I especially liked *The House on the Cliff*) or *Don Sturdy in Lion Land*.

In third grade, my best friend was Joe DiMaggio Jr., the pudgy son of the Yankee Clipper. The two of us sometimes got into trouble. One day, Mrs. McQuigg, our stern teacher, showed the class a film that, if memory serves, was called *One God* and was meant to teach cultural relativism by showing rituals from different cultures around the world, all with the same meaning—a river baptism in the U.S. South, an immersion in the Ganges, and so forth. Joey and I couldn't, for the life of us, stop giggling. We were kept after school and grilled about our religious backgrounds—Joey was being raised as a proper Catholic, but I had to admit that I didn't know "what" I was—religion had never come up, as my parents were secular, atheist Jews. And the two of us were nearly expelled. Our class also had a memorable social studies segment on Plains Indians, in which I chose to be "Chief White Eagle" and proudly sang a song I'd made up, beating on a homemade tom-tom: "Over hills and over plains, me White Eagle. I hunt for my family, me White Eagle." But because of the compulsory chapel that started in the fourth grade, my parents switched me to the nearby Fieldston Lower School, a progressive school run by the Ethical Culture Society, which turned out to be a far better fit.

By 1953, I was in the seventh grade of Fieldston Middle School along with some one hundred mostly Jewish and mostly well-to-do classmates, plus a minority of kids from poorer families on scholarships. One of the five or so Black students, Charlie Jones, the son of a Pullman porter, was a friend of mine. Charlie often came over after school to play at my house, but one Saturday he invited me to meet him at the subway exit in Harlem near where he lived so we could play a pickup game of basketball in a playground. I was the only White kid, and after the game Charlie's parents walked me back to the subway entrance, exercising a caution that Charlie and I didn't fully understand. At the end of the year, the school told a tearful Charlie he wasn't going to return in the fall. Someone had scrawled the complete words of a pop song ("Answer me, oh my love, just what sin have I been guilty of. . . .") on the windowsill of a classroom, and the next day in the auditorium, as part of a talent show, Charlie performed that very song. Whether or not it was that single incident that caused his dismissal, I was very sad at the loss of my friend.

More generally, that year was a time for mischief, and although I was shy, I gleefully participated. We were sufficiently mean to our homeroom teacher that, if memory serves, he left the school the next year. A few of us boys formed SPET—the Society for the Prevention of Embarrassment to Teachers—listening unmercifully to his every word in order to catch any possible error (whether grammatical or factual or just imagined), at which point a hand would shoot up and the call of "SPET" would ring out: "But yesterday, you said the book began, 'It was the worst of times, it was the best of times'!" We used to pass around copies of *Mad* magazine, which had just been founded, with a cartoon of Alfred E. Neuman on the cover, pointing out to each other our favorite pages. We also managed to disrupt our home-ec classes—cooking and sewing, each of which lasted six weeks (with boys separated from girls). In cooking classes (which always began with an intensely boring game of Vitamingo—developed by the federal government during World War II to "interest the students in their own diets"), I partnered with Charlie, who said he liked sugar, so we added three cups instead of one to the angel food cake we were baking. When the subject was sewing, a few of us would, on signal, floor the pedals of our sewing machines to make a terrific racket while yelling, "Buffeting! Buffeting!" in imitation of a film we'd all just seen called *Breaking through the Sound Barrier*. Our teachers were not impressed.

That year was also a time of national anxiety. I served as some sort of cadet or monitor in the New York City Office of Civil Defense, getting an official ID card and an army-style garrison cap. The climax came in the form of a massive drill on September 23, 1953, when the *New York Journal-American* published a special edition headlined "2 A-BOMBS HIT CITY. Killed 1,104,814. Injured 568,393. East Side in Ruins, 1,690,000 Homeless. Thousands Flee into Westchester. . . . We Retaliate: Bombers Attack Enemy." We had been taught to "duck and cover" by an animated film featuring Bert the Turtle, so as soon as the air raid sirens sounded we all crawled under our desks, made ourselves small, and pulled our shirts over our heads.

In this relatively privileged setting, I began hearing from friends who took the subway to school about gangs of "Porto Ricans" who'd mug them, tough kids from a different world, with switchblades. Meanwhile, one of my friends liked to pose a gnawing existential-mathematical teaser: "Can you imagine exactly how many people in this city, right at this very moment, are actually doing it?" We were fourteen and, though we knew the city's total population, could never agree on the calculation. And then one day, he told us about how he'd screwed up his courage to visit the "Porto Rican whore" who waved at him from her stoop as he passed each day in Washington Heights on his way home from school. "Primera vez?" she had asked him. "Hell, no!" he'd replied, lying through his teeth. That's how I came to hear of Puerto Ricans.

I spent endless weekend hours playing one kind of ball or another—throwing a baseball back and forth (I can still hear the buzz it made before it thumped into my glove) in the backyard of Eric Werthman as he related his nighttime "adventures" in midtown Manhattan where he would sneak into Birdland and other jazz clubs. (Eric's father, Bernie, our enthusiastic music teacher at school, tried to teach us the leitmotifs of *The Ring*, playing them on the piano.) Or shooting basket after basket (we didn't call them "hoops" in those days) behind the home of Allan Shedlin, whose wealthy father owned a vinyl plastic factory in the Greenpoint neighborhood of Brooklyn that he took me to visit one Saturday—we played catch with a baseball on the sidewalk with some of the Puerto Rican workmen during their lunch hour.[3]

One classmate I both admired and felt sorry for was a quiet, modest boy named Lewis Leavitt. He lived with Yiddish-speaking parents, who may not have spoken English, and was apparently afflicted with some sort of physical disability that made intramural sports and phys ed classes—which were a breeze for me—a painful indignity for him. In my view, he was by far the brightest person in our class. In eighth and ninth grades, we often discussed books we were reading together—ones that were not part of school assignments. I remember our excited conversations before algebra class about C. W. Ceram's *Gods, Graves, and Scholars* (Schliemann's discovery of Troy, Champollion decrypting Egyptian hieroglyphics) and Paul de Kruif's *Microbe Hunters* (from van Leeuwenhoek and Pasteur to Walter Reed and Paul Ehrlich).[4]

Throughout my high school years, after my family moved to a dead-end lane off 231st Street, looking out at the Hudson River, there was a dour G-man stationed in front of our house next to a black sedan, wearing suit, tie, and fedora. His task, I was told, was to surveil (or simply intimidate?)

---

3 Eric became a psychotherapist and filmmaker (notably, *The Drummer*, starring Danny Glover, about PTSD among veterans of the Iraq War); Allan became a teacher, school principal, and child advocate.

4 Many years later, Sally and I happily reconnected when Lewis and his wife, historian of medicine Judith Walzer Leavitt, hosted us for dinner while we were lecturing at the University of Wisconsin, where he directed the Waisman Center on Human Development. As a professor of pediatrics, he specialized in research on childhood trauma and children with developmental disabilities and was working on projects such as a Sesame Street series to promote respect and understanding among children living in Israel, the West Bank, and Gaza.

a neighbor at the other end of the street. I learned the story because my father often got a ride to his dental office at 16 Union Square West with the unhappy victim of this surveillance, the owner of a typewriter repair shop further downtown, on Fulton Street. Martin Tytell was a typewriter genius, who had gotten mixed up in the aftermath of the trial of State Department official Alger Hiss, known at the time as "the Trial of the Century"—every adult I knew had taken sides. In 1949, Richard Nixon, an outspoken member of the House Un-American Activities Committee (HUAC), had pursued Hiss as a Communist and a perjurer, after Whittaker Chambers, a former Soviet spy and then senior editor at *Time*, produced typewritten copies of State Department documents and microfilm strips allegedly supplied by Hiss, which became known as "the Pumpkin Papers" (because Chambers had briefly hidden them in a pumpkin).

A Woodstock typewriter, allegedly once owned by Hiss and matching the typed documents, was at the heart of the prosecution. After a hung jury in the first trial and because the statute of limitations on espionage had run out, Hiss was finally convicted on two charges of perjury. He appealed and his lawyers asked Tytell if he could build a typewriter whose imprint was indistinguishable from the one in the first trial, in order to demonstrate that Hiss had been framed by the FBI. During two years of painstaking work, Tytell succeeded in building a Woodstock with the identical idiosyncrasies (very slightly raised or off-center letters, etc.), but the appeal was denied for other reasons. In his 1976 memoir, John Dean wrote that President Nixon's lawyer Charles Colson told him that Nixon once admitted that "we" (presumably, the HUAC and the FBI) had indeed built the typewriter used to convict Hiss, exactly as Tytell's feat suggested.[5] Needless to say, neither we nor Mr. Tytell appreciated the special protection afforded to the block where we lived.

My approach to high school dating had its strange moments. Three times I remember leaving my date in the lurch because her father corralled me into a discussion that I couldn't say no to. Once it was with a Freudian psychoanalyst named Bill Pike, who had only one good ear since being wounded while serving in the Abraham Lincoln Brigade during the Spanish Civil War—he wanted to talk about *Totem and Taboo*. (I still dream

---

5   John W. Dean, *Blind Ambition: The White House Years* (New York: Simon and Schuster, 1976), 54. Tytell gives the details in "The $7,500 Typewriter I Built for Alger Hiss," by Martin Tytell, as told to Harry Kursh, *True*, August 1952.

about Peri Pike—the high school version—from time to time.) Another time it was Richard Neubauer, who had fled the Nazis and argued with me that, if my generation didn't act soon, a new anti-Semitic Holocaust would overwhelm the United States.[6] But the most memorable such incident was a last-minute New Year's Eve date with the daughter of Philippe Halsman, whose photos of Marilyn Monroe, Alfred Hitchcock, Winston Churchill, Pablo Picasso, his close friend Albert Einstein, and others had graced the cover of *Life* and who was a long-time collaborator of Salvador Dali. Janie, whom I hardly knew, waited out the evening in a classy black dress while her father pulled volume after volume from his library shelves, engaging me in the deep family history of my mother's European lineage, the Swees (who, he informed me, were also the Tvis and Zivis) and related topics. Janie and I never did get out of the apartment, and I still feel guilty about how pissed off she must have been.

At Fieldston, I was lucky to have teachers who influenced my life and, especially, my writing—an essential part of anthropological storytelling. Four of them were particularly strong influences: Joe Papaleo, Frances Grant, Ies Spetter, and Elbert Lenrow.

Joe was my imaginative fifth-grade teacher. Some of us boys formed a baseball team called Pappy's Devils for which I was the pitcher. He coached us and arranged our games in Van Cortland Park and then, in the fall of ninth grade, I was as surprised as my classmates to find out that Joe was going to be our English teacher. (I had no idea until years later that he'd counted among his college mentors W. H. Auden and Marguerite Yourcenar.) Balding, casually dressed, and always informal, Joe introduced us to many of the moderns: Hemingway, Fitzgerald, Dos Passos, Ford Madox Ford, and some poets as well. (I really liked Malraux's *Man's Fate* and now, sixty-six years later, still remember its opening: "Should he try to raise the mosquito netting?") Joe always made me feel like an equal rather than a child; he read and criticized my creative writing with seriousness and encouragement. We remained friends throughout high

---

6   Rarely having experienced anti-Semitism directly (though I was well aware of its ominpresence in housing, college admissions, and everyday American life) and having set foot in a synogogue only two or three times in my life (for bar mitzvahs of classmates), this fear of a U.S. Holocaust was not high on my list of personal concerns. I accepted my Jewish identity (as a "racial" or social category), yet I tried, quite unsuccessfully, to argue with my date's immigrant father that 1950s Riverdale was not 1930s Nuremberg.

school and often chatted in the locker room, after I did my part on the soccer, basketball, or track team.

In those conversations, he would sometimes complain that publishers were sending him rejection after rejection, asking him to write a different kind of fiction than what he was submitting. An admirer of Paddy Chayefsky, whose film *Marty* had just won an Oscar, Joe was writing about the world he lived in, the life of ordinary Italian Americans in the Bronx and Westchester, but—to publishers' displeasure, he said—without sufficient guns and sex or the Mob backdrop they were looking for. Joe was also close to Bill (William Melvin) Kelley, who like me, but a couple of years older, ran the 440 on the high school track team, was president of the student council, and went on to Harvard, where (unlike me) he slept through his classes, writing at night with long-distance encouragement from Joe; for me, Bill's novels—*A Different Drummer*, *dem*, and (my favorite), *Dunfords Travels Everywheres*—described better than anyone (aside from James Baldwin) the ways Whitefolks in America thought about Blackfolks.[7] The year I graduated from Fieldston, Joe moved to Sarah Lawrence College, where he chaired the Writing Seminar and English Department for more than thirty years (inviting the young and largely unknown E. L. Doctorow to join him). He published his first stories in the *New Yorker* and then in the *Paris Review*, the *Atlantic*, and *Playboy*. Two novels followed, an American Book Award, and a Guggenheim. He was a teacher who radiated honesty, wisdom, generosity, humility, and humor.

Frances Grant was special in a very different way. A proper grey-haired New Englander who favored tweed suits, she was justifiably proud of having been a student at Boston's famous Latin School and, in 1917, Radcliffe College's first Negro Phi Beta Kappa—and in the particularly challenging discipline of classics.[8] She had us read Dudley Fitts's recently published

---

7   See, for an appreciation, Kathryn Schulz, "The Lost Giant of American Literature: A Major Black Novelist Made a Remarkable Début. How Did He Disappear?" *New Yorker*, January 29, 2018. That article credits Kelley with being the first person to have used the term "woke" in writing, in a 1962 op-ed in the *New York Times*. Kelley's years in Jamaica and his work as a photographer are discussed in Sean O'Hagan, "A Glimpse into Jamaica's Soul: The Lost Photographs of William Melvin Kelley," *Guardian*, November 25, 2018.

8   Readers should remember that the word Negro was the preferred term for Black Americans until the late 1960s, when it began to be replaced by "Black," and that "African-American"—at first with a hyphen, later without—entered standard use only in the very late 1980s. Many people of Frances Grant's generation continued to prefer "Negro."

Senior year, taking the baton for the anchor leg of the mile relay. We went to the Penn Relays at Franklin Field that year but I was pushed off the track into the infield on the final leg and our team was disqualified.

Poems from the Greek Anthology, which led to fascinating discussions of the Pre-Socratics, and I remember her declaiming "Ozymandias" to us. Of all my high school readings, the Greek tragedies—various works by Aeschylus, Sophocles, and Euripides—were, perhaps, my favorites. How she loved antiquity! Recently I learned from an interview she gave not long before her death in 1982 that she had spent much of her pre-Fieldston life teaching at a vocational school for Negroes in New Jersey:[9]

---

9 "Interview with Frances O. Grant, October 1977," *The Black Women Oral History Project*, vol. 4, from the Arthur and Elizabeth Schlesinger Library on the History of Women in America, Radcliffe College, edited by Ruth Edmonds Hill (Westport, Conn.: Meckler, 1991), 361–421. I also found in *Negro Yearbook: An Annual Encyclopedia of the Negro, 1914–1915*, ed. Munroe N. Work (Tuskegee, Ala.: The Negro Year Book Publishing Co.), 25: "Frances O. Grant, a colored girl, graduated at the head of a class of fifty-eight from the Girls' Latin High School of Boston, and won the Griswold Scholarship to Radcliffe College for the highest standing in scholarship and character."

"Belief in yourself—in this I go back to my early [fore]parents—and some pride in your own heritage, was so necessary in those days, when the students had been brought up to feel that Negroes didn't do anything, didn't have anything, couldn't go anywhere." When that school closed, she found herself, in her sixties, jobless. And then, "this job came up for Fieldston. . . . I went up to talk with Mr. Tate [the headmaster], and we had a very interesting talk, and he said, 'You know, we're under great pressure to have a Negro teacher in the upper school.' I said, 'But Mr. Tate, I do hope somehow or other that you hire me because you think I can teach Latin, not because I'm Negro.' I stayed there eight years. Those eight years were very, very wonderful years."

The things I, as a high school student, didn't know about this dignified, self-confident mentor! She told her interviewer, "I like good wine, I like good whiskey," and described one of her many summer trips: "Got to Paris in 1925, all Europe was talking about Josephine Baker, and she was in the Folies Bergères, let down on a big platter of bananas. We used to see her, too, wandering around the streets with her pet leopard. You could sit at the café on the Rue de la Paix and see everybody you ever heard of: Langston Hughes, Mercer Cook . . . the people who were going to figure later on in the Negro [Harlem] Renaissance."

All those years she was teaching us, she was subletting the apartment of her long-time friend Langston Hughes. Imagine what I could have asked her, if I had been less clueless. . . .

Then there was Ies Spetter, who was not yet forty when he led our compulsory weekly ethics classes and who tried to teach us about human rights, in part through his own life story. Born in the Netherlands, he had witnessed Nazis throwing Jewish children from an orphanage into a truck. He joined the Dutch Resistance and, in 1943, was captured, tortured, and sentenced to death. Sent to Auschwitz and then to Buchenwald for execution, he managed to escape (weighing sixty-eight pounds, he said), eventually to bear witness at the Nuremburg trials. He moved to the United States in 1951, got a PhD from the New School, and was soon heading the Ethics Department at Fieldston. He was often frustrated at the casual indifference of most of my classmates to his efforts to excite us, but I'd like to think that his stories and example, as well as his determined earnestness, in some way encouraged my own work on human rights many decades later.

Finally, Elbert Lenrow, in whose senior seminar I was privileged to sit and about whom my classmate, novelist Nicholas Delbanco, recently recalled:

> His was an established reputation, and we knew we were lucky to be in the room where Mr. Lenrow taught his fabled class. The course was a survey of sorts, and an ambitious one; we read selections of Greek tragedy and comedy, the *Odyssey* and *Iliad*, the *Aeneid*, Chaucer, Dante, Shakespeare, Goethe's *Faust*. . . . Mr. Lenrow's aesthetic was a discriminating one.
>
> He was, I learned later, a balletomane and opera buff, one of those bachelors of independent means who taught not for the paycheck but for the reward of it, and he managed to bring Michel de Montaigne and John Stuart Mill and Samuel Taylor Coleridge to life. We read Albert Camus and Ernest Hemingway also, but his heart was in the classics. . . . Mr. Lenrow was big-stomached, sparse-haired, and . . . wore glasses—often as not on the bridge of his nose or perched athwart his forehead while he peered around the room. . . . He was exigent, impatient, and could be brusque. In retrospect it's clear, however, that he gave us the gift of attention, suggesting in his seriousness that we could be serious too.
>
> Our teacher sweated easily, and I can picture still the half-moons at the armpits of his shirts. They were expensive shirts. He asked us to write sonnets and Socratic dialogues; he made us read aloud from masterworks as well as the apprentice efforts we clumsily composed. . . . Whether we were reading *Beowulf* or "The Rime of the Ancient Mariner" or "Dover Beach," he brought the texts to life. I was impressed by each of my teachers of English, but Elbert Lenrow stood unchallenged as and at "the head of the class."[10]

What Nicky chose not to report was that at the very moment he was spending his days with us, Mr. Lenrow was—two nights every week—teaching a course at the New School called The Twentieth-Century Novel in America and exchanging long, frantic, and intimate literary letters with his former pupils Jack Kerouac and Allen Ginsberg. (He taught

---

10 Nicholas Delbanco, *Why Writing Matters* (New Haven, Conn.: Yale University Press, 2020), 4–5. Nicky was the most faithful visitor to my bedside after my spinal injury, often coming over to chat (I can't remember about what). Later, I enjoyed the many novels he wrote, starting with his first, *The Martlet's Tale* (1966).

that class for twenty-five years and also had as students Howard Nemerov, Mario Puzo, and other literary luminaries.) Unlike Nicky, I remember Mr. Lenrow admiring more recent novels and explicating his friend Tom Wolfe's *Look Homeward Angel* with a seriousness that made me care about it enough to enthuse to my father about its charms and longueurs. (I recently saw a letter Kerouac wrote—"Dear Mr. Lenrow"—soon after having published *On the Road*, regretting his sudden fame, and wishing he could once again "creep into the backseats of your class at New School and nobody noticed and I enjoyed what you said about American writers because you spoke so beautifully."[11])

I also remember that Mr. Lenrow drove up to Fieldston each morning in a red Karmann Ghia.

Once, Mr. Lenrow had the kindness to invite me to his elegant apartment on Central Park West, where I was suddenly surrounded by thousands of books and vinyl records, floor to ceiling. He took me over to a long shelf of books on Richard Wagner and pulled out a volume of Wagner's correspondence with Anton Pusinelli that he had translated and edited. Then, he walked over to his massive grand piano, sat down, and played Debussy, before offering me tea and chatting for a couple of hours.

Recently, I've learned through email exchanges with Fieldston classmates that several of them, including Nicky Delbanco, had also been invited for similar visits: The poet and English professor Rachel Blau Duplessis wrote that "it was a glimpse of a real world, and probably worldly person, a gifted teacher. I think he knew what he was doing by opening that portal: we had a real life to come was the message." Or again, environmentalist Ruth Galanter wrote that "I am forever grateful for the time one of our classmates chastised me for reading mystery stories, so I asked Lenrow in 'conference' if it was really bad that I was reading them, and he put on his best professorial air and said sternly 'you must NEVER allow ANYONE to tell you what you may read.'"[12]

---

11 Elbert Lenrow, *Kerouac Ascending* (Newcastle upon Tyne, UK: Cambridge Scholars Publishing, 2010), 52.

12 During June 2020, after not communicating with one another for sixty years, a number of Fieldston classmates began a lively online exchange regarding current school policies abut "diversity," "affinity groups," and official statements about the murders of George Floyd, Breonna Taylor, and others. These exchanges encouraged me, as well as many of my classmates, to reflect on our 1950s experiences and were a key motivator in my decision to write this memoir.

Miss Grant, then in her eighties, described her continuing relationship with Mr. Lenrow long after they'd both retired. Unsurprisingly, it centered on words and literature and taste.

> Bert Lenrow and I have a delightful situation over the [*New York Times*] crossword puzzle; we work on it on Sundays. He has had serious bouts with Will Weng and Maleska [the *NYT* crossword puzzle editors], and I may say most unsuccessful ones, because his letters are the kind that they don't want to answer. But we carp at what we feel is an increasing disregard for the rules and abbreviations, and things of that sort, but we realize that we're going into an entirely different world. I talk with Bert an hour and we discuss the movies and the various things on television, the places and the various ones, and we compare them sometimes with the literary background that we have, and we have a good deal of conversation in that way.[13]

One other influential "teacher" was a different sort: "Smitty" (Alton Smith), my zany, irreverent coach for soccer and track. A jazz lover, a man who took great care never to step on a crack and who called many of my teammates by his own pet names ("The March Hare," "Eric the Red"), he had graduated from Fieldston a dozen years earlier, after a several-month-long suspension during the war for doing an effective impression of Hitler (in fake German) from a balcony on the quadrangle. He inspired fierce loyalty and affection from his players and taught us the meaning of teamwork. I must have spent more time with him than any other of my high school teachers. At one point, he hired as assistant a refugee from the 1956 Hungarian Revolution who had played with the gold-medal-winning Mighty Magyars, but after some weeks, the man's English didn't go beyond urging us to kick with our "eenside fuut" and he soon moved on. I had always seen Smitty as somehow anti-intellectual and a loner. And then, in our senior year, he startled me by bringing a beautiful woman to one of our soccer matches and introducing her as (I think) his wife, and an opera singer.

The summers gave me a different kind of education. My parents had met as teenagers on the shores of Lake Mohegan, not far from Peekskill, an hour up the Hudson from New York. In the early 1920s, a group of

---

13 "Interview with Frances O. Grant," 414.

anarchists (and sympathizers with the Russian Revolution) had pooled their money and established a summer colony on the shores of the lake, camping out in tents the first year, then building their own (mostly summer) houses. My grandparents' families, the Swees and the Prices, were among them.

In 1929, a terrible accident brought the two families together and my mother, then a teenage neighbor of my father in the Colony, always said it was her support through the lengthy aftermath that cemented their budding relationship. On May 18, a screaming headline in the *New York Times* read: "TWO KILLED, 62 HURT IN YANKEE STADIUM AS RAIN STAMPEDES BASEBALL CROWD. . . . HUNTER COLLEGE GIRL AND MAN ARE TRAMPLED TO DEATH. TANGLED MASS OF BODIES." The article, which filled much of the front page, reported that "the two killed were pinned under a struggling mass of humanity. One was a 17-year-old Hunter College girl, Eleanor Price, who had taken her small brother to the game." The *Herald Tribune* noted that "'Babe' Ruth rushed to the open bleacher in an effort to stem the wild rush for shelter. Fighting and pushing his way through the crowd he found the woman crushed beneath the trampling feet. He fought his way back to the field but the woman died in his arms before aid could arrive." The next day's *Times* ran a story headlined: "BOY TRIED TO SAVE SISTER IN STAMPEDE" and reported that the fourteen-year-old George Price "was knocked down and trampled. He suffered concussion of the brain and internal injuries and still is in serious condition." Eleanor was my father's only sister; the *Times* reported that she "was known as a bright student . . . interested in literature . . . [who] contributed more than 80 poems" to the *Echo*, the Hunter College magazine. A collection of her poems was published as a book in 1930.

My father never spoke about his sister's death. But one day many years later, I found a Louisville Slugger signed by Babe Ruth in our garage and asked my mother about it. The Babe, she explained, had visited my father in the hospital, a few days after the stampede. Though I was close to my father, he never spoke of that day, even when the two of us returned to the scene in 1952, a quarter century after the event, to watch my idols, the Brooklyn Dodgers, defeat the Yankees 6–5 in the fifth game of the 1952 World Series. I think he went to his grave feeling guilty about not being able to save his sister.

During World War II, our family was already spending summers in one or the other grandparents' homes, so Mohegan Colony—with its leftish, raucous, immigrant Jewish, working-class (often Brooklyn in the winter) ambience—became the center of my own summers, well into adolescence. There were artists, writers, and musicians—Richard Wright lived there while working on *Black Boy* and had conversations with my father. I remember talking with Earl Robinson, who had recently written "The House I Live In," made famous by Frank Sinatra and later sung by Paul Robeson, Mahalia Jackson, and Josh White. Like many others in the Colony, including the fathers of some of my playmates (and the actress Lee Grant, our neighbor), Robinson was blacklisted during the early fifties, as other fathers and mothers of my friends were jailed, while Ethel and Julius Rosenberg were tried and electrocuted. It was a time of much whispering and anxiety among my parents' close friends, most of whom were socialists and staunch admirers of FDR and voted for New York's Liberal Party.

I was only eight when my father, having heard that trouble was brewing and wanting to teach me a lesson about our country, took me down to the crossroads on Lexington Avenue in Mohegan, where he gripped my hand as we watched a line of flatbed trucks with baseball-bat-wielding

Age 3, with my father and sister in Mohegan.

toughs shouting Nazi slogans and swigging from bottles as they drove on toward Peekskill. Many wore military gear or American Legion caps and a few waved rifles. Paul Robeson, who'd always been presented to me as a hero, was to give a concert, with Pete Seeger and the People's Artists as opening act, all to benefit the communist leaders of a Harlem civil rights group then under arrest in New York. But before it could begin, the mob attacked. The concert was canceled, Robeson was whisked to safety, and the event was rescheduled. A week later, when Woody Guthrie joined the performers, fifteen thousand people, including many from the Colony, showed up. Pete Seeger performed "If I Had a Hammer" (which he later said was "almost for the first time"). On this second try, the concert proceeded but afterward the mob attacked the buses and cars. Over one hundred people were seriously injured, and hundreds of others bloodied.

Woody Guthrie wrote "Streets of Peekskill":

> Jimmy Crow & racial hate cant stop me, . . .
> Bring brotherly love to Peekskill wunna big day.
> Hitler's forty million could not hold me . . .
> Gonna stop old Hitler at Peekskill wunna big day.
> I'ma gonnta sing & dance around Peekskill. . . .
> Bring my union love to Peekskill wunna big day.[14]

And Howard Fast (well-known novelist and member of the American Communist Party), who was writing *Spartacus* at the time and was the organizer of that first concert, wrote a memoir describing the second evening.

> It was night time now. And now, for the first time, . . . I realized that it was very likely that all of us would die there that evening. Our lines leaned against the truck, half of us bleeding, all of us sobbing, our clothes torn, our scalps open, our faces scarred—and already it seemed that the nightmarish battle had gone on forever. . . .
>
> They were screaming at us in a full frenzy now, a frenzy of sick hate and bitter frustration. . . . "Every n—— bastard dies here tonight! Every Jew bastard dies here tonight!" . . . The mob was rolling toward us for the second attack . . . and they poured down the road and into us, swinging broken fence posts, billies, bottles, and wielding knives. Their leaders had been drinking from pocket flasks and bottles right

14 Joel Feingold, "Remembering Peekskill," *Jacobin*, 2017, https://jacobinmag .com/2017/06/peekskill-riots-woody-guthrie-paul-robeson-anticommunism.

up to the moment of the attack, and now as they beat and clawed at our lines, they poured out a torrent of obscene words and slogans. They were conscious of Adolf Hitler. He was a god in their ranks and they screamed over and over, "We're Hitler's boys—Hitler's boys!" "We'll finish his job!" "God bless Hitler and f— you n—— bastards and Jew bastards!" "Lynch Robeson! Give us Robeson! We'll string that big n—— up!" . . .

We locked arms, the better to support each other, and as that whole great mob rolled down upon us, well over a thousand of them now, we began to sing, "We shall not—we shall not be moved!" . . .

It is a full hour and a half now since the fighting began, and there has been time enough for the news of what is happening at Peekskill to be wired to every corner of the nation. The press is here to see the great lynching, every New York newspaper, their crack writers and photographers, but not one policeman and not one state trooper—not one.[15]

More than seventy years have passed but that scene seems, in its way, frighteningly prophetic.

When I was nine or ten, my father gave me Arthur Mann's recently published *The Jackie Robinson Story* and I read it compulsively five or six times in the subsequent weeks. In the racially segregated world in which I lived, it provided hope—the hagiographic tale of a Black boy, grandson of a slave, son of a sharecropper in Cairo, Georgia, who grew up, struggling against discrimination all the way, to be a football, basketball, track, and baseball star at UCLA, an officer in the segregated World War II Army (where he was unjustly court-martialed for refusing to move to the back of a bus in Texas, years before Rosa Parks), and, after a heated three-hour meeting with Branch Rickey, general manager of the Brooklyn Dodgers, about whether he was "man enough" not to fight back at the racial slurs he would engender (and he endured more than just slurs), became, in 1947, the first Black player in the major leagues. The book recounted Robinson's struggles against prejudice (and often violence) from his teammates, opponents, and the public, his attempts to win them over, and his successes as Rookie of the Year (1947) and National League MVP (1949). The book, as I remember it, was centered on the issue of racism and, from its White, liberal perspective, what it felt like to be Black in 1940s

---

15 Howard Fast, *Peekskill USA: Inside the Infamous 1949 Riots* (New York: Civil Rights Congress, 1951), part 2, Kindle.

America. I followed Jackie's life, and those of the Black teammates who soon joined him, religiously—star pitcher Don Newcombe (who was afraid of flying and had to be hypnotized before road trips), relief pitcher Joe Black, catcher Roy Campanella, second baseman Junior Gilliam, and left fielder, Cuban-born Sandy Amorós. They were my heroes, my metaphor for a better world.

Sometime in the early fifties, my father also gave me a copy of *The God That Failed*, which chronicled the reasons why Arthur Koestler, André Gide, Richard Wright, and a couple of others whom I'd been reading had renounced their earlier enchantment with communism. During much of that fraught Cold War period, when winters were marked by air-raid drills in school and fear of the A-bomb, I instead focused during the summers on Jackie Robinson's base-stealing heroics and the Boys of Summer, whose every move I followed on the radio.[16]

During those politically tense years, with the Army-McCarthy Hearings going full speed, I found an unexpected mentor on summer evenings. Softball games and swimming occupied most of my days, and listening to Dodgers games many of the nights, but one or two times a week, I joined my friend Freddy Magdoff and his father, Harry, for discussions of a book he'd decided to lead us through: Josué de Castro's recently translated *The Geography of Hunger*. Harry Magdoff was a proselytizing socialist, an affable and encouraging man, who edited *Monthly Review* and later wrote the best-selling *Age of Imperialism*. Right-wing suspicions about his Soviet connections were never completely put to bed; he became a defender of the Cuban Revolution and at least an acquaintance of Che Guevara. But for me, he was just Freddy's father and, in the way he engaged the several boys who gathered on his screen porch in the twilight, carefully explaining the book that argued that hunger and poverty were man-made results of politics, not overpopulation, he ranks among my finest teachers.

Another memorable, less edifying, recreation of those summers: once a week around sunset, my sister, Joanie, and I, along with friends from

---

16 In the late 1950s, Robinson became one of the first African Americans to have a radio talk show, the *Jackie Robinson Show* on WRCA. Its sponsor was Rheingold Beer, the favorite working-class beer of New York, based in the Bushwick section of Brooklyn and named (it is said) because the conductor of the Met's *Ring* cycle in 1883 compared its color to that of *Das Rheingold*.

neighboring houses, would follow the DDT truck, dancing and skipping, twirling, and running after the slow-moving, cloud-producing machine, enveloping ourselves in the sweet smell and dense fog, designed to keep mosquitos at bay. Rachel Carson's *Silent Spring* was still a decade away and neither we nor our parents had any idea that this immersion in deadly pesticide wasn't just healthy fun.

My teenage years brought a change in summer experiences. Age fourteen, I went to the sleep-away Shaker Village Work Camp, near Pittsfield, Massachusetts. According to Wikipedia (which gets it about right), the camp was designed "to give urban youths the opportunity to learn skilled hands-on work through folk crafts, [and was known] for its efforts to preserve Shaker architecture and culture, for its role in the American folk music revival of the 1950s and 60s, and for its influence on the 1960s counterculture movement." Boys and girls lived in separate Shaker-built buildings, which we spent a lot of time restoring to their spare eighteenth-century splendor, took care of livestock (cows, pigs, horses, chickens, and turkeys), learned Shaker crafts (my sister still has the Shaker basket I made of bent wood and copper nails), and sang folksongs. Pete Seeger, Odetta, and others visited, and we learned "Michael Row Your Boat Ashore" almost as soon as it was rescued from the 1867 *Slave Songs* songbook. We also learned a good bit about the Shakers, whose primitive socialism was attractive to the people who ran the camp, and sang their songs ("Tis the Gift to Be Simple," and others).

But I also had a more personal reason to be interested in the Shakers. From my father's father, Max, I had learned about the life of his older brother George Moses Price, who lived long enough to dandle me on his knee I was told and who, quite unexpectedly, had been closely involved with the Shakers. In 1882 at the age of eighteen, in the wake of the pogroms that had begun the previous year, he had been the first of his family to emigrate, from Poltava (Ukraine), in Russia's Pale of Settlement, leaving behind his "parents whose poverty brought them to the brink of starvation." He had been "grossly disappointed" by his Russian high school, having imagined it as a place "where a person would be judged not by his wealth, fame or race, but by his knowledge and character," but finding, instead, "that prejudice, ignorance, religious bigotry and lust for bribery reigned supreme. . . . The Russian Realschule had nothing in store for the

Jew. . . . It is impossible and unthinkable that a Jew should regret leaving Russia, . . . my wicked homeland."[17] How he loved America! It would take a serious student of his many learned books and articles, written in Russian and English (and translated into other languages, including Japanese), to corroborate the stories my grandfather and my father (named after this uncle) told me. What Max said was that his brother George, who knew no one when he landed at Castle Garden at the southern tip of Manhattan (a decade before Ellis Island opened), was eventually taken in by the Shakers, who did not practice sex between the "brothers" and "sisters" in the sect but rather perpetuated their communities by adoption.[18] In George's case, he stayed with them for three years, getting well-schooled in English and other American skills before deciding to make a life on his own when, at twenty-one, he reached the Shaker age of choice. Max said George was forever grateful to those strange sober folk.[19] I think of him whenever I hear "Appalachian Spring."

Max had just been born when George fled Poltava, and it was George who helped him get settled in New York in 1898 at the age of seventeen, graduate from the University of Pennsylvania Dental School, and meet his wife, Adah (Nanny to me), who had immigrated in 1906 with her family from Odessa, in the wake of the bloody 1905 pogrom in that city. (Max told me he'd been brought up in Georgia, "like Stalin," but on a watermelon farm—presumably his family had been forced to resettle from Poltava after the 1880s pogroms.)

My father's early years were spent on a tobacco farm in the Connecticut River valley, where he briefly attended a one-room school. Max had been forced to abandon his Flatiron Building dental practice temporarily for reasons of health, so my father and his sister and brother grew up for

---

17 Leo Shpall, translator, "The Diary of George M. Price," *Publications of the American Jewish Historical Society* 40, no. 2 (1950): 173–81, citations are from 173–75. The original was written in 1882 in Russian, with the author identified as "Г. М. Прайс" (G. M. Price).

18 The unbelievably inhumane conditions at Castle Garden and the other immigrant holding centers are described in "The Memoir of Doctor George M. Price," *Publications of the American Jewish Historical Society* 47, no. 2 (1957): 101–10.

19 After leaving the Shakers, George went on to get his MD (1895, NYU), become a public health luminary, the chief investigator of the disastrous 1911 Triangle Shirtwaist Factory fire, author of books on tenement sanitation, the modern factory, Russian Jews in America, and the labor movement, and an inveterate fighter against sweatshops. He headed New York's Union Health Center from 1913 until his death.

a few years milking cows, before moving back to the Bronx, not far from Yankee Stadium. One of my father's early memories concerned a visit to the farm, soon after the Russian Revolution, by Max's sister, a Soviet physician in a delegation attending a conference in New York. (Might it have concerned the 1918 flu pandemic?) What my father remembered was that Max and his sister talked in Russian all night and into the morning, when she left, never to be heard from again. Max told him that their discussions had been about the Revolution.

Max and Nanny, when not speaking English, spoke Russian; they were relatively formal, drinking tea she prepared from the silver samovar the family had carried with them, he always placing a cube of sugar in his mouth before the first sip. My mother's parents also spoke Russian but preferred Yiddish as their private language. Pop dug his own tomato and vegetable garden in Mohegan; Mom (who had grown up in several shtetls in Vilna Gubernia [modern Lithuania and Belarus] and immigrated with her parents at the age of thirteen in 1905) loved to tell me scary bedtime stories about wolves and horse-drawn sleighs, witches and devils. My mother's side of the family was the more literary one: my grandmother's brother Avrah Meisha Dillon was a published Yiddish poet, theater critic, and journalist, and part of New York's *Di Yunge* movement; he was also (privately, of course) gay. Pop was a true Voltairean, always trying to instill in me antireligious Enlightenment values, including tolerance, the quest for knowledge, and the love of books. Both sets of grandparents, like many immigrants of their generation, refused to teach their children Old World languages, insisting that they grow up fully American.

During the summers, Nanny and Mom both participated in Hadassah, the women's movement that supported the birth of the state of Israel, and often went to meetings in the Colony. The men in the family, as far as I remember, were far more interested in World War II and its aftermath—I have strong memories of both of my mother's brothers and my father's only brother coming home in 1945 showing off their uniforms and medals from the Army, the Navy, and the Army Air Force and speeding recklessly around the Colony in the olive-green Jeep one of their buddies had commandeered.[20] *Stalag 17* was one of the first movies I really enjoyed.

---

20 My father had hurried to enlist as soon as war was declared but was rejected because he had a chronic pilonidal cyst.

(To this day, I have never felt comfortable in Germany—prejudices die slowly.)

When I was fifteen, I had a more international experience: Camp Rising Sun, a utopian experiment for boys aged fourteen to sixteen in the Hudson River Valley. As Wikipedia puts it: "Participants come from all over the world and are chosen by merit. Instead of being asked to pay for tuition, campers are requested to pass along, to someone else, the benefits they gained." Before camp started, my family hosted that year's camper from Poland for a week, and I got an earful about life behind the Iron Curtain. (Andrejz took the longest hot showers of anyone I'd ever seen—back home, it was from a bucket.) When camp ended, we hosted Munthe, the better-off Danish participant. My best friend that summer was Ezra Griffith, a soccer-playing companion from Barbados, who had just moved to Brooklyn, who went on to Harvard and became a distinguished professor of psychiatry at Yale. At camp, lots of soccer, discussions that lasted late into the night, and a healthy whiff of how large was the world, shared by campers of many colors and languages and from every continent.

My final two high school summers were spent out west, as already described, and ended with the submission of my application to be in Professor Kluckhohn's freshman seminar on the Navajo at Harvard.

COLLEGE DAYS

The week of freshman orientation was something of a blur, settling into a dorm suite with four strangers, most from the Midwest (I recall playing Prokofiev's fifth repeatedly, on my new record player, as its dissonances symbolized for me the openness of the future); learning to take meals in the cavernous Freshman Union, with its baronial stone fireplaces, antlered chandeliers, and ornate wooden walls lined with the heads of bison, deer, and moose shot (I think) by Teddy Roosevelt; joining the soccer and cross-country teams (before dropping out after the early weeks, deciding that academics rather than sports was what I was there for); taking an aptitude placement test in chemistry—my mother wanted me to be a doctor—that placed me in an accelerated class that covered two semesters in one, with me truly struggling to get a C+;[1] and remaining sufficiently intimidated by the grandeur of Harvard that I was afraid for the whole fall semester to venture up the impressive steps of Widener Library.

During that first busy week, I was given an appointment in the basement of Peabody Museum to be interviewed by Clyde Kluckhohn to see if I could get into his freshman seminar. It was a very large room, with discarded airline seats lining the walls. Kluckhohn, sunburned and chain smoking, cradled on his lap a folder with my SAT scores, my written application, and some other papers. After glancing through them he suddenly looked up to indicate a young woman who'd just entered at the room's far end. "Isn't she beautiful! She's Polynesian," he whispered, trying to impress me with her exoticism. And I was indeed impressed. Only later did I learn that she was Dolores Newton, born in Brooklyn and the only Black American in the anthropology graduate program.[2]

---

1   The first day of class, the professor announced that he graded strictly on a curve. "Look to your left. Look to your right. One of every two of you will get an A or a B; the other will get a C or a D." I looked around me and saw all these boys with fancy slide rules sticking out of their shirt pockets. I knew I was done for.

2   In those days, Harvard was overwhelmingly White—eighteen Black freshman out of something like one thousand entering students. The entering class at Radcliffe had one Black woman—see Kent Garret and Jeanne Ellsworth, *The Last Negroes at Harvard: The Class of 1963 and the 18 Young Men Who Changed Harvard Forever* (New York: Houghton Mifflin Harcourt, 2020). I remained friends with Ezra Griffith, whom I knew from Rising Sun and who hung out with the Boston West Indian community, and had memorable

Dolores Newton among the Krikati (Brazil), 1964. In a 2021 email Dolores explained that this photo, shot by her anthropological colleague in the field Jean Carter (Lave) "was taken somewhat as a gag as we were amused by the gift to us of the carton of dried milk—we set it out prominently, my foot pointing to it—from two Catholic priests who came by."

That seminar really made my year. The other classes I took were large, impersonal lectures: Hum 5: Ideas of Man and the World in Western Thought taught by philosopher Rogers Albritton, a survey of French literature, the infamous fast-track chemistry, and twentieth-century U.S. history. For the seminar program, Harvard had commandeered a three-story wooden building and each one—David Reisman's sociology, Jerome Bruner's psychology, Kluckhohn's anthropology, and so on—had its private room, lined with bookshelves. The ten of us with Kluckhohn were each

---

political discussions—that first year or the next?—with Ghanaian George [Ayi Kwei] Armah, who later wrote *The Beautyful Ones Are Not Yet Born*, and Chukwuma "Zik" Azikiwe, son of Nigeria's independence leader and first president of the country and himself, later, a Nigerian diplomat.

given a key to the outside door of the building and the door to the seminar room and were encouraged to come and go any time of the day or night. Kluckhohn placed his whole Navajo (Diné) library in the room, as well as some classics in anthropology, and encouraged us to read as much as we could. After the first few weeks, when we met with him—individually or, occasionally, in groups—he gave us specific assignments for the year.

With his sly humor, Kluckhohn paired me with a Radcliffe student, Penny Reynolds (who later became a scholar of Russian history and married a Roosevelt), and gave us the year-long assignment to write an analysis of Navajo marriage, using the books and articles that were on the shelves as well as the unpublished fieldnotes of his students (of which there were many over the years, including Alexander and Dorothea Leighton, pioneering medical anthropologists and psychiatrists), most of whom had lived in the *hogan* (round Navajo house) of a couple named Dave and Tessie Skeet and all of whom had written, in their daily logs, about the relationships in that family. The file drawers filled with fieldnotes were in another office, for which he also gave us keys. I found these notes fascinating, a window into an unfamiliar, exotic, and attractive way of life, as viewed by anthropologists. By the end of May, Penny and I had produced an eighty- or one-hundred-page study of Dave and Tessie's marriage, set in the context of what had been published about Navajo marriage in general. I don't have a copy to look back on, but I'd bet it was written in a dry, impersonal social science style—I was already on my way toward unlearning what my high school teachers had taught me about good writing, trying instead to master the drab social science style of the late 1950s. My outside-the-class (often summer) reading—D. H. Lawrence, Faulkner, Richard Wright, Hemingway, Peter Matthiessen, James Baldwin—was being kept in a separate intellectual basket.

At the end of the spring semester, Kluckhohn met with me and asked about my plans for the future. Shyly, I imagine, I said I was thinking about becoming an anthropologist.[3] Kluckhohn, whose undergraduate degree

---

3 More than half of the ten students in that seminar ended up as professionals—George Collier as professor at Stanford, Ives Goddard at the Smithsonian, Don Bahr at Arizona State, and Dilli Pirrotta who soon married Don and was his lifelong companion in studying the world of the Tohono O'odham Indians. Al Begay, a Navajo and the only American Indian in our freshman class, was also in the seminar but dropped out of Harvard before he graduated.

had been in Greek and who had been a Rhodes scholar in classics at Oxford, gave me quite an earful.

> In that case, don't make anthropology your field of concentration. Choose classics or history. Anthropologists are only semiliterate—they spend half their time in the library, but the rest in the field, which they tend to prefer. You can learn everything you need about anthropology in a couple of years of graduate school. The important thing now is to get a good education in the humanities. But every summer, even if you have to beg, borrow, or steal to get the money for it, get out somewhere in the world where you can do anthropological fieldwork and then write up the results.

So, I chose to major in History and Literature, with France as my subfield.

That summer I took my first foreign trip, flying in a prop-driven Lockheed Constellation to Amsterdam, buying a tall Dutch bike with saddlebags, and riding through Belgium all the way down to Paris, with my sleeping bag as companion. Then, a train to Annecy, and a week biking through the Alps with a Moroccan schoolteacher I met in a youth hostel. (The first night, we were impressed by an enormous vegetable we'd never seen, growing in front of a house, and asked the woman standing there what it was—"*un gros artichaut*," she said. We bought it from her, scrounged the hostel's kitchen for the biggest pot we could find, and savored the newfound delicacy.) Then I took a train to Bordeaux and rode my bike to Arcachon, where I spent July and August as a camp counselor for ten-year-olds and had a summer romance with a French counselor named Monique.

When I returned to Harvard, I was called to the office of Evon Z. Vogt, an affable and generous anthropology professor and a protégé of Kluckhohn, who told me that in July, while working at his typewriter on the Navajo reservation, Kluckhohn had suffered a fatal heart attack. Vogtie, as he asked me to call him, soon became my primary undergraduate teacher.

Vogtie was leading the graduate seminar in anthropological classics required of entering PhD students—*The Andaman Islanders, Argonauts of the Western Pacific, We the Tikopia, The Nuer*, and others—and proposed to give me a one-on-one reading course on those same books, for which I was to write a reaction paper on each week's reading.

During one of our weekly meetings, Vogtie accepted a transatlantic phone call that he'd apparently initiated earlier—"Hello, EP," he said to E. E. Evans-Pritchard, professor of social anthropology at Oxford, as I sat and listened. "We're in the market for a British-trained social anthropologist. Who've you got?" And that's how David Maybury-Lewis came to Harvard as assistant professor the following fall.[4]

Meanwhile, my courses on French literature included one on Marivaux from a visiting professor from the Sorbonne and another on eighteenth-century French novels, and for History and Literature, I read Vico, Machiavelli, and Erich Auerbach's *Mimesis*. I took a class in sociology with Talcott Parsons, who had studied at Heidelberg and translated Max Weber, but found it dry and abstract. I also took John Wild's course in the Philosophy Department on existentialism, which strongly attracted my sophomoric spirit. And I followed with great interest the *New York Times* reports that fall on Fidel Castro's antics at the Hotel Theresa during his stay in Harlem.

At the beginning of the spring semester, I was chosen (along with my friends Renato Rosaldo, George Collier, Jane Fishburne [later, Collier], Don Bahr, Dilli Pirrotta, Jane Fearer, and perhaps others) to be in the Harvard-Cornell-Columbia summer fieldwork program, and I devoted a reading course with Vogtie to getting ready for fieldwork on the Cornell-Peru project in highland Vicos. Several of us in the program also hired a moonlighting Berlitz teacher to give us a crash course in spoken Spanish a couple of evenings a week.

On the way south, flying with Renato, a refueling stop in sweltering Tegucigalpa, a night in Panama, and on to Quito, high in the Andes, where I stayed with him for a few days before he went off to Riobamba, his summer site, and I continued on to Lima and the highlands of Peru. One day, we flagged a taxi and asked, as casually as we could, for a brothel. "Do you want *el rancho grande* or *el rancho pequeño*?" We chose and were driven outside of town, down a long dirt road. We told the driver to wait. As we walked through the swinging doors into a large, dark room, a band struck up, some girls appeared, a couple of tough-looking men came out to welcome us—and we looked at each other and hightailed it back to the taxi. What did we expect?

The summer of 1961 confirmed my anthropological dreams. Living

---

4 However shocking this may seem, when widespread advertising of positions, followed by interviews and campus visits of short-listed candidates have been de rigeur for decades, this is the way hiring worked at the beginning of the 1960s.

with a Quechua-speaking family high up in the Andes (I could see snow-capped Huascarán, one of South America's tallest peaks, and the Cordillera Blanca in the distance), sleeping in a potato storage house that I shared with guinea pigs, eating multicolored potatoes rolled in red-hot ají (chili peppers), working in fields up at twelve thousand feet where we watched condors floating in the azure sky, chewing coca and drinking high-proof sugarcane alcohol with my Vicosino companions, attending fiestas, and observing and interviewing about the local institution of *watanaki* (trial marriage), supposedly handed down since Inka times. Twice there were distinguished visitors and I walked down to the hacienda center to see them: Vogtie stayed for a couple of days and Teddy Kennedy, as part of his brother's Alliance for Progress, spent a day handing out PT-109 tie clips to Vicosino officials who tried to figure out what they could possibly be for.

At summer's end, a sightseeing trip to Cusco (over the Andes from Lima, with plastic oxygen hoses to suck on in the unpressurized DC-3) and Machu Picchu (by almost-empty train), a visit to sweltering Puerto Maldonado in the Amazon (again, by DC-3, this time with no seats), and overnighting in Quinze Mil, a mining town where I was awakened from my hammock by a gunfight in the street.

Back at Harvard, I spent the first couple of weeks in Stillman Infirmary, quarantined with a case of hepatitis I'd picked up in Peru, in the same room as the son of the U.S. ambassador to that country. We had fun exchanging stories about the Radcliffe participant in the Vicos project, a statuesque woman whom Teddy Kennedy openly hit on and tried unsuccessfully to seduce, once they were both ensconced in the ambassadorial residence in Lima at the end of the summer.

I've been unable to locate my fieldnotes, which may still be somewhere in a basement of the Cornell University Vicos Project Archives, but I did retrieve a copy of the sixty-seven-page report I wrote when I returned. It strikes me as surprisingly professional—straightforward, empirical, and honest, sticking closely to the data. Social science triumphant.[5]

That year, I did another reading course with Vogtie, a second course on existentialism, a stimulating class on twentieth-century French litera-

---

5   Unlike me, Steve Nelson, a Cornell participant in the Vicos summer program, kept his fieldnotes and has written them into a memoir of his experience, *Gettin' Home: An Odyssey through the '60s* (Createspace, 2018). My nineteen-year-old self figures in some of his tales and photos.

Vogtie visiting Vicos, RP on horse.

Atop the so-called "Throne of the Sun God," Machu Picchu, wearing my Vicosino hat, at summer's end.

ture given by a young (not yet famous) Fredric Jameson, and an absorbing year-long course on great philosophers, from the pre-Socratics to Heidegger, taught by Paul Tillich. I also did an unmemorable junior tutorial with W. M. Frohock, the dour chairman of the Department of Romance Languages and a specialist on Rimbaud. (In November, out of the blue, he invited me to a private lunch at Chez Henri, ordered a bottle of chilled Chablis, which I'd never before tasted, and tried, unabashedly, to set me up with his daughter, Natalie, who was soon to return for Christmas break from a college in, I think, Alaska. I thanked him but claimed that I was otherwise committed.)

I lived in Adams House, considered the artsy Harvard residence. My entryway abutted a Roman Catholic church and Bow Street, where Dolly, a skinny, well-dressed, middle-aged sex worker, walked her dog. Joan Baez sometimes came by, sitting on the steps with her guitar, singing. During my sophomore year, Edward Said was the resident tutor, parking his green Jaguar out front, and escorting very classy-looking women into his rooms. Junior and senior year, David Maybury-Lewis (and his wife, Pia, and two young sons) occupied the resident tutor's suite, where bows, arrows, and other artifacts from his stay among the Akwe-Xavante decorated the walls. (I was delighted because, despite Harvard's strict parietal rules—visits from women only between 4:00 p.m. and 7:00 p.m. on weekends, etc.—David's rule was that if we didn't wake up his kids, he would turn a blind eye.) That corner of Cambridge was much shoddier than it later became, fading toward Central Square where one encountered street people who rarely ventured into Harvard Square. But even Harvard Square was a bit threadbare in those days, with my philosophy "section-man" (a graduate student who directed the weekly group tutoring sessions) sitting at all hours in the Hayes-Bick, a greasy-spoon cafeteria, where a cup of coffee cost, if I remember, five cents.

The friends I hung out with, many from Adams House, were mostly serious students (though they had their prankster side as well): Mike Cornog (whose father was principal of New Trier High School in Winnetka, Illinois, and who became headmaster of a New England private school), Tom Martin (whose father was a Harvard English professor and who became a law professor), Bobby Reischauer (whose father was U.S. ambassador to Japan and a Harvard professor, and who became director of the Congressional Budget Office), David Lelyveld (younger brother of *NYT* journalist Joseph Lelyveld, and who became a distinguished South Asianist), Joe Dodge (who became a law professor), Bentley Layton (who became a professor of religious studies at Yale), Phil Stubblefield (who became an ob/gyn physician), Dick Schacht (who became a Nietzsche specialist and professor of philosophy), Hampy Howell (who became a psychotherapist), plus others from anthropology: Renato Rosaldo, George and Jane Collier.

During sophomore year, looking for excitement and feeling invulnerable, a few of us pulled a stunt that could easily have gotten us expelled. On a lark, but with careful planning, we stole the bronze statue of the Ibis from the tower atop the Harvard Lampoon castle, just across the street from Adams House. (Our idea was to strike a blow against the rich kids—the final club, prep school boys.) Midnight: armed with flashlights for signaling, two friends and I surveyed the surrounding streets for passersby; another (the smallest of the team), equipped with a rope, a pipe-cutter, and an old broom clambered up the brick wall to the tower, and another waited on the street with a large empty sack as the heavy bird was lowered down. We hid the creature for many months in the attic of a team member's father who was on sabbatical leave and eventually dropped it in the dead of night in front of the offices of the *Harvard Crimson*. (Grand larceny, a felony in Massachusetts, applied to stolen property valued at greater than $250 and carried a prison sentence of five years and a fine of $25,000. Since the statute of limitations was ten years, I assume we're now safe.)[6]

6　The *Harvard Crimson* newspaper, rival of the humor magazine the *Lampoon*, ran several stories on the incident, beginning on December 2, 1961. "Broom Replaces Ibis As 'Lampoon' Symbol": "The Lampoon's sacred Ibis, perched for these many years on the 'Poon Castle, has been stolen. In its place resides a broom. 'Poon president Jack Winter '62 claims he has a good idea who stole it—including the names of three individuals—but won't press charges if the $7200 bird is returned quickly. A spokesman for *Gargoyle*, the College's humor magazine, which by rumor is implicated in the theft, merely pointed out that this is Ibis-mating time."

A couple of years later, "'Poon to Welcome Ibis Back Today": "The Harvard Lampoon will welcome its long-lost Ibis back to the top of its building in a ceremony at 2:30 p.m. today. Usually reliable sources on the Lampoon revealed last night that the story of the bird's rediscovery will be recounted at the celebration this afternoon. The bird, a rare metal variety of Three-klornis aethlepicus, disappeared in the fall of 1961."

And then, in a historical retrospective in 1968, the *Crimson* recounted: "The Ibis, formally known as Threskiornis aethiopica, was apocryphally donated to the Lampoon by William Randolph Hearst in 1901, when the new Lampoon building was completed. Since its first happy years with the 'Poonies, the Ibis, sometimes known as Threskie, has had several leaves of absence, many of them accountable to a century-long feud between

A couple of my friends got involved in psychologist Timothy Leary's LSD experiments, boasting about their multicolored experiences. Somehow, I was never interested, though I did take a rather boring and very straight psych class (Human Motivation) senior year, to fulfill a requirement, with the young Richard Alpert, who along with Leary was dismissed from Harvard only weeks later and eventually became Baba Ram Dass.

And then, in the spring of junior year, two life-changing events:

- winning a $500 NSF award to go to Martinique for a summer of anthropological fieldwork, and
- meeting Sally Hamlin, a Radcliffe freshman from Cincinnati, on a blind date.[7] We went to a Rock Hudson / Doris Day movie in Harvard Square called *Lover Come Back*, and within weeks I was dreaming of a lifelong relationship. (I felt truly relieved to set aside the "dating," much of it centered on consensual groping, that I had been engaging in for the previous two and a half years with girls from Pine Manor Junior College, Newton College of the Sacred Heart, Wellesley, Pembroke, Smith, Vassar, and more—the hormones were raging at the time.)

In Martinique, I planned a study of fishing magic as a scientific test of one of Bronislaw Malinowski's most famous theories—why people

---

the Harvard Crimson and the Harvard Lampoon. . . . In 1961 the Ibis disappeared . . . suddenly. After giving up on the Crimson, the Lampoon kidnapped the president of the *Gargoyle*, a rival publication, and then the president of the Mountaineering Club, whose ability to scale great heights was admired, feared, and suspected. . . . [In 1963] a large white package, tied with heavy string was left . . . at the Crimson."

7   Sally had graduated from Cincinnati's premier public high school, Walnut Hills, which sent several of her classmates to Harvard and Radcliffe (and another, "Jimmy" Levine, to Juilliard). Her mother, a Radcliffe graduate, was a homemaker before becoming the director of a scholarship program at the University of Cincinnati. Her father, a Harvard graduate, was a university librarian whose ancestry traced back to the *Mayflower* and on to the twins Cyrus and Hannibal Hamlin (b. 1769), each of whom had a son—Cyrus's named Hannibal and Hannibal's named Cyrus. The younger Hannibal was Lincoln's first vice president and the younger Cyrus (a missionary who founded Robert College in Istanbul and was later president of Middlebury College) was Sally's great-grandfather. Her Hamlin grandfather was a Congregationalist minister on Cape Cod. Sally was close to her maternal grandparents, Swedish immigrants who lived in Medford (he was a butcher in Boston's Faneuil Hall and a devout Red Sox fan), and she saw them frequently on weekends while she was at Radcliffe.

*Petite Anse
(mid-1990s).*

performed "magic." He had argued that risk and uncertainty fostered anxiety, which in turn caused people to engage in magical practices; he "proved" it by noting that when Trobrianders fished in their calm lagoon, where the return was consistent yet unspectacular, they performed no magic, but that when they went out in their outriggers to fish the high seas, where the returns were sometimes enormous, sometimes nil, and the physical risks of not returning at all were very real, they performed extensive rituals to assure success.

I flew down the islands to Martinique and explored the island by road-taxi (densely packed minivans or old school buses) for a few days. And then one morning, hiking up to the top of a hill, my breath was taken away by the sight of a spectacularly beautiful, isolated fishing village rimming the blue-green Caribbean, Petit Anse.

Arriving in the village, I walked over to some men near the shore, said I wanted to stay, and was quickly welcomed. During that summer, I was essentially the village's first real encounter with a White person—French gendarmes came annually to check fishermen's canoe licenses but that was about it. I lived and ate with a family, the Nauds (Christophe and Eva, the parents of twelve children), who showed me great kindness, and I soon befriended Emilien, one of the strongest fishermen in the village, who was courting one of the daughters, Merlande. I fished with Emilien most evenings and soon earned the respect of the fishermen who drank in the local café after we came in from the sea. My entrée hinged partly on an elaborate magic trick.

During the war, my father's brother, Nat, an Army Air Force pilot who'd been shot down over the Pacific, shared a hospital room for some weeks with a professional card sharp. When I was a teenager, he taught me a few of the tricks he'd picked up from him. Having learned how to "force" a card, I could, for example, ask someone to "pick a card, any card," to show it around to the dozen or so other drinkers in the café, to replace it in the deck, and to reshuffle. I would then go to the hearth, take some ashes, and rub them on my naked chest where the identity of the card would miraculously appear—2D for the deuce of diamonds, or whatever card I had earlier marked with a bar of soap on my body. It never failed to impress.

There was no electricity or water in the hundred or so small houses in Petite Anse, and no cars. A sole crank-up telephone served the whole community in case of emergencies. Bread arrived by fishing boat each morning. Store-bought necessities—rice, sugar, rum, onions, matches—were purchased locally, from tiny shops attached to houses, with storekeepers replenishing their goods by fishing canoe from the capital. Most purchases were on credit, scribbled in a notebook and paid up whenever cash was available. Ground provisions came from kitchen gardens or higglers who headed-in baskets over the hills from the north. Cooking was on charcoal. Chamber pots were dutifully emptied early each morning into the sea. Men fished from three in the morning till noon, mended nets and other equipment in the afternoon, and hit the rumshops by twilight, before retiring soon after.[8] The largest and most modern house in

---

8   During the "summer" months, while I was in Petite Anse and the large pelagic fish—swordfish, marlins, dorados, and tuna—were absent in Caribbean waters, men fished mainly with drop-nets rather than hooks and lines and they took to sea in the afternoon, returning after dark.

the village was owned by Amédée, the crippled *quimboiseur*, master of the magic that permitted a fisherman to catch more than his neighbor.

My fieldnotes from that summer are largely data oriented, as I had been taught they should be. But my letters to Sally—often many pages— capture the flavor of that summer better than anything I could write today.[9]

> [early July 1962] Dear S. In the last five years there've been four enchanted nights that have had a quality unlike anything else I've known—one spent on the floor of Monument Valley, Utah, with Navaho wind gods sweeping across fantastical red rock formations, another at the bottom of the Grand Canyon, a third alone on a beach in the shadow of a Loire chateau, and one high, high up in an Andean canyon, camping with the descendants of Incas and watching the flocks of llamas move in the moonlight on the valley floor below. Last night made a fifth.
>
> At four o'clock, we left the land behind—Emilien, his crewman Hector, and a young boy, Em's nephew. We dropped our nets in the sea off Diamant and tied ourselves to a float to wait for the fish to come. Slowly, very slowly, the sun sank behind the mornes [mountains] and the Western sky became flaming red, then rose and pink, and finally bluish-black. The sea washed against the fragile gommier [canoe] as we ate mangos in the salt spray without a word, each man thinking his own thoughts. Venus appeared and then other stars until we were floating under a magnificent, star-specked dome, watching lights on shore twinkling through the clear air.
>
> Em told me the nets would be ready when there was a great "fire" in them at the bottom of the sea. And soon there was. Looking over the side of the canoe, we saw the nets glowing phosphorescent through the crystalline water. Each dip of Hector's oar sent beautiful blue and white sparkles, larger than a firefly and more enchanting, spinning away in a whirlpool. The nets were hauled in, and I traced a phosphorescent "S" on my foot in blue sparkles, like Candide carving Cunégonde's name on trees.
>
> Slowly, we rode the waves back, and as we rounded the point and

9 She was spending the summer in New Hampshire, where James Conant, former pres- ident of Harvard, and his wife had hired her to take care of two grandchildren who were staying with them while their parents were going through a divorce. (I quote here from the letters that, for sentimental reasons, she saved in a bag in my mother's attic. More of these letters are reproduced in Richard Price, *The Convict and the Colonel* [Boston: Beacon, 1998].)

Emilien fishing.

could see Petite Anse, flames leaping from yellow torches told us
that other canots had already returned. We beached the canoe, lit
our torch, uncoiled the nets, spent an hour removing our fish, and
returned to bed. . . .

[August 3, 1962] Last night I went fishing again with Emilien. It was
even more beautiful than the last time and much more pleasant
because Em and I disembarked for one of the two hours of waiting between dropping and hauling in the nets, to search for mangos on shore.
We found two heavily laden trees and carried, in our pockets, shoes,
and hats, 57 mangos back to the waiting matelot, Hector, who was
rowing just offshore in the canoe. We spent the next hour watching
the sun set and the stars appear, and eating 15 mangos apiece. It was a
delicious evening. As we returned home through the phosphorescent
water, we rounded the point and there, hanging just above the western

horizon, was the new moon, orange and mysterious. Em and H traced large, deliberate crosses on their chests as they saw la lune.

[early August 1962] This morning I was alone for 3 hours at work with a paintbrush. Emilien asked me to paint the name on his canoe— Notre Dame—while he repaired his nets. I did the best I could, though it is pretty crude. He seemed pleased and also asked me to paint on four crosses, which I did. Perhaps I'm spending too much time fishing and not enough on magic. I've been going to sea for five hours each evening. Last night, our nets got fouled in some rocks and were ripped to shreds. Now, hours of repair work. . . .

[August 1962] Last night we dropped our nets around a point to the west, just in sight of the lights of Fort-de-France. Gosh, it looked big! I remember so well how small FdF seemed the first time I saw it just a few weeks ago. Apparently, it has grown considerably. . . . There was hardly any talking in the canoe last night so I amused myself with many and varied thoughts. Just as I was reprimanding myself for not being more bold and asking more questions . . . I began aimlessly bailing the boat with a half-calabash and Em cried out for me to turn over the bailer. By chance—the way I find out most things—the world of "things that bring bad luck" was opened up to me. Turning over a bailer, cross- ing one's arms in a canoe, and much else turns out to be forbidden—like walking near a pigeon-pea bush before going to sea. And a menstruat- ing woman who steps over a net or touches a canoe is as dangerous as a dog who pisses on same. So, in spite of my shyness I learn things. As we sat rocking under the stars, I thought of how nice it is to have some- thing you feel you can do well, and I slowly realized how I am begin- ning to think of myself as an anthropologist. It's a strange and pleasant feeling to realize for the first time that maybe you've got a métier that is already somewhat within your control.

Emilien has two uncles (his father's brothers) who are the most magically powerful men for miles around. Amédée, the great quim- boiseur, has become my friend. His brother, Amélius, who is said only to do "evil," is terribly jealous of the famous sorcerer who cures people and canoes from the whole island. The evil uncle once told Emilien in confidence, that if he had the books of magic his brother has, the sun would never rise again!

[August 23, 1962] Early morning. Amédée has shown me many of his secret formulas though there are others about which he remains vague and private. He also showed me one of his livres—Le Grand et Petit

Albert. His strongest magic, however, comes from notebooks handed down, supposedly, from the original Martiniquans, the Caribs. He has a little chapel in his house where he goes through all sorts of hocus-pocus. His new house, the largest and most modern in the village, is built thanks to a grateful fisherman from faraway Bellefontaine who, using one of his "Carib" potions on a seine net, pulled in U.S.$9,000 in one day and gave $1,000 to him. . . . My quimboiseur friend is not particularly impressive-looking or sounding. He has the air less of a physician than of a country veterinarian. Local fishermen all call him Papa. . . . A lot of his trade is with lycée students from FDF who come before exams. I'll try to learn what to do so the two of us can get all A's next semester.

7 PM. I've just chalked up my ninth hour of the day with Amédée. I'm feeling things out with him that I never would have dreamed possible a few weeks ago. Today I saw and taperecorded a séance. Papa gave me various formulas and promised to show me his really secret, ancient book next Tuesday. For the moment, I'm abandoning going to sea. Papa insists that the "Livre Caraibe" he'll show me Tuesday is his source for recipes to help students get good grades on exams! . . .

I watch clients come and go and listen as they obtain advice and remedies. His house is chock full of gifts from grateful clients. There's a $96 transistor radio given by a storekeeper who continues to send Papa 1,500 francs a month; there's a large alarm clock; there are many small gifts from students who have passed their bacs thanks to the magical "rings" he makes for them to wear; and there are bottles and bottles of champagne on top of the sideboard. So far, most of his "livres" turn out to be 19th-century French mystical texts, though Le Grand et Petit Albert is supposed to go back to the thirteenth century. On Tuesday I will finally see his famous book of "Carib" formulas, which he insists were translated from Latin.

[August 27, 1962] Amédée also told me he won't be able to get his secret book until Thursday afternoon, so I'll have to wait till then to begin copying the magic formulas (if he really comes through with it—I hope so much he will!)

[August 30, 1962] It is becoming increasingly difficult for me to see Papa. He has clients from FDF almost all day long, many of them bus or taxi drivers. In the waiting area outside the house, barefoot fishermen, hats in hand, mingle with smartly dressed FDF businessmen and lycée students. . . .

What a joy life would be if school were able to capture the excitement and fascination with learning that I sense here.

One August morning after a particularly successful fishing outing the night before, I accompanied Emilien on the spectacular trip by fishing canoe from Petite Anse to Fort-de-France, skimming through turquoise waters, capped by the whitest of foam, passing deep green forests and mountains, with the Mont Pelée volcano reaching for the sky in the distance. After I watched him sell his fish to a market woman by the side of the canal, we went ashore for haircuts (Emilien's barber working on my head only with the greatest reluctance, saying he'd never before cut the hair of a White man), and I wandered into the venerable Librairie Alexandre while Emilien purchased some fishing gear nearby. I bought a dozen books about Martinique—Michel Leiris's *Contacts de civilisations*, Eugène Revert's *La magie antillaise*, Élodie Jourdain's pioneering study of Martiniquan Creole, a couple of books of creole folktales, and a half dozen books of local poetry, among them Aimé Césaire's *Cahier d'un retour au pays natal* and *Cadastre*, as well as Lilyan Kesteloot's just-published study of Césaire's work. (As best I remember I had never heard of any of these authors except Leiris, whose book I'd read in Widener Library in preparation for the trip.) I read and reread the *Cahier* several times that summer.

Once I returned to Harvard, excited by the books I'd found in Martinique, I proposed to Professor Frohock, who was still my official advisor, that I write my senior thesis on Césaire's *Cahier* and its author. Although Frohock was a specialist in twentieth-century French poetry, he said he'd never heard of Césaire, but if I would lend him some sample works, he would take it up with his colleagues in the Department of Romance Languages. I offered him copies of the *Cahier* and *Cadastre*, one of which had a photo of Césaire on the back. A week later, the verdict was handed down: having looked over the poems, the department (which included Fredric Jameson) had decided that Césaire's work might be of anthropological interest but that it was not of sufficient significance *as literature* to merit a senior thesis at Harvard. I was upset enough by this incident, which I interpreted as racist and ethnocentric, to make an arrangement for H. Stuart Hughes, who was chair of History and Literature and a historian of modern France, to serve as "paper" advisor while Vogtie, in anthropology, actually supervised my thesis, "The Magic of the Sea: Anxiety and Ritual in Martinique"—an essay that never mentioned Césaire.

Besides thesis writing, I spent my senior year taking a diversity of courses. I remember one from Erik Erickson in psychology, a class on literature from India (*Shakuntala* . . .) and another on literature from the Far East (*The Tale of Genji, The Dream of the Red Chamber* . . .), Larry Wylie's seminar on French civilization (with Sally), and, to fulfill a science requirement, a terribly boring one in physical anthropology called Human Growth and Aging. I also applied to the National Institute of Mental Health, which at the time supported graduate training in anthropology, for a five-year fellowship—which I won.

In the course of all this, I persuaded Sally to marry me (despite the vehement objections of her church-going parents).[10] In June, we set off together for three months of fieldwork in Martinique followed by a year in Paris, where I took the first year of my graduate fellowship and Sally, a French major, did her junior year at the Sorbonne.[11]

One thing that strikes me looking back at that senior thesis is that although it includes the necessary scientific data to demonstrate its argument, it doesn't eschew lyricism in its style. Describing the village, it begins, "Set in a broad hollow, its back to steep hills, Petite Anse opens on the sea. Rich countryside begins at the edge of the narrow beach and runs up into the heavily forested slopes above. Seven hundred Creole-speaking Negroes live in wood and cement houses which cluster along the shore and spread unevenly back into the hills. Although their grandfathers were slaves, the fishermen of Petite Anse are a proud and independent people."

So, Vogtie (and Harvard social science) had not succeeded completely in wringing out the attempt to be literary, at least at the undergraduate level. Indeed, Professor Hughes, one of the official readers of the thesis, commended it by writing, "A remarkable thesis in almost every way, particularly since it did not fall into the common social-science defects of style."

---

10 My own parents liked Sally from the first. My father suggested that we simply elope. In similar fashion, they accepted my desire to become an anthropologist. They were supportive throughout my life in the choices I made.

11 Sally had been awarded Harvard's 1963 prize for the Best Sophomore Essay in French. She'd been wavering between majoring in French literature and art history (in which she'd taken a freshman seminar and several courses).

LÉVI-STRAUSS

In October 1963, after a wonderful second summer of fieldwork in that same Martiniquan fishing village (which also served as an extended honeymoon), Sally and I took a banana boat from Fort-de-France to Rouen and thence a train to Paris. Alfred Métraux—the Swiss-born South Americanist who was a pillar of French anthropology, a specialist on the peoples of the Andes, and the author of a major book on Vaudou in Haiti—had accepted to mentor me for the year. Arriving at the Gare du Nord, where Métraux was to meet us, we instead found Claude Lévi-Strauss, then in his fifties, who explained that Métraux had taken his own life not long before.

Lévi-Strauss kindly offered to step in as my teacher, and, after a month-long debacle with the student housing office at the Sorbonne, he helped us find a place to live for the year—a wonderful sixth-floor walkup apartment on the Place des Abbesses in Montmartre that belonged to an archaeological colleague who was off in Lebanon digging for the year. (Fully furnished, with gas heaters in two of the three rooms, it had an outside-of-the-kitchen window box that served as fridge.) He also gave me a paying job—I was never sure it wasn't like the dictionary-copying in Conan Doyle's "Red-Headed League," but I certainly learned a lot. It consisted of writing one-page English-language summaries of what I deemed to be the most significant articles in the first ten issues of the recently founded journal *L'Homme*. He explained that he wanted to use my summaries in an advertising brochure to encourage subscriptions.

The first time I met him in his office at the Laboratory of Social Anthropology that he had recently founded, on the Place d'Iéna, Lévi-Strauss encouraged me to follow several courses, in addition to his own. One was a survey of anthropological classics for beginning doctoral students, taught by his former student Claude Tardits, an Africanist (and war hero), in which I reread *Argonauts* but for the first time Fustel de Coulanges, Durkheim, Mauss, Griaule, Balandier (*Afrique ambiguë*), Lévi-Strauss (*Le Totemisme aujourd'hui* and *La Pensée sauvage*), and other French authors. Lévi-Strauss especially recommended the evening seminar in ethnopsychiatry taught by Georges Devereux, the Hungarian-born, American-trained psychoanalyst whom he had just persuaded to join him teaching in Paris. Devereux, who had done a pioneering study of dreams among the Mohave Indians, ran his seminar as a stream-of-consciousness lecture, spending most of the year on the Homeric epics and Greek tragedy, writing copious notes on the blackboard in Greek. I often felt bewildered. However, I did retain the lesson that psychoses, such as schizophrenia, were universal but that their manifestations in different places were different and eminently cultural. Throughout those evenings, I knew I was in the presence of a genuine European intellectual. (A few years later, I read his provocative *From Anxiety to Method in the Behavioral Sciences* [1967], which—even if a bit too psychoanalytic for my taste—became a book I often recommended to graduate students at Yale and Johns Hopkins.)

Each week I attended Lévi-Strauss's seminar on the Rue du Bac at the old École Pratique des Hautes Etudes (where he held the chair of Comparative Religion of Nonliterate Peoples), along with a gaggle of fashionably dressed female groupies, some in furs, and his several doctoral students. His message from week to week was consistent: nothing is more important than precise ethnographic knowledge—what he called "the science of the concrete." (He had just published *La pensée sauvage*, with its first chapter entitled "The Science of the Concrete" and a picture of wild pansies—*pensées sauvages*—on the cover.)

Each week, a doctoral student, fresh back from the field, would present their findings. One day, a woman who had been on the Hopi reservation drew a diagram on the blackboard of the Blue Flute ceremony, as part of a structuralist analysis. At a certain moment, she explained, masked male dancers entered the plaza (I think it was in Shungopavi), some of them representing bees. Lévi-Strauss, sitting off to the side, jumped up: "What kind of bees?" She smiled: "The kind that go 'buzz, buzz, buzz.'" "*Mais, non!*" objected the professor, shaking his head. "The Hopi recognize twelve [or was it seven or fifteen?] species of bees. There are the Xs [he used the Hopi word], which have black bottoms and yellow tops and are nocturnal. There are the Ys [again the Hopi word], which have extra-long antennae and only fly at dawn. There are the Zs that live in the trunks of mesquite trees. . . ." And so on through the series. "This matters to the Hopi because they use the bees to think with—in this context they are metaphors, they form contrast sets. If you don't know which bees are involved, how can you hope to understand the meaning of the ceremony?" The woman was reduced to tears.[1]

---

1   I hope it's clear that the quotations are from my memory.

The week's main public events were the master's lectures at the Collège de France—he was at the time in the midst of writing *Le cru et le cuit* [*The Raw and the Cooked*], the first volume in his tetralogy on the mythology of the Native peoples of the Americas. The lectures were quite like his books—logical, measured, pellucid, yet filled with imagination and allusions to opera, mathematics, linguistics, and literature. One day I remember his concern with details spilling over from his magisterial lectures to his seminar. He asked everyone sitting around the table to take a slip of paper and write the first color that came to mind after he pronounced a word. First, he said *"cru."* Then, after collecting the slips, he said *"cuit"* and collected those. The next week he explained that he was designing the cover of his forthcoming book and that the results were that the letters in *"Le cru"* were to be an alternation of red (for raw meat) and green (for raw vegetable), while those in *"Le cuit"* would all be brown (for anything cooked). And so it turned out.

But I really lived for Friday afternoons, when I met Lévi-Strauss alone for an hour in his office. He led me through the Americanist classics, which he insisted were at the heart of anthropological knowledge: Boas, Lowie, Radin, Eggan, and more. Ethnography (Boasian rather than Malinowskian), the more detailed the better, was the love he instilled in me.

As is well known, at the beginning of World War II, Lévi-Strauss had fled France and Naziism (on a refugee ship described by fellow passenger Victor Serge as "a sort of floating concentration camp" that took thirty days, dodging German U-boats on the way, to reach his famous forced sojourn of six weeks in Martinique[2]) for eventual exile in New York, where he was quickly offered a position at the New School and became part of that city's flourishing anthropological community. It was there,

---

2   Victor Serge, *Mémoires d'un révolutionnaire* (Paris: Seuil, 1951), 401. It was on this freighter and in the Martinique "concentration camp" of Lazaret that Lévi-Strauss met and befriended André Breton, André Masson, and Wifredo Lam and where, after his liberation from the camp, Breton famously met and began to promote the work of Aimé (and Suzanne) Césaire. See Claude Lévi-Strauss, *Tristes tropiques* (Paris: Plon, 1955), chapters 2, 3, and 35; André Breton, *Martinique: Charmeuse de serpents* (Paris: Jean-Jacques Pauvert, 1972); and Eric T. Jennings, "'The Best Avenue of Escape': The French Caribbean Route as Expulsion, Rescue, Trial, and Encounter," *French Politics, Culture & Society* 30, no. 2 (2012): 33–52. Jennings notes that "Vichy officials, interrogating him upon arrival in Fort-de-France, plainly told a bewildered Claude Lévi-Strauss that he was Jewish, not French" (43).

he often said, that he learned anthropology for the first time. "All that I know about ethnology, or think I know," he reminisced, "I learned during those years in New York, and entire days spent one after the other in the reading room of the New York Public Library, where I read ethnology from morning till night."[3] Indeed, in an often-retold story, it was into his arms that the fatally stricken Franz Boas collapsed at the Columbia Faculty Club the following year. His close friend Métraux recorded a telling conversation the two had in 1947 in New York, just before Lévi-Strauss's departure to begin a new life in Paris. In his journal, Métraux (who had passed a frustrating morning with anthropologists at the American Museum of Natural History) wrote down their joint conclusion: "In the United States, anthropology is a social disease that affects people who can't take their own civilization."[4]

At the time, this judgment contained more than a ring of truth. The world of Boas and his students was, indeed, one of people who did not fit the normal expectations of European academics—and they stood outside the usual expectations of American academia as well.

> Each one in this circle [Ruth Benedict, Margaret Mead, Zora Neale Hurston, Melville Herskovits . . .] was in some way an outsider. [It was] a network of marginals, argumentative and diverse, a deeply nonconformist German-Jewish immigrant surrounded by an African American, women who loved women, and still more Jews and immigrants. . . . The anthropology of this group was contrarian, fresh, and transgressive, a vehicle for reimagining race, nationalism, gender, sexuality, culture, deviance and norms themselves.[5]

I have never been an outsider in the sense that Lévi-Strauss and Métraux conjured for those 1940s Boasians. But unlike most of my classmates at Harvard, I lived for my summers of fieldwork in foreign lands. It was, perhaps, my way of being at once in the United States and radically elsewhere, remaining at least ambivalent about "my own civilization," if not fully smitten by the social disease of alienation. In a 1959 interview,

---

3   From Pierre-André Boutang's film, *Claude Lévi-Strauss par lui-même* (2008).

4   "L'anthropologie est, aux Etats-Unis, une maladie sociale qui atteint les gens incapables de supporter leur civilisation" (Alfred Métraux, *Itinéraires 1 [1935–1953]: Carnets de notes et journaux de voyage* [Paris: Payot, 1978], 171).

5   Ira Bashkow, "Lines of Thought: The Man Who Opened Up Anthropology in America," *Times Literary Supplement* June 5, 2020, 4–5.

while speaking about the importance of cultural relativity, Lévi-Strauss once again brought home this unease or ambivalence, characterizing anthropologists (not just American ones) in general: "It is often said—and I don't know if it's always the case but it probably is for many of us—that the thing that pushed us to be anthropologists is a difficulty to adapt to the social environment in which we were born."[6] As I write now, having lived roughly half of my life outside the United States, I think that this most French of intellectuals was onto something.[7]

In our weekly meetings during 1963–64, I struggled to understand what I saw as contradictions in Lévi-Strauss's thinking. Through my readings of his work and from his lectures, I had been led to believe that the structuralism he championed was ahistorical, largely synchronic rather than diachronic. This was partly due to the contrast he famously made between "primitive" societies ("bathing in a historical fluid to which they choose to remain impermeable") and "modern" ones ("that harness history as the motor of their development"), and his analogy of the clock (mechanical, repetitive, with low or feeble entropy) versus the steam engine (thermodynamic, with high energy).[8]

But at the same time, I was struck that in the analysis of particular ethnographic problems, he clearly felt that understanding history and diachrony was crucial. Early in his career, in an article in a journal of philosophy, he had written: "If anthropology and history once begin to collaborate in the study of contemporary societies, it will become apparent that here, as elsewhere, the one science can achieve nothing without the help of the other."[9] And several years later, he added that "both history and ethnography are concerned with societies *other* than the one in which we live. Whether this alterity is due to remoteness in time (however slight), or to remoteness in space, or even to cultural het-

---

6   Georges Charbonnier, *Entretiens avec Claude Lévi-Strauss* (Paris: Plon, 1961), 19–20.

7   In a series of lectures toward the end of his life, Lévi-Strauss expanded these musings: "Anthropologists must adopt a perspective that places them outside their own cultural tradition without ceasing to be inside it, while trying to enter into the most intimate essence of the observed culture that will always remain inaccessible to them" (Albert Doja, "Celebrations of Lévi-Strauss's Heroic Legacy," *Journal of the Royal Anthropological Institute* (N.S.) 26 [2020]: 864–71, quote from p. 868).

8   Charbonnier, *Entretiens*, 37–46.

9   Claude Lévi-Strauss, "Histoire et ethnologie," *Revue de Metaphysique et de Morale* 54, no. 3–4 (1949): 363–91.

erogeneity, is of secondary importance compared to the basic similarity of perspective."[10] In any case, in our weekly meetings, he treated me to lessons in history that Vogtie, who was oriented more to functionalist British social anthropology (and quite un-Boasian), would never have contemplated.

Early on, Lévi-Strauss asked me to share what I was writing, and the first thing I showed him was my senior thesis. He helped me see that there were really two parts to it, the test of Malinowski's venerable theory of magic and the ethnography and history of Martiniquan fishing magic itself. For the first, he suggested adding a lot of bibliography and a more thorough review of the theoretical literature. I added materials from Kroeber, Leach, Lévi-Strauss, and others, and presented it to him, in English, in my best impression of social science. The next week, he told me he was having it translated for *L'Homme*.[11] And then came the historical part. Lévi-Strauss found fascinating that I had chronicled the use in contemporary fishing magic of French pharmaceuticals from centuries past. He encouraged me to figure out the history of Martiniquan fishing magic, sending me to the library of the School of Pharmacy, where I spent countless hours poring over codices from the seventeenth and eighteenth centuries, and to the library of the Natural History Museum, where I researched the history of plant names. Eventually, I was able to show that the recipes and rites used by my fishermen friends were mostly developed in the seventeenth century in interactions between enslaved Africans, the original Carib population, and French settlers.[12]

Lévi-Strauss's reaction to my summer report from Peru was also an encouragement to historicize, to read the sixteenth-century Spanish and Inka chroniclers in the library of his beloved Musée de l'Homme, just up the street at the Place du Trocadéro, searching for the history of Quechua marriage from the time of the conquest to the present. Under his guidance, I put this together with my own Vicos research, and he sent it to his friend George Peter Murdock, who had recently founded

---

10 Claude Lévi-Strauss, *Anthropologie sturucturale* (Paris: Plon, 1958), 23.

11 Richard Price, "Magie et pêche à la Martinique," *L'Homme* 4 (1964): 84–113.

12 Richard Price, "Fishing Rites and Recipes in a Martiniquan Village," *Caribbean Studies* 6 (1966): 3–24.

Ethnology. "Trial Marriage in the Andes" became my second published article.[13]

What a paradox! The anthropologist who probably did less fieldwork than any major contemporary cared more about ethnography (as well as history) than any anthropologist I'd ever met. "Why not admit it?" he once said to an interviewer, "I was fairly quick to discover that I was more a man for the study than for the field."[14] Understanding Lévi-Strauss's vast intellectual legacy depends, in my view, on realizing that the master's big ideas grew out of thinking about the minutiae buried in the most traditional of ethnographic and historical tomes. As Marshall Sahlins wrote, "He developed an ethnographic knowledge of the planet unparalleled by any scholar before and unlikely to be duplicated by anyone again."[15] That ambition—the idea that ethnographic knowledge is worth its weight in gold, as well as his insistence that ethnographic knowledge needs to be historicized—was the most precious gift that an experienced elder could give to a young, aspiring anthropologist, especially to one who likes to think of himself as an ethnographic historian.[16]

{Film clips from that year. Our month-long stay at the one-star Hotel du Panthéon, moving up a flight of stairs each week to an even cheaper room as our funds dried up. Getting to know the Boul' Mich and the Latin Quarter by heart. Settling into our sixth-floor walkup on the Place des Abbesses, with a Portuguese concierge handling our mail. Stand-

13 Richard Price, "Trial Marriage in the Andes." *Ethnology* 4 (1965): 310–22. There is an anomaly I cannot explain. In the acknowledgments of this publication, as in those of the "Fishing Rites" article, I do not thank Lévi-Strauss, although he is the person who supervised my historical research for each.

14 Didier Eribon, *Conversations with Lévi-Strauss* (Chicago: University of Chicago Press, 1991), quoted in Edward Rothstein "Claude Lévi-Strauss, 100, Dies; Altered Western Views of the 'Primitive,'" *New York Times*, November 4, 2009.

15 Marshall Sahlins, "On the Anthropology of Lévi-Strauss," 3 Quarks Daily, November 3, 2009.

16 Lévi-Strauss continued to show us personal kindness for the rest of his life, helping Sally in the 1980s with art dealer contacts when she was writing *Primitive Art in Civilized Places*, writing the occasional job recommendation for me, sending page-long, handwritten letters of appreciation whenever we sent him a book we had written. We last met in his office in 2005, where Sally interviewed him for her research on the Musée du Quai Branly, and he offered sprightly observations and asked characteristically penetrating questions. He was ninety-seven.

ing in line each morning for croissants or baguettes at the boulangerie that we could see from our balcony. Exploring the array of cheeses and fowls and crustaceans on display in the shops on the rue Lepic. Learning to cook from the 1958 edition of *La cuisine de Madame Sainte-Ange*. Getting past the high-heeled prostitutes lining the streets between our apartment and Place Pigalle, who reached out to me even when Sally and I were together. Sally waking in winter darkness to descend deep into the métro en route to her 8:00 a.m. class at the Sorbonne, while I kept warm under the covers. Eating lunches at the university restaurant in the 5e arrondissement—serious meals, including wine, in exchange for a state-sponsored coupon. Using the odiferous public pissoirs on the boulevards and the "Turkish toilets" in cafes. Seeing the screaming headline in the *Corriere della sera* on a rack outside a *tabac* on the Boulevard de Clichy and realizing it meant that President Kennedy had been shot. New Year's Eve with a whole bottle of champagne and a midnight showing of *Some Like It Hot* at the Studio 28 cinema up the block. Sally in her yellow sundress coming home from class on a spring day, saying a man had shoved his naked penis against her in the crowded metro. Wandering the Boulevard de Clichy with its carnivalesque offerings—mermaids swimming in tanks, fire-eaters, shooting galleries. Walking up the winding streets from Abbesses to Sacré Coeur and joining the crowds gazing out with all of Paris spread before us.}

ANDALUSIA
SILENCING THE PAST

French universities offered several-week-long breaks at Christmas and Easter. In mid-December 1963, Sally and I drove our Volkswagen Beetle convertible (a marriage gift from my grandfather Max)[1] down to Madrid, picking up on the way Vogtie's daughter Skee, who was doing a year abroad in Grenoble, and a Harvard friend David Riggs, who later became professor of English at Stanford. In the Spanish capital, we met up with Renato, who was doing a year of philology at the Complutense. Sally and I remember wandering the streets with Renato, who had an acceptance postcard addressed to the University of Chicago for a degree in philology in one pocket and one addressed to the Harvard anthropology department in the other and was trying to decide which one to drop in a mailbox. (He eventually chose the latter, which I'd done a few days earlier.) Our destination was the pueblo of "Los Olivos" where our friends George and Jane Collier, whom I'd known since freshman year, were spending the year with their newborn son, on a Fulbright, before returning to Harvard for graduate work.[2]

George and Jane, by then experienced fieldworkers from several summers in Chiapas, Mexico, were conducting research in this small, nucleated pueblo, a maze of contiguous whitewashed houses, nestled in the hills of western Andalusia. By the time Sally and I returned during Easter vacation, we were already typing fieldnotes and laying plans for a longer stay that summer, after the Colliers had left. In early June, we moved in with a family that we'd met through George and Jane. The first page of our fieldnotes describes how they "had prepared our living quarters royally: a large double bed with a mattress [filled with cork], an antique washstand, newly whitewashed walls, a worktable, chromolithographs of mountain scenes and of a religious figure on the walls, a fancy wooden toilet seat for our personal use, and a window grate covered with multicolored flowers." The Colliers had very generously left us all their fieldnotes and we settled immediately into an intensive summer of research on *noviazgo*, one of the earmarks of the pueblo, which had unusually formal, patterned, and

---

1 When I was a sophomore at Harvard, Max had given me his discarded DeSoto sedan, with push-button transmission. He'd also gifted me his three-volume set of *Das Capital*.
2 For their publications, the Colliers chose this pseudonym for the pueblo and we have always followed suit.

Los Olivos, 2017.

lengthy practices of courtship. Living with a family that had four children in various stages of noviazgo, we collected information on more than three hundred historical cases of courtship dating back to the late nineteenth century.

Our host family was presided over by Felipe, a strong farmer of few words, and Felisa, who was garrulous, often talked to herself, and like almost all the middle-aged women in the pueblo dressed exclusively in mourning black. Conce, the eldest daughter, was in the final stage of formal noviazgo with a man named Luis. Every evening after dinner, around eleven, he would show up and sit at the table and chat, *peleando la pava* (whispering sweet nothings) about the weather, the harvests, upcoming fiestas, and more, while Felisa chaperoned the conversation. Whenever she dozed off, the *novios* would take the opportunity to touch hands, briefly. The novio of the next oldest daughter, Amparo, was in Spanish Morocco doing his military service. Pepi, the youngest daughter, was in an earlier stage, still meeting and chatting with her novio each evening before dinner *a la esquina* in plain sight of the house; it wasn't yet time for Esteban to ask Felipe's permission to enter the house and take part in the after-dinner sit-downs. Aurelio, the muscular son who, like his father, spoke little, had a novia in a neighboring town, whom he saw only on weekends.

Besides our interviews about noviazgo—many conducted with Amparo, the best-educated member of the family—and our socializing with novios throughout the village, I often worked in the fields, especially with Conce's novio and his brother Andrés, threshing wheat, cultivating fruit trees, and harvesting cork. I remember hiking with them and their heavily laden burros through the night over the mountains of the Sierra Morena to mining and market towns where they would sell their fruits and vegetables in the morning. I spent most evenings with men just back from the fields, enjoying too many rounds of white wine and simple tapas at one of the two village bars, before returning home for the evening meal.

Sally and I were very impressed by the quantities of food consumed. Breakfast: fried bread and coffee. Around 2:00, *cocido* (a hearty stew of beans, chickpeas, vegetables, fatty pork, and bacon), served with hunks of bread and wine, always followed by gazpacho and then dessert. *Merienda* at 6:30: chorizo, ham, bread, wine, and fruit. Dinner at 10:30: another heavy meal, usually cocido (or rabbit or bacalao), with bread and wine, followed by flan and fruit. Not to mention the specialties served for the frequent fiestas and occasional marriages.

Years later, the Colliers returned to conduct further fieldwork, which led to a major book by each of them. Meanwhile, Sally and I produced articles on courtship and its implications for social stratification—densely ethnographic and typical, in style, of the Harvard/British social anthropology models Vogtie had taught me.[3]

Ever since I read a draft of George Collier's dense and thoughtful book, *Socialists of Rural Andalusia*, I have had disquieting thoughts about the Los Olivos fieldwork. The book tells how George and Jane (and by impli-

---

3 George A. Collier, *Socialists of Rural Andalusia: Unacknowledged Revolutionaries of the Second Republic* (Stanford, Calif.: Stanford University Press, 1987); Jane Fishburne Collier, *From Duty to Desire: Remaking Families in a Spanish Village* (Princeton, N.J.: Princeton University Press, 1997); Richard Price and Sally Price, "Noviazgo in an Andalusian Pueblo," *Southwestern Journal of Anthropology* 22 (1966): 302–22; Price and Price, "Stratification and Courtship in an Andalusian Village," *Man* 1 (1966): 526–33. Jane Collier's *From Duty to Desire* includes an excellent chapter on changes in courtship patterns and attitudes since our 1964 fieldwork (67–112).

cation also Sally and I) failed to understand the role of the Spanish Civil War in shaping the picturesque pueblo where we briefly resided. The puzzle the book poses, but never fully answers, is how much our vision of a relatively homogeneous, apolitical, culturally conservative Spanish pueblo in the 1960s was a function of the regnant structural-functional theoretical models of the day, rather than being the result of an effective silencing of the past by the pueblo's own inhabitants, who were living under the oppressive blanket of Generalissimo Francisco Franco's military dictatorship. More simply, how could we, as apprentice anthropologists, have so completely missed history . . . even as we believed we were actively engaging it?

In 1964, Los Olivos appeared to be a sleepy agricultural pueblo of some six hundred residents. As we wrote, "With falling farm prices, the olive and cork groves which surround the community are becoming decreasingly capable of supporting its population, which has been dwindling [from a high of over eight hundred] since the 1920's. Those people who have stayed retain a traditionalism in customs and values that stands out even in this relatively backward region."[4]

This description also fit the Colliers' view at the time. But, unlike us, they took the question further, continuing their pursuit of the pueblo's history and uncovering what had been an effective conspiracy of silence during the 1960s. George's analysis of archival records, from baptisms to court cases and the minutes of the town council, eventually revealed that Los Olivos had in fact been a highly politicized and stratified pueblo in the 1920s and 1930s, one in which people's cultural practices, including age at marriage, differed significantly according to their class position. And he discovered that "although Los Olivos passed the Civil War years far from the Republican-Nationalist front and was never involved in armed conflict . . . thirty-eight Socialist men—12 percent of the town's adult males— were killed within the first year of the war, and their family members were terrorized and humiliated [with many forced into exile]."[5]

During the 1970s and early 1980s, particularly in the post-Franco era,

---

4   Price and Price, "Stratification and Courtship," 526.

5   G. Collier, *Socialists of Rural Andalusia*, 140. George uncovered horrific realities: there were three mass killings and various other assassinations of Socialist men. Their wives and daughters, heads shaved, were paraded through the streets after having been forced to drink castor oil. By the end of the war, more than fifty local men had been either killed or jailed.

the Colliers sought out those surviving Socialists and their children, who in the wake of the Civil War had fled Los Olivos and settled elsewhere in Spain, interviewing them about the war and its devastating effects on their lives. *Socialists of Rural Andalusia* documents the whole twentieth-century history of Los Olivos from the perspective of political economy, carefully following full birth cohorts as well as numerous individuals, as much as the surviving oral and written records permit. The book persuasively shows how national politics played out through local class-based interests in radically transforming the shape of Los Olivos several times during the turbulent first half of the twentieth century.

I do not have a definitive answer to the question of why both we and the Colliers missed better understanding this history and its implications during our initial fieldwork. But it does seem clear from *Socialists of Rural Andalusia* that the relative cultural homogeneity and conservatism (including patterns of courtship) of the town that we knew in the 1960s was the result of the town's population at that time being made up largely of the victors of the war (the majority of the vanquished having either been killed or gone into exile during the previous thirty years). "It is as though the postwar years, extending into the 1950's and even the 1960's, were locked in a negative dialogue with the Republican years, continually affirming values and ideology opposite to those of the Republican era, which no one dared to voice."[6]

In 1964, politics was simply not a permitted idiom in the pueblo. For example, when we asked why certain individuals had never married, people replied in terms of personality traits—this or that spinster was domineering or sexually shameless or this or that bachelor was excessively shy or a closet homosexual—not, as the Colliers later found, that these people were, in many cases, from Socialist families. "Idioms of honorable personhood replaced the language of politics and conflict in this discourse. . . . We failed to comprehend silence—the refusal of enemies to talk to one another—as the idiom of bitter resentments dating from the 1930s. . . . Life appeared all too normal in the uncontested discourse of the victors."[7]

The Colliers' subsequent research showed that class conflict had strongly marked Los Olivos in the 1920s and 1930s. But the Levantamiento served to silence political discourse. "The Falangists not only did

---

6   G. Collier, *Socialists of Rural Andalusia*, 2.

7   G. Collier, *Socialists of Rural Andalusia*, 166, 7, 166.

away with the revolutionaries; . . . they won control of people's minds."[8]
The result was the context of apparent tranquility that both the Colliers
and we so innocently encountered in Los Olivos in the early 1960s.[9]

Our discipline's 1960s theoretical paradigm, which George Collier
points out "stressed consensus more than conflict and exchange more
than exploitation,"[10] may well have played a role in our failure to penetrate
the pueblo's silencing of its past—but I remain unsure about its ultimate
force. I know that I had already developed a serious interest in history
and process and, thanks to my Harvard education and Lévi-Strauss's urging, already approached ethnography very much with history in mind. I
like to think that had Sally and I spent even a little more time in 1964 Los
Olivos—our fieldwork lasted only ten weeks and was narrowly focused
on courtship—we might well have learned much more about civil war
events in the pueblo and their consequences.[11]

My fieldnotes mention the time I asked my friend Luis

> what happened locally during the Civil War and he said people were
> killed like rabbits by the Falange—who swept through the pueblo in a
> wild revenge-killing spree after the *socialistas* had destroyed the inside
> of the church. And, he added, in 1940, 41, and 47, more people still
> died of hunger than had been killed in the war. Everyone in Los Olivos
> ate grass, he said—I have since heard other people refer to these lean
> years in similar terms—Luis said also that Franco's motto of 25 Years
> of Peace ought to be 25 Años de Hambre. He promised to talk to me
> more of these subjects later on. (21)

Or again, "We talked with Francisca, aged 78. She talked some about

---

8   G. Collier, *Socialists of Rural Andalusia*, 210.

9   It may be worth mentioning that our picture of a relatively peaceful, homogeneous
pueblo fit that found in other anthropological studies of the period—see, for example, Ju-
lian Pitt-Rivers's classic *People of the Sierra* (Chicago: University of Chicago Press, 1954).

10 G. Collier, *Socialists of Rural Andalusia*, 6.

11 In fact, those ten weeks of work on courtship and stratification were really more like
six or seven, since my final weeks were heavily devoted to another project—an ethnography of the local barber-toothdrawer (also the pueblo's mailman) who had inherited
his dental practice from his grandfather. My dentist father fed me helpful questions, and
our flurry of letters back and forth helped mightily in the research. These findings were
published as Richard Price, "Un barbier-arracheur de dents en Andalousie," *L'Homme* 7
(1967): 97–102, in *Bulletin of the History of Dentistry* 20 (1972): 7–13, and (in Spanish) in
Boletín de Información Dental (Madrid) 42, no. 324 (1982): 63–67.

the War, in which her son was taken away in a truck and shot in Aracena. She said that many men were shot right up against the wall of the ayuntamiento here" (50).

And another excerpt:

> Two days ago, I spent the morning with Luis [in the neighboring town of Aracena] ostensibly selling *habichuelas* [green beans] from his *huerta* [garden]. Since we unloaded the beans in a lump only five minutes after we set up our stand, we had the morning free, and spent it talking about women, visiting bars, and loafing around. Across the street from the main entrance to the market is a cafe, run by two brothers from Riotinto, both staunch communists. We spent a good while with them, whenever there weren't other people too close. Besides ranging over various world political topics, they told me anti-regime jokes, mimicked a *guardia civil* [federal policeman] in a highly unattractive way, while his back was turned; showed me how you can turn a 50 peseta piece sideways and cover the bottom part of Franco's portrait until it looks for all the world like a rat or a mole; pointed out particularly ridiculous passages in the day's *ABC* [Madrid newspaper], particularly ones telling how Franco received some Vatican ambassador or other, and laughed at a picture of the minister of agriculture kissing the Pope. They said that they both had read widely . . . and could have good administrative jobs—in a bank or the like. But their past prevents them from anything but running a bar. They are watched like hawks and can rarely talk about politics. Their father was taken off and shot after the war. Their store of anti-regime games and jokes was endless, and fun. (40)

Finally, there are hints in my notes about socially ostracized families in the pueblo.

> [The noviazgo of] Andres and Paca faces extreme opposition from his parents. This involves Paca's family, who, I have been slowly finding out, is one of those very few families in Los Olivos that is partly ostracized socially for one reason or another. They are known as la familia de R . . . after the father who is called R . . . , which I think is some sort of rodent. I have gotten only partial information on why the family is thought so badly of, so far. [Her mother] is said to be a malicious, vile gossip who mixes in everybodies business and says many nasty things about people behind their back. The father, who if anything is considered less charitably, is said to have a novia in every town in the sierra.

They have no really close friends, it is said, because "la gente no quiere mucho amistad con ellos." As I find out more I will write it. (36)

George summed this up by writing, "When we asked, neither we nor the Prices learned much from villagers about politics or the Civil War. One young man never followed up on his promise to Richard Price to tell him about the Civil War killings in the village, and though Price recorded antiregime banter in one of the mining towns, past politics was not a topic he pursued."[12]

The main story told in *Socialists* seems solid. And the village-centered "ethnographic-present" fieldwork that was the anthropological mode in the 1960s may well have served to limit our understandings of the larger picture. But our experience shows something else that's worth underlining: a repressive regime can go a long way toward silencing the past, even in the collective consciousness of honest people like that of most of our neighbors in Los Olivos.

George is right that Sally and I didn't put what, in retrospect, looks like two and two together. We didn't connect the occasional case of social ostracism that we witnessed to the events of the civil war, nor did we sufficiently consider the consequences that the devastation of the war had caused on the town's population (or its marriage practices). Was this simply because of the functionalist social anthropology models of the time? Or might a few more months of solid fieldwork have opened our eyes to what had really happened? I lean heavily toward the latter view, but we'll never know for sure.

---

12 G. Collier, *Socialists of Rural Andalusia*, 6.

BACK TO HARVARD

Return to Harvard for graduate school, where the sparkling white, fourteen-story modernist, Minoru Yamasaki–designed William James Hall now housed the Department of Social Relations, encompassing sociology, clinical psychology, and social anthropology. That combination had been melded together right after the war by Clyde Kluckhohn (anthropology), Talcott Parsons (sociology), and Henry Murray (psychology), and our entering class of graduate students, the first in the new building, got its fill of interdisciplinary training. There was a year-long course that trotted out star professors in each field; so, for example, we were exposed, right from the horses' mouths, to Stanley Milgram's famous obedience experiments, David McClelland's motivational theories ("nAch" and all that), Thomas Pettigrew's ideas about racial prejudice, and more. We all took statistics and probability from the inspiring Fred Mosteller. And those of us in social anthropology got a classics-in-anthropology course (running from Tyler and Radcliffe-Brown to Leach and Lévi-Strauss). I also took a remarkable seminar on Maya Indians organized by Vogtie and cotaught by Alfonso Villa-Rojas (visiting from Mexico), senior archaeologist Gordon Willey, Tatiana Proskouriakoff (decipherer of the Mayan hieroglyphics), and ethnoscientist Brent Berlin. Renato and I wrote a joint (completely unmemorable) term paper—a Lévi-Straussian analysis of the *Popol Vuh* (the Quiche Maya epic).

But what really made my year was learning, by chance, that Sidney Mintz, a Caribbeanist anthropologist from Yale, was a visiting professor at MIT, and I hastened over to his office hours to meet him, since at that time Harvard did not offer the option of a PhD in anthropology with a focus on the Caribbean. As in most elite departments in the United States, anthropology was still viewed as the study of people who, in that pre–politically correct era, were classified as "primitive," and the Harvard department limited its PhDs to students who had carried out at least three months of fieldwork in a non-Indo-European language. (As Mintz once joked, "If they don't have blowguns and you can't catch malaria, it's not anthropology.") This rule meant that a student could not get a PhD in anthropology at Harvard with a dissertation about (for example) Martinique, or anywhere else in Afro-America, since linguists were still classifying Caribbean creole languages as the bastard offspring of Indo-European languages such as English, French, Portuguese, or Dutch. But I found a loophole. Sally and

I were planning to spend a summer or two working on Vogtie's Chiapas project, where the Zinacantecos spoke a Mayan language called Tzotzil. Having met the requirement, I would then be free to do dissertation field-work in any creole language I liked.

During that first meeting, when I told Sid I wanted to be a Caribbean-ist, he did his best to dissuade me, arguing that, however good I might be as an anthropologist, I would never earn the respect of my colleagues. "Believe me," he said, "that's been my experience. Anthropology is about American Indians or Africans or Melanesians. It's got to be exotic. The Caribbean seems too much like a broken-down version of ourselves. Anthropologists don't take it seriously. You'll get much farther in the profes-sion if you work with American Indians." But I was able to persuade him that I was serious, and we began to plan a Caribbean-oriented reading course. As we gradually became friends, I wanted Sally to meet him too. One memorable visit was when she cooked up a storm for a lunch in-vitation in our apartment, only to be told, when he arrived, that he had recently become a follower of Weight Watchers and would only like a bowl of Campbell's soup.

The first week he gave me two books: Alejo Carpentier's *The Kingdom of This World* (a novel!) and C. L. R. James's *The Black Jacobins*, both about Haiti, where he had done fieldwork. I was quickly hooked. I also showed Sid my senior thesis, and, together, we worked out a plan for me to study the history of artisanal fishing throughout the Caribbean. He helped point me toward often-obscure sources, and I eventually crafted a paper that focused on fishermen in something like the way he had done more extensively for peasants, showing how their specialized roles when enslaved created a breach in the system that permitted their easier tran-sition to freedom.[1] Sid also had me read extensively on the hottest Ca-ribbeanist anthropological topic of the day, the nature of the Caribbean family, and I eventually wrote a lengthy review of that (extremely dry and boring) literature, which, after much delay, was published in a Brazilian journal.[2] But in between these writing tasks, Sid encouraged my reading of Caribbean classics. I well remember, halfway through Fernando Or-

---

1 Richard Price, "Caribbean Fishing and Fisherman: A Historical Sketch," *American Anthropologist* 68 (1966): 1363–83.

2 Richard Price, "Studies of Caribbean Family Organization: Problems and Prospects," *Dédalo (Revista de Arqueologia e Etnologia da USP)* 14 (1971): 23–59.

tiz's *Cuban Counterpoint: Tobacco and Sugar*, running out to Harvard Square in the midst of a snowstorm to buy a cigar to create the proper ambience, eventually turning green with nausea as I finished that marvelous text.

Sid urged me forcefully to be generous and eclectic in my book-buying and subscriptions to professional journals, grooming me as a professional. Sometime during the course of that year, I decided that "Bush Negroes" (as Maroons were then called)—the descendants of self-liberated enslaved Africans in the Dutch colony of Suriname—would become the focus of my dissertation research. Sid, who said he'd always wanted to study these people but had never had the chance, encouraged me.

He had me read the work of Melville Herskovits, the founder of Afro-American Studies, who had considered Suriname's six "Bush Negro tribes" to stand at the "African" end of his "Scale of Intensity of New World Africanisms" (with the population of Harlem—which he sometimes glossed as "the Negro quarter of New York City"—at the other, most assimilated, end).[3] I read about the research that Dutch anthropologists had recently undertaken among the Ndyuka (Okanisi) Maroons of eastern Suriname. And Sally and I poured over the magnificent photographs by French geographer Jean Hurault of proud Aluku Maroons who since the late eighteenth century had lived just over the border from Suriname in Guyane (French Guiana).

My work with Sid was really what got me through that first year of graduate study. He'd been trained in Columbia's still-Boasian department, with Ruth Benedict as one of his favorite teachers. His historically minded, Marxist-inflected brand of anthropology struck quite a contrast to the predominantly British orientation of social anthropology at Harvard. Otherwise, I spent much of that year dealing with people in anthropological subfields that had no interest for me, such as A. Kimball Romney, who was promoting a technique called componential analysis, or John Whiting, a culture-and-personality specialist who advocated using "factor analysis" and the Human Relations Area Files to test hypotheses

---

3 Herskovits published his "scale of intensity" repeatedly in the 1930s and 1940s and wrote that "after Africa itself it is the Bush Negroes of Suriname who exhibit a civilization which is the most African." Melville J. Herskovits, "The Negro in the New World: The Statement of a Problem," *American Anthropologist* 32 (1930), 145–55; quotation from 149.

such as the idea that people who lived in round houses were more likely to be polygynous.

One classmate I rarely spoke with was a Catholic priest named Greg Dening, who later left the Jesuits, got married, and became Max Crawford Professor of History at the University of Melbourne. Many years later, he began a review of one of my books by giving his own version of that year:

> Richard Price and I spent a wretched year together at the beginnings of our postgraduate degree in anthropology at Harvard in 1964. Well! "Wretched" is my word. You will have to ask Richard for his. But in retrospect, I think, for a most historical anthropologist and a most anthropological historian like Price, it was a most unhistorical year. That made it wretched for me at least. We were in the hands of a preacher of a brand of anthropology called Componential Analysis and of an enthusiast for the Human Relations Area Files (HRAF). Kinship was without process and narrative in Componential Analysis. The thousands of observational texts in the HRAF were without context and the seeing "I". To my prejudiced eye, that was being unhistorical.[4]

Sally and I lived high up in a studio apartment in the brand-new Peabody Terrace graduate-student housing towers, looking out on the Charles River. The elevators reeked of the dirty diapers that mothers were hauling down to the basement washing machines. George and Jane and their one-year-old son lived in an apartment in a wooden house around the corner on Banks Street; once, during the big power blackout in November, Sally and I walked down fourteen flights of stairs and used the crisis as an excuse for a relaxed candlelight visit. In May, Sally finished her degree requirements and was in the first class to get a Harvard, rather than Radcliffe, diploma. (We didn't attend graduation.)

That year we often double-dated with Renato, as he was falling in love with Shelly Zimbalist, a brilliant Radcliffe senior. (I remember eating dinner at Shelly's parents' home in Great Neck, Long Island, watching her father, a lawyer, downing a whole water glass of Scotch with his meal.) Shelly, a close friend of the Colliers, entered Harvard grad school in anthropology a year behind us and shared many of our own experiences, for example spending a summer in Los Olivos for a study of mourning

---

4 Greg Dening, "Review of The Convict and the Colonel: A Story of Resistance and Colonialism in the Caribbean," *Rethinking History* 4 (2000): 220–23.

With Chep Apas.

rituals; she had already preceded us during summers in Zinacantan as part of Vogtie's project.[5]

During the spring, Vogtie arranged for a Zinacanteco named Chep Apas to be flown up for a few weeks of intensive Tzotzil-teaching to those of us who were in the Chiapas Project. He lodged for a week or two each with the Vogts, the Colliers, and (if memory serves) two other Chiapas-veteran couples, Vickie and Harvey Bricker and Frank and Francesca Cancian. Late in his stay, Renato and I decided he should experience more than the domestic and academic side of U.S. life. He deserved, we thought, to have some fun. So, one evening, we took Chep out on the town. When he arrived at our apartment dressed as usual in his colorful Zinacanteco clothing, we were able to persuade him, with some difficulty, to leave his beribboned hat behind and to cover his colorful shirt and tasseled scarf by wearing a trench coat that I lent him.

---

5 Shelly and Renato, who, like George and Jane, became professors at Stanford, did fieldwork under very challenging conditions with Ilongots in the Philippines, and each wrote a pathbreaking book: Renato Rosaldo, *Ilongot Headhunting, 1883–1974: A Study in Society and History* (Stanford, Calif.: Stanford University Press, 1980); and Michelle Z. Rosaldo, *Knowledge and Passion: Ilongot Notions of Self and Social Life* (Cambridge: Cambridge University Press, 1980). Shelly's edited book with Louise Lamphere, *Woman, Culture, and Society* (Stanford, Calif.: Stanford University Press, 1974), to which Jane contributed a chapter, remains a landmark of feminist anthropology.

We took the MTA directly to Boston's red zone and sat down quietly at a bar, within view of the counter where a go-go dancer was going through her routine. Before long, Chep heard some men speaking Spanish at a neighboring table, ran over, and whipped open his trench coat, proudly announcing, "Soy Zinacanteco!" Mumbling some excuse to the puzzled Puerto Ricans, we pulled the trench coat back and quickly left the bar. Afterward, Chep told us that the dancer was amazing . . . he'd never before seen a woman's thighs.

In June, Sally and I drove all the way from Cambridge to southern Mexico, to participate in the Chiapas project for the summer. It had been a year since the Freedom Summer and the signing of the Civil Rights Act, and it was only a few weeks before the Voting Rights Act was signed into law, so it shouldn't be surprising that with Massachusetts plates and a Harvard sticker on our red VW convertible, we ran into some trouble in Laurel, Mississippi.[6] First, we were targets of a shotgun blast that left a hole in our windshield. Then, when we checked into a motel, the manager inquired suspiciously what we were doing in that part of the country. When we told him that we were going to work with Indians in Mexico, he said, "You're doin' good, we might as well give the country back to the injuns 'cause otherwise the niggas are gonna take it over." Before we left the next morning, we messed up the room by overturning the bed and throwing around the furniture. The only way we knew how to respond.

The summer was enjoyable, living in Muktahok, an outlying Tzotzil-speaking village of the municipio of Zinacantan, sleeping in a corn-crib (with two adolescent boys on a platform right above us, watching through the cracks for action in our sleeping bag), and eating endless tortillas and beans. The bathroom was a cornfield—one hand would hold a corncob in lieu of toilet paper and the other a rock to chase the dogs waiting for something to eat. Our fieldwork was designed to produce a network-analysis study of the community (another at-the-time trendy method in social science).[7] Renato was one of the other students whom Vogtie scattered among the hamlets of Zinacantan that summer.

---

6 My mother had attended the 1963 March on Washington (where MLK gave his "I Have a Dream" speech) and would attend the anti–Vietnam War march in Washington in 1965.

7 Richard Price and Sally Price, "Aspects of Social Organization in a Maya Hamlet," *Estudios de Cultura Maya* 8 (1970): 297–318. Never having taken a real course in Spanish,

Two men from Muktahok needed to contest some land rights issues with officials in Mexico City, and we agreed to take them on our way north at summer's end. I remember showing them how to flush the toilet and turn on the light in their hotel room on the Isthmus of Tehuantepec; in the morning, I found the light still on—they figured that was what it was for. In Mexico City, we took them (wearing, as always, their Zinacanteco outfits) to the National Museum of Anthropology, where they pretended to converse with the mannequins who were dressed as Zinacantecos and where some American tourists aggressively tried to buy their hats.

Back in Cambridge in the fall, with more freedom in my choice of courses, I went over to MIT twice a week for a class in which Noam Chomsky led us through his just-published *Aspects of a Theory of Syntax*, sat in on David Maybury-Lewis's lectures on Brazil, and got to know visiting professor Munro ("Ed") Edmonson, whose work in Mayan literature and Black New Orleans folklore was inspiring. Advanced graduate students Pierre and Elli Kongas Miranda held evening salons in their apartment, where we were introduced to the Aarne-Thompson method of comparative folktale analysis and Terry Turner presented a long deconstruction of a jaguar myth of the Kayapo. With gentle pressure from Vogtie to continue working in Chiapas, I also participated in an NSF-sponsored training course in interpreting aerial photography, even flying out to Palo Alto with a few others for a week at the Itek Corporation, a defense contractor that specialized in spy cameras used for aerial reconnaissance in Vietnam. Vogtie and his wife, Nan, also hosted parties for Chiapas project participants at their suburban Weston home, sometimes with square dancing, and Sally remembers attending at least one "ladies' luncheon" that Nan hosted for graduate students and faculty wives. Meanwhile, Sally worked for Vogtie editing his magnus opus, *Zinacantan: A Maya Community in the Highlands of Chiapas*, for publication at Harvard University Press. In preparation for our work in Suriname, we hired a graduate student from the Netherlands to teach us Dutch in the evenings, using a book called *Een goed begin*.

But the bulk of that year was devoted to continuing work with Sid.

---

my command of the language—honed among Vicosinos (whose first language was Quechua), Zinacantecos (whose first language was Tzotzil), and rural Spaniards in Andalusia—is somewhat "country" and uneducated, if serviceable. (Sally had taken an evening course in Paris, in preparation for our work in Los Olivos.)

Every second Saturday, Sally and I drove down to New Haven to spend the day with him, talking about books and other mutual interests. On each visit, he'd give me a large stack of things to read. The next time we'd discuss them, and he'd send me off with another stack. As my interest in working in Suriname became stronger, I made a deal with Vogtie: during the summer of 1966, Sally and I would return to Zinacantan for six weeks where I would do research on the use of aerial photos in studying agriculture, if he, in return, would finance a several-week trip for us to Suriname to explore the feasibility of longer-term fieldwork there. After I did my bit with the aerial photos we headed to South America.[8]

On our way, we picked up a string hammock in the Yucatan and then flew to Suriname from Mérida with a brief but memorable stop in Papa Doc's Haiti. Our plan was to visit the Mirebalais Valley, where Herskovits had done his research for *Life in a Haitian Valley*. But first, we needed official permission to venture into the countryside. We spent about six hours in a Port-au-Prince police station, the walls lined with photos of firing squads and their victims, trying to get the necessary pass for an overnight stay. But the pass we were finally given required us to be back in the capital by sundown, so we never got to the Mirebalais Valley—or even very far from Port-au-Prince.

Once arrived in Suriname, we set to work securing permission to carry out fieldwork among the Saamaka, then some twenty thousand people living in seventy villages along the Upper Suriname River.[9]

---

8   Richard Price, "Land Use in a Maya Community," *International Archives of Ethnography* 51 (1968): 1–19; "Aerial Photography in the Study of Land Use: A Maya Example," in *Aerial Photography in Anthropological Fieldwork*, ed. Evon Z. Vogt (Cambridge, Mass.: Harvard University Press, 1974), 94–111.

9   In 2010, the people previously referred to by outsiders as Saramaka requested to be recognized as Saamaka, their own pronunciation of their name.

SURINAME IN THE SIXTIES

Our first two weeks were a bureaucratic marathon, countless hours sitting on wooden benches in lonely government waiting rooms in Paramaribo, the colonial capital. It was clear early on that our fate depended directly on District Commissioner Jan Michels—a man who, we later learned, Saamakas called Tu-Buka-Goni (double-barreled shotgun) because he spoke out of both sides of his mouth. Michels eventually gave us the go-ahead on the condition that we not spend time with the communities forcibly displaced by the recently constructed hydroelectric dam built by Alcoa to furnish electricity for its new smelter downriver. He kindly offered to arrange our transportation to the paramount chief's village and to provide letters of introduction, replete with official seals.

With our upriver departure set for the following week, we began to be bombarded with well-meant advice by everyone from old government hands who had visited the interior to storekeepers, the East Indian family who'd rented us a room, and the chief of police who had impounded our passports "just in case." We were not taken in by their tales of a jungle teeming with snakes and jaguars and rivers swarming with bloodthirsty piranhas. But we did take the advice of merchants who had outfitted previous mining and scientific expeditions to the interior, purchasing knee-high boots (essential protection against snake bite, they said), U.S. Army surplus nylon-and-net zip-up hammocks like those being used in Vietnam ("against vampire bats and malarial mosquitos"), and certain types of cloth and rum that they claimed were preferred by "Bush Negroes." Once in Saamaka, we quickly learned better. We never once donned the clumsy boots (instead going barefoot throughout our stay) or slept in the coffin-like hammocks. The only resemblance between the cloth we'd bought and that used by Saamakas was that it contained stripes, and the 150-proof rum was much stronger than anything Saamakas drank or even used for libations.

On the morning of our departure, we set out in a government jeep for the sweaty, bumpy ride that brought us after several hours to Alcoa's massive hydroelectric dam at Afobaka. The district commissioner's three Saamaka boatmen were there waiting for us and helped transfer our gear, now covered (like ourselves) with red-brown bauxite dust from the road to a government motor canoe for the trip upriver. It was only as the boatmen pointed the slim craft out into the artificial lake that we looked back and saw the immensity of the construction, the broad sweep of concrete in between hundreds of meters of high packed red earth, looming up from the fetid water.

At last, we were on what Saamakas were still calling "the river," negotiating a tortuous path lined on either side with the bare grey tops of forest giants, standing as skeletal sentinels in a vast space of death. As we followed the course of the twisting, ancient riverbed, far below us, the Saamaka steersman would point and call out to us the name of each submerged village, buried forever beneath the muddy waters—houses, shrines, cemeteries, gardens, and hunting grounds, places where great battles had been fought and famous miracles effected.

After four or five hours in the eerie silence of the lake, we heard a low roar that grew louder as we approached. Suddenly, we broke into the exuberance of the bright green forest and plunging waters of the most famous rapids on the Suriname River, Mamadan (Mother of All Rapids). The river rushed at us from all sides, the foaming water coursing through numerous channels and plunging over giant boulders. After the boatmen poured libations on shore at the shrine to the gods of the rapids and the sea, we spent a fitful night's sleep on an island in the midst of this liquid plenitude.

It was still early the next morning when we arrived upstream at Abenasitonu, one of the first of the Saamaka villages that had not been sunk by the dam. Our gear was deposited in the wooden house of the Moravian schoolteacher, who was away on summer vacation, and we were told to wait there while the boatmen continued several days upriver to the village of Asindoopo to ask Gaama Agbago, the paramount chief, whether they could bring these Whitefolks into Saamaka territory. Four days later, the boatmen returned with formal permission to proceed, and we set out again upstream.

At the time, no outsiders—whether from the government or elsewhere—ventured into Saamaka territory without this nod to the principle that the *gaama*, on behalf of his people, maintained full territorial control. The government's unilateral decision to build the Afobaka dam had, of course, slashed a deep wound into this long-respected sovereignty. But in 1966, any non-Saamaka setting foot in their territory still did so as a guest of the Saamaka People. For them, the treaty that their ancestors concluded with the Dutch crown in 1762 not only ended decades of bitter warfare but also established three inalienable principles:

Sally on the river.

freedom (from slavery), independence (from the colonial society—the right to govern their own society as they wish), and control over their own territory, stretching from Mawasi Creek (some fifteen kilometers downstream from the dam) to the headwaters of the Suriname River. Gaama Agbago was fond of repeating the litany, "From Mawasi on up, the forest belongs to us."

During the rest of the upriver journey, we stopped for brief visits in village after village, seeing bits and pieces of a way of life that looked more exotic than anything we'd ever imagined—libations being poured before a gabled coffin as women shrieked in mourning, men sporting shiny gold earrings, bright patchwork capes, embroidered neckerchiefs, umbrellas, variously curved machetes, tasseled calfbands, multicolored beaded sashes across their chests, and hats that varied from berets and fedoras to panamas and pith helmets—evoking for us visions of seventeenth-century pirates of the Caribbean. Between villages, sometimes for an hour at a stretch, we glided next to forest walls of breathtaking beauty, seeing only the occasional fisherman or a woman paddling a small dugout canoe laden with garden produce. Over and over, we passed through foaming rapids, marveling at the boatmen's skills and knowledge of every twist and turn and rock in the river. Throughout the voyage, we pestered them about Saamaka words, building on our knowledge of Sranantongo (the coastal creole), which we had learned from a Dutch radio course and which they spoke as a contact language. I was already getting used to being called Lisati (the Saamaka pronunciation of Richard) while Sally's name, easier for Saamakas to pronounce, remained intact.

On the afternoon of the third day, we arrived at Tuliobuka (Mouth of Two Rivers) where, over a mighty rapids on our right, the Gaanlio flowed into the Suriname. We entered the left-hand, quieter flow of the Pikilio, which led to the gaama's village several kilometers upstream. A messenger had been sent ahead that morning to alert him of our arrival, but we were told to wait in the canoe until we received permission to disembark. After a half hour baking in the sun, we were led ashore and into Gaama Agbago's council house, a kind of throne room that took our breath away. Michels had told us that during the reign of Agbago's immediate predecessor, visitors literally crawled through the doorway until being signaled to rise. The Herskovitses wrote about their arrival in what they called "the Court of the Granman" in 1929, greeted by multiple shotgun salutes and much "hallooing of the women," and they devoted more than half a dozen pages of their book to a description of the council house and its ceremonial stools, umbrellas, and other accoutrements. (Even in 2015 a blogger wrote of visiting the Saamaka "King" in his "Royal Palace.")

Our boatmen ostentatiously wiped their feet on the large doormat and bowed down as they entered, and we followed suit. The gaama was reposing on a large, cushioned steel chair, flanked on either side by a dozen wicker armchairs set on a platform. He wore a fedora, a tailcoat made from a bright Union Jack, green and blue pinstripe pajama pants, and red high-top basketball sneakers, unlaced. In one of the armchairs, a young man, who we later learned was a foster child of the chief, was casually thumbing through a Dutch movie magazine.

The gaama motioned to us to come forward and indicated the two adjoining armchairs. After an exchange with the boatmen about the trip, he recounted some of the history of outsiders visiting Saamaka territory and poured a libation of rum, informing the ancestors of our arrival and asking them to protect us during our stay. Hearing that we'd lived in Martinique, he told us how, in his youth, he had shipped out on a steamship from Belém and how he and his fellow sailors, on shore leave in Fort-de-France, had been arrested and spent time in jail in the wake of a political assassination. He boasted about the size of that ship and gave a vivid imitation of the sounds of its powerful, chugging engines and foghorn.

When we were finally given an opening to explain the reason for our visit, I summoned up my best effort at Sranantongo to outline our goals, saying we wished to learn how Saamakas lived and mentioned gardening, hunting, woodcarving, and of course language. But because the several weeks we could stay on this visit would be far too short, I said, we wished to return some months hence and stay for two years. Later, we realized that I'd been far too direct—as newcomers we had little sense of the subtleties of Saamaka etiquette, let alone the linguistic tools to produce it. The gaama answered graciously but noncommittally, offering us the use of a wood-frame guesthouse he maintained for government visitors and inviting us to join him in a ride back to the coast in three weeks, when he was due in Paramaribo for official business. We presented him with several of the gifts we had brought, and our meeting was over.

The next morning, we met again with the chief, asking him whether we might arrange to eat our meals with a local family—as we'd done in previous fieldwork in Peru, Martinique, Spain, and Mexico. He answered cordially but refused, explaining that people moved around a great deal to forest camps and spouses' villages, and offering instead to obtain for us whatever food we needed. He had apparently heard from the boatmen how mosquitoes had been attacking us through the open mesh of our Yucatecan hammock and generously offered us a sturdy Brazilian substitute.

Our first days in Asindoopo, a village of several hundred people, included frequent periods of boredom and frustration. Complete outsiders, we were tolerated as amusing curiosities by some and as possible sources of tobacco or trinkets by others but also left alone for long periods. No one seemed to want to take responsibility to engage us. Despite our requests, no one agreed to teach us anything about canoeing or cooking or gardening. I spent most mornings fishing in the river and most afternoons with a group of young men playing soccer at the nearby Moravian mission, after which they drank beer and listened to calypsos and soul music on a battery-driven phonograph while pouring over a deck of Hollywood pinup playing cards. Sally, visiting village women, was frustrated by quick shifts from cordiality to hostility when she asked questions about harvesting rice, sewing clothes, or carving calabashes. Our handwritten notes from the period report such gems as "Bought one fish from a little boy for 2 fishhooks, but Sally dropped it in the river as she was cleaning it. No one saw." Children sometimes burst into tears at the mere sight of us—once, when a little boy cried at seeing me, one of the gaama's wives teased him, "Better get used to it. That's what you'll see when you go to the city." When young men or women took us to nighttime dances in nearby villages, our Saamaka clothes evoked loud hooting and clapping as people pulled and adjusted them to show us exactly how to wear them. Women must have corrected Sally's tying of her waistkerchief a hundred times. And late evening visitors to our house would encourage us to get into our hammock if we were tired, saying they would just stay and watch.

Slowly, however, we began to forge relationships. Abatili, a thirty-some "grandson" of the gaama who lived in Dangogo, the gaama's natal village a few kilometers upstream, and one of my new soccer-playing friends, took a special interest in us and began sending us small gifts—a bird he'd shot, a carved comb, two eggs. As one of the gaama's official boatmen, he took advantage of his access to an outboard motor to bring us to Dangogo several times. There we met his grandmother Nai, who gave us a bucketful of oranges on our first visit and with whom we participated in a large memorial feast in honor of her deceased mother a few days later.

Dangogo was divided between a hilly site, where Nai, her brother Captain Kala, Abatili, and their closest relatives lived, and a flatter part of the village across the river. Between them rushed a rock-strewn rapids, and on either shore, there were flat rocks where women cleaned fish, washed hammocks, did their dishes, and engaged in relaxed conversation. Just downstream, on either side, were numerous canoes, all intricately carved on their prows, sterns, and seats, tied up to stakes on the sandy banks. On both sides of the village, large clusters of houses, separated by lines of bushes, belonged to particular kin groups, each with its own ancestor shrine. Fruit trees—oranges, limes, breadnuts, mangos, guavas, coconuts, *palepu* palms brought back from Guyane—calabash and cotton trees and many varieties of medicinal plants dotted the village.

With the gaama's permission, Abatili took us by paddle for a four-day visit to Kpokasa, his sisters' garden camp on the upper Pikilio. Kpokasa was our first glimpse of a world dominated by natural beauty, plentiful crops, game, and fish—a world treasured by Saamakas as an escape from the tensions of village life. During our stay, we were included according to our abilities and stamina in hunting, cutting roofing materials, house-building, rice harvesting, and food preparation along with the close-knit family group including Abatili and his wife, as well as his three sisters. Naina was a premenopausal woman with striking facial cicatrizations who seemed somewhat skeptical about the two new visitors; Akobo, in her forties, expressed enthusiasm about teaching us Saamaka things; and their younger sister Beki was pretty much a full-time mother for her two sons—a ten-year-old, perpetually misbehaving, and a lively one-year-old still often tied onto her back with a length of cotton cloth—and an out-going four-year-old daughter named Moina.[1] Naina's thirty-year-old son Dosili was also there with his young wife and his daughter Seena, whose mother had died giving birth to her. In the evening, we all ate our meals together (women in one group, men in another, but within hearing dis-tance) and, when folktales were told around the smoldering fire, we even managed to contribute a crude version of Cinderella in our fast develop-ing but still rudimentary Saamakatongo.

Our notes from that stay record beautiful nights, our hammock slung in an open-sided shelter under the full moon with, off in the distance, mysterious, somewhat frightening sounds. I took the precaution of slip-ping my machete under our hammock, but they turned out to be agoutis calling out one night, howler monkeys the next. (We never met the jungle beasts we imagined roaring, though later—twice during our time in Saa-maka—jaguars came within a few feet of our house in Dangogo at night and were shot by Dosili.)

Upon our return from upriver, we talked to Abatili about the possi-bility of living in Dangogo instead of Asindoopo, which, because of its political role and relationship to the outside world, we thought would give us an atypical view of Saamaka life. He agreed to help us make this request to his grandfather.

When the gaama interrogated him about our stay in Kpokasa, Abatili

---

1 The dedication page of Sally's first book has a photo of Moina as a five-year-old and then, only ten years later, as a young mother—*Co-Wives and Calabashes* (Ann Arbor: University of Michigan Press, 1984).

described how many "hands" of rice Sally had cut, what kinds of birds I had shot, how we'd participated in rice hulling and housebuilding, and how we had eaten food from the same pot as his sisters. Apparently satisfied, Agbago said that the next day we would all go to Dangogo and pick out a site for our future house. He also announced that he was taking a government plane to the city in four days, so we would need to leave Saamaka at that point as well. He was clearly skeptical that we'd ever return, despite our having left a cash deposit with Abatili for the house that was to be built in Dangogo during our absence.

Throughout our stay, Gaama Agbago was generous, showering us with gifts almost daily—enamel basins filled with cocoa, tea, condensed milk, cookies, and sugar from the city and kilo upon kilo of rice from local gardens. He included us in the distribution of hunting kills—portions of tapir and wild boar that were routinely presented to him when any man on the Pikilio made a significant kill. One evening, he sent a wrap-skirt to Sally and a bottle of cold Parbo beer to me from his kerosene-powered refrigerator.

By the time our three-week stay upriver was over, we had participated in a variety of rituals—a funeral, a feast for the ancestors, the installation by the gaama of a new village captain, ceremonies for snake gods and forest spirits, and numerous rites at the ancestor shrine. We had seen a good deal of spirit possession. We had visited a number of neighboring villages, often being given a raucous welcome by dozens of women and children clapping and hooting all around us. We had attended secular and ritual dances, some lasting all night. We had gathered much preliminary information about gardening, learned the names and locations of the forty-three villages that had disappeared underneath Alcoa's lake, and begun to understand the rudiments of material culture, from calabash carving to house construction. More importantly, our initial use of Sranantongo had shifted into a workable command of Saamakatongo.

The final page of our joint notebook from that summer contains a list of what to bring when we returned: a 12-gauge shotgun, fishing gear, a machete, a small hammock for Sally to use in the menstrual hut, dozens of two-ell lengths of cloth, and a kerosene lantern, as well as a portable typewriter, paper, and carbon paper. Our visit to the Pikilio had lasted several days longer than that of the Herskovitses, who wrote *Rebel Destiny* on the basis of their trip, but we were well aware that we'd hardly scratched the surface.

On our way downstream, a couple of kilometers above the site of Mamadan, our canoe slid down through a final rapids to meet the flat brown waters of the artificial lake. Although the surrounding forest was still as green and vibrant as when we'd come upstream, the "Mother of All Rapids" had disappeared forever beneath Alcoa's rising waters.

Sally and I have written a book that describes in detail our first two years of fieldwork with Saamakas (1967–68), based very closely on the thousands of pages of notes that we kept, so there's no need for me to repeat that narrative here.[2] That experience remains a bedrock of our marriage and our joint identity.[3]

Our stay in the village of Dangogo was predicated on our obeying two taboos, spelled out publicly by gods and oracles and often reiterated by village officials: Sally's involved female pollution and mine involved Saamaka history. Sally would have to go to the menstrual hut upon the first sign of blood each month and obey a long list of related rules, and I would have to avoid ever discussing anything having to do with "First-Time" (i.e., seventeenth- and eighteenth-century) history. Nor were we to walk on the path across the river that led by the shrine to the Old-Time People (those who shed their blood for freedom) or travel upriver to the creek where the Saamakas' ancestors had lived during the wars of liberation. During our first two years living with Saamakas, anthropology was allowed, history strictly forbidden.

But Saamakas and their gods had not fully considered the extent to which their coveted early history, the stories of their formative years fighting the Whites, was embedded in their everyday lives and memories. The near daily prayers at the local ancestor shrine, at which I was welcome, called upon a myriad of First-Time people, whose feats and foibles were evoked; references to First-Time permeated the proverbs and sacred

---

2   Richard Price and Sally Price, *Saamaka Dreaming* (Durham, N.C.: Duke University Press, 2017).

3   And those years confirmed what I'd already learned in Martinique: as another anthropologist put it recently, "for anthropologists of Black people in the Americas, *field*work is never completely out of sight of another set of fields—cotton, cane, tobacco, rice" (Savannah Shange, *Progressive Dystopia: Abolition, Antiblackness, and Schooling in San Francisco* [Durham, N.C.: Duke University Press, 2019], 9).

With a pataka
I'd just caught.

songs that I recorded; sicknesses and other afflictions were mitigated by rituals intended to placate offended First-Time people who were causing them. In Saamaka, early history was never far from the surface; it was simply not something that I could ignore. By the time we left in 1968, I knew that someday I would return to work more directly on the secret history that I already understood lay at the heart of Saamaka identity.

Despite feeling enormously privileged to have lived in Dangogo and made Saamaka a precious part of our life, we often reflect that our time there deprived us of many of the defining experiences of our generation in the United States and the rest of the world.

I have only sporadic memories of my relationship with my draft board during the Vietnam War but well remember the fear of being called up to fight in a war I strongly opposed. The USA officially sent in ground combat troops for the first time only in 1965, when I was already a married student in my first year of graduate school, which gave me, in effect, a double deferment. But at some point, when we were in Saamaka, a letter reached me calling me up for the draft, with a date to report, somewhere in the Bronx. I had no choice but to fly back to the States, where I was able, with the help of a letter from Harvard administrators, to argue that my fieldwork in Suriname, supported by a grant from the National Institute of Mental Health, constituted "being enrolled full time with satisfactory progress," which satisfied current law. And by the time I'd finished my degree, we'd had our first child, which further exempted me. I do, however, remember long days in Saamaka mulling over whether we should go to Canada, as some of our friends were doing, or simply stay in Saamaka forever, to avoid Vietnam.

During 1968, the shortwave radio we had in the field was powerful enough to pick up weekly news broadcasts beamed from Paramaribo in the Saamaka language by Dyangalampu, Gaama Agbago's Western-educated son. So that was how we learned of the assassinations, two months apart, of Martin Luther King and Robert Kennedy—both times Sally heard the news while she was in the menstrual hut. When the Soviet Union invaded Czechoslovakia, we tried to share the radio news with friends in Dangogo—Dosili shook his head in amazement for several days at the idea of waking up one morning, say in Dangogo, and finding tanks positioned all around the village. But we heard nothing of the My Lai massacre nor the rise of the Black Panther Party nor the violence at the Democratic Convention in Chicago nor the uprisings that marked May 1968 in Paris nor Tommie Smith and John Carlos raising their fists at the Mexico Olympics until our return to the States. If 1960s Saamaka has become a sort of dreamscape for us, our memories of that remarkable period in the United States come largely through the filter of Saamaka-language bulletins on a scratchy little radio deep in the South American rainforest.

We have always felt that, in a real sense, we missed the sixties.

CHAPTER EIGHT

YALE
(1969–1974)

In late 1968, returning from Saamaka, we realized that few of my class-mates remained in Cambridge, and because I wanted to work with Sid, we decided to settle in New Haven.

We rented a place with an extra bedroom, a mile from campus, because a young man we knew well from Dangogo, Adiante Franszoon, fiercely motivated to get an education and some job training, had persuaded us to bring him to the United States.[1] We bought a TV with earphones so Adi could pick up some English from watching the NBA and other programs while we were working and, when we weren't, helped him learn the rudiments of reading and writing. I spent the year writing my dissertation, in the midst of the political turmoil that was roiling the nation, and I applied successfully for a position as lecturer (to be converted to assistant professor as soon as I finished my dissertation) in the Yale Department of Anthropology. The salary was $9,000. Sally indexed our Saamaka fieldnotes and worked on two jointly authored articles, one on Saamaka cicatrization and the other on patterns of naming.

Having asked Yale for my first year off, I obtained a post-doc in the Netherlands. When we arrived in Amsterdam, I began to work with Suriname specialists as well as in archives and museums while Sally, pregnant with our first child, typed my dissertation for presentation at Harvard, finishing the last page just days before the birth. At the University of Amsterdam, anthropologist Andre Köbben, who had conducted fieldwork among the Okanisi (another Maroon people in Suriname, then known as Djukas or Ndyukas), directed a year-long seminar where we got to know several young Suriname specialists who became lifelong friends (Bonno and Ineke Thoden van Velzen, Silvia de Groot, and Surinamers Charles

---

1 Adiante later became a prize-winning student in the New Haven Adult Education program, gaining his high school equivalency in record time, and went on to complete a degree at New Haven Community College. When I joined the faculty at Johns Hopkins in 1974, Adi moved to Baltimore, too, rooming with graduate students and earning a BA in economics at the University of Baltimore. For years now, he has been supporting himself with the woodcarving skills he learned in Saamaka, producing high-quality furniture with Saamaka-style carving and selling it on the web and, on Sundays, at Washington's Eastern Market. Google him!

With Sally and André Köbben, after the thesis defense of Silvia de Groot.

Wooding and Humphrey Lamur). Sally often brought our son Niko along to the seminar in a baby carrier.

We visited Humphrey, who was a demographer, and his family in the Bijlmermeer, the futuristic urban project that was already becoming a ghetto, getting a view of Suriname immigrant life in the motherland. But we spent much more time with our anthropologist colleagues Bonno and Ineke in their stately home in Bosch en Duin and with Silvia, who lived with her husband (a distinguished physicist) in an elegant apartment on the Prinsengracht. Altogether, it was a fruitful year, learning more about Suriname and Maroons and, of course, life in the Netherlands. (For example, not long after we moved into our apartment a man in suit and tie knocked on our [red, wooden] door: "Perhaps, as foreigners, you weren't aware," he said politely, "but the Residents' Association expects you to scrub down your front door at least once a week.")[2]

Before leaving Europe, we made a brief visit to Los Olivos, bringing nine-month-old Niko, to catch up with our old friends.

---

2   As a Surinamer, Adiante had a Dutch passport, so he spent the year in the Nether-lands and then returned to New Haven when we did.

In the fall of 1970, we returned to New Haven so I could begin teaching at Yale, where I was designated the department's Latin Americanist. (Yale had for the first time admitted women students the year before.) We moved into Sid and Jackie's townhouse next to Yale's gymnasium while they were away for the year in Paris. Our neighbors included Hal Conklin, a colleague whose work I admired. The beginning of the semester was difficult. I contracted hepatitis and was quarantined in a bedroom, so Sally met my first classes, but in early October she gave birth, three months early, to our daughter, Leah.[3] We were fortunate to have Adiante living with us, since he took care of Niko four hours a day; together the two of them became faithful fans of Sesame Street. Once I recovered, I lectured on Peoples of South America and gave a course called Anthropological Approaches to Religion, but I can't remember much else in the blur of waking up every two or three hours, when it was my turn, to feed a couple of thimblefuls of milk to Leah, who remained fragile throughout the year. (I also remember that my personal reading included Audre Lord, Maya Angelou, LeRoi Jones, Julius Lester, Piri Thomas, and Alice Walker and that I subscribed to *Jet* to try to keep up with Black opinion.) Sid and Jackie both wrote us occasional letters from Paris. (In one, Sid reported that when he met Lévi-Strauss, the maître told him he remembered us as "two China dolls.")

For our second year at Yale, we moved to a rented summer cottage on the beach in East Haven, with an unlimited sandbox for the kids. Department meetings were sometimes rather tense, as were those of the three-man committee on which I served that chose four female candidates—including Emily Ahern (later, Emily Martin) and Leith Mullings—to join the all-male department. Once, I was chastened by Cornelius Osgood, a New England patrician who had been one of the founders of the Yale department in 1937 and who sat next to me at the department meetings, for having hair that extended over my shirt collar and another time for the fabric of my slacks (double knit, which my mother thought was fashionable). After those meetings, I would come home, take a chunk of meat out of the freezer, walk out to the surf, and cast for sharks in Long Island Sound.

The class I created on Maroons throughout the hemisphere had ter-

---

3   She was born at two and a half pounds, before developing lungs. One nurse suggested that we should wait to give her a name, and doctors told us that if she lived she was likely to be mentally retarded. The obstetrician did not bill us for the birth.

rific students—Virginia Dominguez (later, president of the American Anthropological Association and advocate for internationalism), Drexel Woodson (later, Haitianist and professor at the University of Arizona), Gary McDonogh (later, prolific urbanist and professor at Bryn Mawr), Ira Lowenthal (devoted Haitianist who has spent his life there as a social and political development consultant/program manager), Ken Robinson (from Bermuda, later a Rhodes scholar and distinguished lawyer), and Scott Parris (later, economics editor at Cambridge University Press).[4] And I also cotaught, with Hal Scheffler, the class on anthropological theory that was required for entering graduate students. In addition, I cotaught a class on anthropology and ethics, considering issues of colonialism, imperialism, the Vietnam War, and anthropology's place in the world, with Gary Witherspoon, who was visiting Yale for the year. With his Navajo wife, Nellie, Gary was raising sheep on the farm they'd rented north of New Haven, and they often invited us for fry bread and other Navajo delicacies.

That year, we celebrated Christmas in New Haven at a party given by Dutch sociologist Harry Hoetink, who was a visiting professor, and his wife, Ligia, at which Harry disguised himself as Sinterklaas and turned the evening into a properly Dutch event with satirical poems and presents for each guest. Harry was one of the world's leading Caribbeanists and an immensely cultured scholar in the old European tradition. We immediately hit it off, and during the several years that we later spent in the Netherlands, we often passed Sunday afternoons together, eating Dutch *pannekoeken met appelstroop* in a restaurant by a canal and dreaming about moving some day to the Caribbean—Harry and Ligia thinking about her original home, the Dominican Republic, and the two of us about Martinique. We had countless detailed discussions about the financial planning and other logistics that would allow us to make those moves, though in the end, we were the only ones to actually put our plan into practice. Harry was as central a player in our life as anyone has ever been, both personally and intellectually, until his death in 2005.

During those first two years at Yale, often with Sally, I wrote a number of articles on specific aspects of Saamaka life—emigration patterns, cic-

---

4 That class led to my first book, *Maroon Societies: Rebel Slave Communities in the Americas*, ed. Richard Price (New York: Doubleday/Anchor, 1973) now in its third edition (Johns Hopkins University Press).

atrization, woodcarving, naming, and play languages.[5] But, in addition to teaching, I also devoted a good deal of my time to university—and national—politics. Arriving at Yale in the fall of 1970, the trial of Bobby Seale and the Black Panthers was underway down the street from my office. There was tear gas in the streets, protests and confrontation, and the university was heavily involved. At the same time, Yale—like Harvard—had decided to increase its admission of Black students exponentially, from a mere handful to something like 150 in one year. Two years later, I was asked to organize and run an orientation program for incoming minority students—Black, Puerto Rican, Asian, and American Indian—for several weeks during the summer so that they would feel "comfortable" in that elite setting when classes began. I helped choose distinguished faculty, including Sid, to offer classes in the mornings and organized special visits to Sterling Library and other campus high spots in the afternoons. We also hosted cookouts and softball games and I don't remember what else. Meanwhile, as another result of the civil rights movement, and under severe pressure from Black students, Yale (again, like Harvard) decided it was time to inaugurate a program in Afro-American Studies and to recruit Black faculty. Sid agreed to preside over the Afro-American Studies Program on the condition that a Black scholar be chosen after the first year to replace him.[6] I sat on the board that ran the program and learned a great deal from the experience.

Classes were heavily politicized. Bob (Robert Farris) Thompson, a White Texan whom Sid called "Sambo" behind his back, was teaching African art history—beating bongo drums in class and preaching transatlantic connections to enthusiastic crowds of (often Black) students—while he was writing *Flash of the Spirit*. Our families (two children in each) sometimes got together on weekends, and our debates about art and the transatlantic tradition, often confrontational, continued for years, with Bob's notes scribbled with a Trump-like Sharpie on manuscripts in progress.[7] I also recall long and interesting exchanges with

5   See www.richandsally.net for references and downloadable files.
6   Roy Simón Bryce-Laporte, a Black Panamanian sociologist who was the son of St. Lucian immigrants who'd come to build the canal, became director the next year.
7   Sally describes some of the intellectual differences we had with RFT in "Seaming Connections," in *Afro-Atlantic Dialogues: Anthropology in the Diaspora*, ed. Kevin A. Yelvington (Santa Fe, N. Mex.: SAR, 2006), 81–112—available for download from the left-hand column of www.richandsally.net.

Robbie (Armstead) Robinson, messianic organizer of the collection *Black Studies in the University*, in the supermarket where we both shopped.[8] I had memorable dinners with Arna Bontemps, who offered a window into the Harlem Renaissance and made me feel, for the first time, that I had met a true southern gentleman as he described his Nashville home and surroundings. Watching encounters on TV between Mohammed Ali and Howard Cosell with my "bursary student" (what was later called a "work-study student"), sophomore Drexel Woodson, who was the son of an independent roofer in Philadelphia, I got rich insights into Black perspectives; he helped assiduously in an ongoing bibliographic project that eventually resulted in a book.[9] That year, Drex often had a copy of Harold Cruse's *Crisis of the Negro Intellectual* under his arm. There was some hope that the world was changing, finally.

For my third year, I had a paid leave, and we moved into a converted eighteenth-century barn in the woods a few miles from Danbury, Connecticut, an hour or so from Yale. (My mother was scandalized that we were raising her grandchildren in what she saw as an old drafty building without proper heating.) With my strong support, and independently encouraged during a visit to the barn by Jackie Mintz and Emily Ahern, Sally began thinking about applying to graduate school once our children were in school. Meanwhile, we secured a grant for Adiante to transcribe the many hours of field recordings we had made, which allowed him to move into an international student center near Yale and continue his education.

The Watergate scandal was brewing that fall, and Sally several times took three-year-old Niko to Danbury, where they stood on a street corner and handed out McGovern flyers. The day Nixon was reelected, I told Sally, "I need to shoot something!" So we dropped Niko and Leah off with a neighbor, borrowed a shotgun from a farmer down the road, and trudged through the falling snowflakes across the woods until I saw a large deer, aimed, and brought my metaphor down. We dragged it home, and Sally—whose experiences in Saamaka included the preparation of

---

8 *Black Studies in the University: A Symposium*, ed. Armstead L. Robinson, Craig C. Foster, Donald H. Ogilvie, and the Black Student Alliance at Yale (New Haven, Conn.: Yale University Press, 1969).

9 Richard Price, *The Guiana Maroons: A Historical and Bibliographical Introduction* (Baltimore: Johns Hopkins University Press, 1976).

hunting kills—skinned it. I butchered it, and we gave part of it to the shotgun owner, who kept our share in his deep freeze. We enjoyed venison, cooked in the barn's giant fireplace, all winter.

One (abortive) project that year was for Sally and me to write a general ethnography of the Saamaka People. A fading typescript from that never-finished (and impossible to write) book, recently found and dated 1972, begins:

> Whether it's an indication of a certain alienation from our own society, a basic function of the ethnographic process or—as seems likely— some combination of the two, we have always felt life most viscerally while doing fieldwork, whether in Peru, Martinique, Andalusia, Chiapas or, most particularly, Saramaka. For us, in the field, there is a remarkable openness to reality, a switching on of all one's senses, and a fantastic investment in human relations. Life becomes delightfully refreshing.

Despite physical discomforts, periods of boredom, ailments ranging from funguses and dysentery to malaria and hepatitis, and periodic ridicule for being culturally clueless, we really loved fieldwork. Now, despite our temporary sylvan environment, we felt ourselves sinking deeper and deeper into academic life and increasingly distant from Saamaka.

Nonetheless, that year in the country gave me the freedom to write the long introduction to, and complete, *Maroon Societies* and to drive down to New Haven once a week to write, with Sid, a long paper for a spring symposium at Johns Hopkins on creole societies.[10] Resistance and civil rights were very much in the air and both *Maroon Societies* and the Mintz and Price essay sprang in large part from that ambience. The preface that Sid and I wrote for the 1992 edition explains in some detail its 1973 genesis and ends with the reminder that "the inescapable fact in the study of Afro-America is the humanity of the oppressed, and the inhumanity of the systems that oppressed them. That such oppression has by no means ended should be clear to everyone, as it is to us."[11] And that book ends with the comment that "New World it is, for those who

---

10 This was published, after an initial, smaller print-run publication in 1976, as Sidney W. Mintz and Richard Price, *The Birth of African-American Culture* (Boston: Beacon, 1992), and has been translated into various languages.

11 Mintz and Price, *Birth of African-American Culture*, xiv.

became its peoples remade it, and in the process, they remade themselves."[12] Indeed, the book's stress on the creativity of enslaved Africans and their descendants in the Americas brought charges from some Africanists that we were "Creation theorists" and that we—and particularly I—exaggerated the importance of creolization.[13]

If memory serves, it was soon after the Hopkins symposium that I was invited to return to Baltimore to give a lecture. I was shown around the Department of Social Relations, which had three anthropologists on its faculty, and soon after, I received an offer from the dean of Hopkins to join that department as an associate professor. I informed my department chair, after which Yale promoted me to associate professor and matched the salary offer from Hopkins. I wrote the dean to decline his offer.

Before long, the Hopkins dean phoned again and asked what it would take to attract me. Boldly—in the belief that I would soon get tenure at Yale in any case—I said that I didn't want to be an anthropologist in a department of social relations . . . that I would need an anthropology department of my own. "How many faculty would you need?" he asked. Making a quick calculation, I considered the faculty in the thirteen-member Yale department. First eliminating the three archaeologists and two physical anthropologists and then the couple of elderly colleagues who seemed no longer to be actively contributing, I came up with a (generous) figure of seven as the ideal number for a new department focused on social/cultural anthropology. We chatted some more, he thanked me for the conversation, and we hung up.

At the beginning of my fourth year at Yale, thinking toward a long-term future there, Sally and I bought a house for the first time in our ten-year marriage,[14] settling in Hamden, a good school district just outside of New Haven. That year, I cotaught a graduate seminar with Sid called History and Anthropology. When the Hopkins dean phoned again, it was to ask if I was now ready to go for the idea of forming a new department, offering

---

12 Mintz and Price, *Birth of African-American Culture*, 84.

13 For my own views on this controversy, which still rages in some circles, see Richard Price, "On the Miracle of Creolization," in Yelvington, *Afro-Atlantic Dialogues*, 113–45; and "Reflections from the Verandah," in Richard Price, *Travels with Tooy: History, Memory, and the African American Imagination* (Chicago: University of Chicago Press, 2008), 287–308.

14 Other than our 1960s palm-thatch house in Dangogo.

me a full professorship, the chairmanship, and seven faculty positions. I told Sid about my doubts, trying to imagine how I could attract faculty to a department that was just being invented and fearing I might drop out of sight once I wasn't in a prestigious department. He offered to speak with his friend Kingman Brewster, president of Yale. When he did, Brewster told him he couldn't promote me for a year or two—at thirty-three, I was too young—but assured him that he would when the time came. Sally and I felt torn but finally decided to take the risk and told Sid. Then, one evening, as I was trying to get up my courage to ask Sid (who'd been teaching at Yale for more than twenty years and whose wife, Jackie, was associate provost) if he would consider joining me in this venture, he phoned me and asked whether there was any way I might "be willing to bring an old man along." Before long, we took the train to Baltimore together to work out the details with the dean. We were also welcomed by Provost Harry Woolf (who later became director of the Institute for Advanced Study in Princeton) in his elegant, wood-paneled office; he uncorked an excellent bottle of Beaune from his wine cabinet as we chatted.

There was a backstory that I learned many decades later from a history of Hopkins written by Stuart W. Leslie, distinguished historian of science, who recently shared it with me.[15] He describes how historian Jack Greene, Hopkins's specialist in colonial America, had been trying since the late 1960s to launch a program in Atlantic history and culture but realized he needed a Department of Anthropology with a strong historical and Atlantic bent to make it a success. He raised a half-million-dollar grant from the Rockefeller Foundation and in 1973 brought three prominent anthropologists to campus—Sid Mintz from Yale, Bernard Cohn from Chicago, and David Maybury-Lewis from Harvard—to consult about the shape of such a program and to offer suggestions about recruiting a director. "Each consultant had his own list of prospective candidates for chair," Leslie wrote, "with almost no overlap except for Richard Price, a Harvard graduate who had recently joined Yale's department. Mintz, who knew him as a colleague, considered Price 'the very best of his age-group in Caribbean anthropology, and I would hate to see him leave [Yale].'"

---

15 Stuart Leslie's history of Johns Hopkins is scheduled to be published in 2026 for the university's 150th anniversary. The relevant chapter is titled "Jack Greene and the Program in Atlantic History and Culture."

In 1974, we headed south from New Haven to Baltimore (as did Adi), where I became a full professor and the founding chair of the Johns Hopkins Department of Anthropology. Sally explored school possibilities for Niko and Leah, including a memorable interview with the principal of the Baltimore public school for gifted and talented children, whose final word was, "Lady, I don't know what your children are like, but if I were you, I wouldn't send them to any Baltimore public school, including mine." Reluctantly, we gave up the idea of public education and enrolled them in a private school where many of their classmates were Hopkins faculty children. During those first weeks, I several times drove over to Morgan State, a couple of miles (and a couple of worlds) away to visit distinguished historian Benjamin Quarles, who had provided a laudatory blurb for *Maroon Societies* and whose work I admired. I thanked him, told him about the new department, and said I hoped we could collaborate. He said that Harvard had recently called, offering him a professorship, and that he had declined, saying, "I've been at Black colleges all my life. How come you never asked before? No thanks, I have my students to teach."

During those first weeks, I also attended a reception for new faculty at Evergreen House, the Gilded Age Baltimore mansion owned by the university. Stanley Fish, who had just arrived from Berkeley (and was the model for David Lodge's Morris Zapp in *Changing Places* and subsequent campus novels), engaged me in conversation. "I missed the sixties!" he remarked. It took me a minute to realize that he wasn't talking about the 1960s . . . he was boasting about his salary having jumped from the fifties to the seventies. (Yes, in 1974, seventy grand was a top salary—I think mine, as full professor and department chair, was $18,000.)

The dean gave me a couple of choices about where to house the nascent department, and I chose the attic of Maryland Hall, an expansive empty space with sloping ceilings and dormer windows that somehow felt like anthropology to me. I spent time with office-furniture catalogs, choosing everything from chairs and file cabinets to credenzas and a drafting table and buying two large hooks so I could hang a hammock from Suriname in my office. Hundreds of book jackets from the new library acquisitions that were arriving each month provided decoration for a graduate-student lounge, and one long room was outfitted for seminars.

Sid took 1974–75 on leave at the Institute for Advanced Study in Princeton, while I was organizing the department and Atlantic program, though of course we consulted frequently. China specialist Emily Ahern was also hired, with her first year on leave. And Bill Sturtevant, curator of North American Ethnology at the Smithsonian, joined the department as a permanent adjunct member. With our children now (at least partly) school-age, Sally was finally ready to begin coursework for a PhD, and Sid and Emily kindly offered her reading courses on their visits to the department.[1] By the fall of 1975, when our faculty and first full cohort of graduate students arrived, we had already begun to establish what anthropologist David Scott later called "the premier training institution for Caribbeanist anthropologists. . . . [It aimed] to shape a distinctive Caribbeanist anthropology . . . with a sharply critical self-consciousness of the historical peculiarities of the Caribbean as it existed in the anthropological imagination."[2] And as Michel-Rolph Trouillot concluded, the department "occupied a very special place in the history of anthropology in the second half of the century."[3]

It was a fraught and very exciting time in the discipline. As Scott has written,

> The 1970s . . . were years of considerable turmoil in U.S. anthropology. The radical social movements of the 1960s—counter-culture, Civil Rights, anti-war, Black Power, feminism—together created a context of disciplinary anxiety, self-interrogation, and reassessment. As Dell Hymes, for example, suggests in the Introduction to *Reinventing Anthropology* (1972), the edited volume that, more than any other, captures the mood of antagonism and critique characteristic of these U.S. years, it seemed unclear to many that, as presently understood and organized, anthropology could justifiably carry on.[4]

1 She had been accepted for PhD studies at Yale before we decided to move. And once at Hopkins, she won a three-year NSF fellowship for graduate study.

2 David Scott, "Modernity That Predated the Modern: Sidney Mintz's Caribbean," *History Workshop Journal* 58 (2004): 191–210, quote at p. 209; "The Futures of Michel-Rolph Trouillot: In Memoriam," *Small Axe* 39 (2012): vii–x.

3 Michel-Rolph Trouillot, "Big Migrations," *Lingua Franca*, November 1999, 11.

4 Scott, "Modernity That Predated the Modern," 203.

Not accidently, the department we created was heavily female—of the six professors, Sid and I were the only men. We should have known that this might raise some eyebrows. After all, when I was hired at Yale, the department had no female faculty, and it was only in my final year there that it suddenly added four (including Emily Ahern). At a dinner at the home of the chair of the Hopkins History Department in 1974, with a number of his colleagues in attendance, he asked me, with a twinkle in his eye, why anthropology seemed to appeal so much to women. And then, he quickly answered his own question: "It's a field made for dilettantes!" At which point, Willie Lee Rose, distinguished historian of the South and the only female professor in the large History Department, explained why she would never accept a married woman as a graduate student . . . because she might become pregnant (and presumably be unable to function as a professional). Those were the days!

Suddenly, with tenure and feeling more fully in charge, I discarded the collection of neckties I had so frequently been obliged to wear at Harvard and Yale and promised myself that I'd never wear one again—a pledge I have kept, with one exception: in 2006, when President Chirac invited Sally and her spouse to a dress-coded "garden party" at the Élysée Palace to celebrate the opening of the Quai Branly museum. (In a similar rejection of sartorial norms, I have not been to a professional barber since the summer of 1963 in Martinique, when Sally took over the scissors.)

In 1975, the department hired three other colleagues. Kathy Ryan, a Cornell PhD who specialized in Sri Lanka, taught innovative courses, mainly on religion, but after some six or seven years, unable to finish her first book, she became an elementary schoolteacher. Katherine Verdery, a Central Europe specialist who had just completed a PhD at Stanford, was a key member of the department and wrote important books about Romania; she eventually moved to Michigan and then to a distinguished professorship at CUNY. Beatriz Lavandera, a gifted sociolinguist trained at Penn, was kidnapped and severely tortured by the Argentine military when she paid a summer visit to her parents in the late 1970s; she eventually became a professor at the University of Buenos Aires (where she hosted Leah during the summer of 1989). Our work developing the curriculum and dealing with all the other complexities facing a new department transpired in a spirit of good-humored camaraderie. Sid and I turned out to be an unusually compatible team in our new roles, working together to produce a productive and intellectually lively community.

Sid and I both felt that it was important to recruit Black students. Our early PhDs included Jamaican-born Trevor Purcell (later, professor at USF), Charles (Val) Carnegie (later, professor at Bates), and Gertrude Fraser (later, professor at UVA), Haitian-born Michel-Rolph Trouillot (later, professor at Duke, Johns Hopkins, and Chicago), Colombian-born Lucia Forbes (later, professor at Mercy College), and U.S. African Americans Brackette Williams (later, professor at the University of Arizona, director of African American studies there, and a MacArthur fellow) and Don Billingsley (later, international education consultant who taught at Yale and Berkeley). Two of the early PhDs, Patricia Torres and Roberto Melville, were from Mexico and Guatemala, respectively, and became professors in Mexico. Some others, like Kenneth Bilby (later, author of important books about Jamaica and its musics) and Cuban-born Samuel Martinez (later, professor at UConn), went on to become distinguished Atlanticists, others in more far-flung fields—Rob Weller in Chinese studies; Alice Ingerson in forest conservation; Scott Guggenheim and Lanfranco Blanchetti at the World Bank; Clare Wolfowitz in Indonesian studies; Suzanne Siskel at the Ford Foundation and the Asia Foundation; Gary McDonogh in urban studies; Deborah Heath in science and technology studies; Dee Rubin and Debbie Caro in anthropological consulting; Ewa Hauser, director of the Center for Polish and Central European Studies at the University of Rochester; Becky Bateman at the University of British Columbia; Pam Feldman(-Savelsburg) at Carlton; Paul Sullivan, who wrote two extraordinary books about the Yucatan; Chuck Rutheiser in urban studies; Gene Galbraith in international finance; Ira Lowenthal, who has lived in Haiti as an activist anthropologist for a half-century; Jay Hamilton, who has long worked in youth and family services in Hawaii; and Laurie Benton, who in 2020 was appointed Biggs Professor of History at Yale. . . . And there were two very outstanding students who, as far as I know, never completed their dissertations: Scott Parris (who became economics editor at Cambridge University Press) and Lou Rojas (whose father was an ironworker on the Manhattan Project and sheriff of Los Alamos County, and who worked for some years on contracts with the

Navy, investigating ethnic, particularly Hispanic, discrimination, both on board ships and in recruiting).

What a privilege and inspiration to teach, and learn from, such students![5] We've remained friends with many of them to this day.

My colleagues and I had complete freedom to develop a curriculum, all of our students (about six per year) had full financial support, and there was a heady intellectual atmosphere. Unlike the far more hierarchical (and patriarchal) History Department, in which individual professors accepted students to study with them personally, we admitted students together, to study with us all. I taught the seminar in Atlantic History and Culture with Africanist historian David Cohen, who became a close friend—in fall 1975, we organized a mock-wedding of anthropology and history at David's home, with invitations to faculty and grad students in the Atlantic program—and I also chaired the department seminar that brought in speakers from around the world.[6]

Collectively, our faculty decided to keep our seventh position as a rotating slot to fill with a distinguished visitor each year. We hosted Sir

---

5   Some of these students came to us in unusual ways. In our first year at Hopkins, Sid and I spent three intense days at Brooklyn College, where we had been asked by the president to evaluate a troubled Anthropology Department. In the department office, we struck up a conversation with a senior from Haiti, Michel-Rolph Trouillot, who was working at the Xerox machine (and also driving a taxi to make ends meet). That's what led Rolph to join us for his PhD studies. The next year, Drexel Woodson—who, like Virginia Dominguez, had already taken so many undergraduate classes with Sid and me at Yale that we advised them to go to Chicago for graduate school—phoned to say there was a student at Chicago whom we simply had to consider for our program, and he gave me her number. We had already offered all our fellowship slots for the year, but after Brackette Williams submitted an excellent sample paper she'd written, rode the bus from Chicago, stayed with our family for the weekend, and met with Sid, Emily, and me, I pleaded with the dean for an extra fellowship, and that's how she joined our program.

6   The first outside speaker I invited was Cora Dubois. I had gotten to know her at Harvard, where she was only the second woman to achieve tenure in arts and sciences. Suffering from cancer, she spoke movingly about the challenges of being a woman in the male world of upper academe. (I knew that in 1950, she had declined an appointment to succeed Alfred Kroeber as head of the Anthropology Department at Berkeley rather than sign the California Loyalty Oath required of all faculty members.)

Edmund Leach (twice[7]), Fredrik Barth and Unni Wikan, Dell Hymes, Michael Silverstein, Stanley Tambiah, Maurice Bloch, Bill Skinner, and many others. We made it a tradition to take our visitors out to Bo Brooks or another B'more crab house, with students and faculty in tow—Fredrik and Sir Edmund, in particular, got a kick out of using their mallets to smash the shells on the brown-paper tablecloths. Except for Sid, the permanent faculty were all under thirty-five, and we often got together socially with the students, with Ira, Ken, Rolph, and Scott G. serving as DJs for the Caribbean music at dance parties in our home.

Saturdays were special. The Maryland Academy of Sciences was moving to a new building in Baltimore's Inner Harbor, and I had agreed that the department would accept their anthropological collections, for which they had no room and virtually no information on provenience. (Most of the several hundred objects had been collected by the crews of eighteenth- or nineteenth-century Baltimore clippers in their commercial voyages around the world and later donated to the Academy.) In a basement, we spread out five or six large tables, and Sally and I, Bill Sturtevant (one of the world's greatest authorities on material culture), and Edmund Leach (proud of having recently been named a trustee of the British Museum) would examine an object—a mask, a club, a basket . . . —and assign it tentatively to the table marked Africa or Australia or North America, before trying to decide whether it was, say, Navajo or Zuni. Watching the erudition of Sturt and Edmund in action, and argument, was such an education!

Sally and I had eleven very happy years at Hopkins, where I served three terms as department chair and she completed her coursework for the PhD. (Sally took courses with every member of the department, except me, and with every visitor, and wrote her dissertation under Sturtevant.) I also served as editor of Johns Hopkins University Press's Studies in Atlantic History and Culture, which published major books by Gordon Lewis, Barry Higman, Roger Abrahams, Roger Bastide, Harry Hoetink, Rolph Trouillot, Walter Rodney, Ray Kea, and many others. My office door was always open, and I spent a great deal of the time when I wasn't formally teaching chatting with students and colleagues and solving minor prob-

---

7   Arriving for his second visit in the wake of the ceremony in which he had been knighted by the queen, his public lecture analyzed the event in structuralist terms. It was titled "Once a Knight Is Quite Enough."

lems. After each three-year stint as chair, during which I devoted myself pretty much full time to the department and had little time for my own research and writing (except for summers), I was rewarded with a leave year, which we always took as far from Baltimore as possible.[8]

During those years, we had the joy of sharing life with Niko and Leah as they grew into their teens. We carpooled them to and from school (Sally taking more shifts than I); we spent breakfasts, dinners, evenings, and most weekends as a family; and both Niko and Leah developed friendships with some of our graduate students—Gene gave Niko his first harmonica and taught him to play, Gertrude and Leah traded thoughts on Maryse Condé's *Heremakhonon* (or was it Alice Walker's *The Third Life of Grange Copeland?*). Unlike the middle-class stereotype, adolescence led to greater closeness as a family, not less. We watched the gradual gentrification of Baltimore, the arrival (which we deplored) of the glossy Inner Harbor. But John Waters was in his heyday too—we enjoyed his premieres at the Charles Theatre and chats with Edith Massey at her Fells Point store. Greektown served hearty dinners, Bo Brooks great crabs. We also belonged to a small co-op of Hopkins families who took turns buying fruit and vegetables at the downtown wholesale market every Saturday. Baltimore, despite its stark and disturbing racial segregation, was a pretty good place for privileged White people like us to live.

Our carpool partners included Ray Kea, an Africanist colleague and friend in the History Department, and his Danish wife, Inge. Ray was denied tenure—quite unjustly, in my view—and eventually moved to UC Riverside, where he invited Sally and me for a week of lectures some thirty years later. That's where we made the acquaintance of economist Deirdre McCloskey, who, as Donald McCloskey just a few years earlier, had written books that were unusually sensitive to cultural concerns; Scott Parris, economics editor at Cambridge University Press, had sent me two of them with his enthusiastic recommendation. Soon after Deirdre had written *Crossing: A Memoir* (1999), she and I were each invited,

---

8   My colleagues thanked me at the end of each of my stints as chair, once with a stunning Chagall lithograph of Adam and Eve that now hangs in our home in Florida. Our first years in Baltimore did see the publication of my long-delayed *Saramaka Social Structure* (essentially, my 1970 dissertation), which Sid had counseled me to publish, as a gesture of solidarity, in the Caribbean—it finally came out in 1975 from the Institute of Caribbean Studies, University of Puerto Rico; *The Guiana Maroons*, begun when we were at Yale, was also published during this period (1976).

along with a filmmaker, to speak at the opening plenary of the annual meeting of the American Historical Association in Boston. There was an audience of thousands, and it was clear that almost everyone had come to see Deirdre in her flamboyant Bella Abzug–style hat, clutching her tiny dog to her breast.

I hadn't been back to Saamaka since the end of 1968, except for several weeks in the summer of 1974, when I helped recent Yale graduate Virginia Dominguez explore a possible field site in Suriname. But in 1975, Sally and I decided to go for a longer visit, leaving Niko and Leah with my parents. (They were living in Croton-on-Hudson since my father had left his bustling three-chair practice on Union Square to become a "country" dentist, whom everyone called Doc, in this exurb.) On the way down to Suriname that year, we visited Emilien and Merlande in Petite Anse.

A little background. In 1972, Merlande, not normally one to put pen to paper, had written us a letter describing the tragic accident two years earlier that put an end to Emilien's career as a fisherman. Far from the sight of land, he'd slipped while hauling a fighting swordfish over the gunwale of *Notre Dame* and fell backward, breaking his spine. Emilien, she wrote, had been transported to Brittany for treatment, and they feared he would suffer permanent paralysis. Two years and many operations later, he'd returned, with a lifetime disability pension and an interdiction against ever again going to sea.

Around the same time and unbeknownst to us, people in Petite Anse heard a radio report saying that an American named Richard—whom they assumed to be me—had been captured and killed in Vietnam, where the war was raging. They apparently mourned my death, as Sally and I lamented Emilien's fate. For several years, preoccupied with other matters (young children, changing jobs), and somehow afraid to face Emilien, we avoided visiting. And then in 1975, unannounced, we pulled a rental car up to Le Rayon, the little café by the shore that they'd built after Emilien could no longer fish. Who was more shocked and happier? Emilien—who looked as good as ever—and Merlande, sitting outside their café, both of whom thought I was dead? Or the two of us? They sent their adolescent son to his grandmother's house, and we slept in his bed, not far from their own, listening to the waves lap the shore. We stayed for a few joyous days.

On our way back to Baltimore, after that summer in Saamaka, we made a brief stop in Georgetown, Guyana. Although I was feverish with malaria, we spent a couple of interesting days with Guyanese linguist John Rickford, who was teaching at the university and finishing his doctoral research. The local political situation was sufficiently fraught under Forbes Burnham's rule that John took us out for conversations on the windblown seawall, where we invited him to come to Hopkins as visiting assistant professor in 1977, his first U.S. post. (He later became a distinguished professor at Stanford.)

My 1974 and 1975 trips to Saamaka had been devoted to figuring out how to persuade Saamakas to lift their official prohibition so I could explore their early history in depth. These visits encouraged me enough to apply to the National Science Foundation for a grant to fund six months of fieldwork during the summers of 1976 and 1978. In a sense, the older Saamakas we knew best, including Gaama Agbago, had always expected that someday I would work on First-Time—how else could I become a man of knowledge? Nevertheless, they clearly wanted me to do it only when I was really ready—when *they* thought I was ready—and the time finally seemed right.

By our returns to Suriname in 1975, 1976, and 1978, the pace of change in Upper River Saamaka villages had accelerated. Government officials or tourists dropped in and out of once-isolated villages almost monthly, film crews occasionally came and went, Saamaka men often wore long pants in the villages, people were listening to radios, and many—both men and women—were spending time on the coast. We, too, had changed: I was a professor rather than a student and seen by both Saamakas and other Surinamers, who'd been sent copies of my books, as an authority on Saamaka life. And Sally, much to everyone's approval, was no longer childless.

In 1974, when I was in Saamaka briefly, and in 1975, when we were there together, we lived in our house in Dangogo. But during the long summers of 1976 (when our children accompanied us) and 1978, we moved to Asindoopo, the gaama's village, taking advantage of the screened-in wooden house and outhouse left to us by two women from the Summer Institute of Linguistics who were back in the States for a visit. The change was convenient both for our ethnographic projects and, in 1976, for the practicalities of having our children in the field. We were no longer marked as lamentably childless, and people in Asindoopo, both adults and children, received Niko, age six, and Leah, age five, with real warmth, helping them to adopt Saamaka clothing (a little breechcloth for him, a beaded waist tie for her) and inviting them to join in village activities with other children. Niko's agemates in Asindoopo soon had him shooting lizards with a slingshot and spouting words and phrases in Saamaka. Leah had a less happy experience, due to a severe reaction to her pretrip smallpox vaccination, which led to life-threatening dehydration. The mission clinic at nearby Dyuumu was momentarily out of intravenous solution, but they came to our rescue, radioing the capital for a two-seater plane that flew her, with Sally, to the Moravian hospital in Paramaribo for intravenous hydration. When she was strong enough to travel, I flew back with her to New York (while Sally and Niko returned to Saamaka), and she spent the rest of the summer with my parents. I returned to Suriname and hitched a ride on the Missionary Aviation Fellowship Cessna that was ferrying a couple of toilets from Paramaribo to Dyuumu, lying to the pilot, just before he'd said the pretakeoff prayer, that I had no alcohol or tobacco in my bags. (We got news not long after that he had died when his plane went down somewhere over Suriname's rainforest.)

In 1978, Sally and I returned to Saamaka. Living in Asindoopo was particularly useful for my work on First-Time, much of which was with middle-aged Peleiki and the elderly Tebini, who was considered the Saamakas' greatest living historian. With the approval of Gaama Agbago, Captain Kala, and the other Matyau clan elders who had become, in a sense, our spiritual guardians, I was now working with men who had known me, at least by reputation, a decade earlier. Fortunately, there was a growing realization by some elders that if knowledge of First-Time (at least the nonritual parts of it) wasn't gathered together and written down soon, it might well be lost forever.

For these Saamaka men, First-Time—the era of the Old-Time People—differed most sharply from the recent past in its overwhelming inherent power. Stretching roughly up to 1800, First-Time was not more "mythologized" or less accurately recalled than the more recent past, but knowledge of First-Time was singularly circumscribed, restricted, and guarded. It formed the fountainhead of collective identity; it contained the true root of what it meant to be Saamaka.

Once Ameikan, a man in his seventies, remarked in my presence: "First-Time kills people. That's why it should never be taught to youths.

. . . That's why, when you pour a libation at the ancestor shrine, you must be careful about speaking in proverbs [because you may not be aware of all their hidden implications]. There are certain [people's] names that, if you call them, you're dead right on the spot! There are names that can't be uttered twice in the course of a whole year! It is with such things that we were raised."

The imminent danger of First-Time resided, in part, in its specialized uses in social action. The recent past (roughly the last hundred years) that intruded on everyday life tended to affect only individuals, domestic groups, and, occasionally, whole village units. First-Time, though called upon less frequently, related to larger and older collectivities, most often the "clans" that traced their ancestry matrilineally back to an original group of rebel slaves. First-Time most often came alive in the restricted but highly charged arena of interclan politics. It was the migratory movements of the First-Time people that established land rights for posterity; it was the details of how they held political office that provided the model on which modern succession was based; and it was the particular alliances and rivalries among the wartime clans that shaped the quality of their descendants' interaction in the present. Any dispute between clans—whether over land, political office, or ritual possessions—immediately brought knowledge of First-Time to the fore. In these settings, when corporate property and prestige were at stake, such knowledge became highly perspectival; the point of knowing about a First-Time event was to be able to use it in support of one's clan. To cite a simple but exemplary case: the members of the Matyau clan described with meticulous detail the way that Gunguukusu, the Watambii clan ancestor, greeted their own man Ayako on the occasion of their first postrebellion reunion in the forest. Since Saamaka etiquette requires the "guest," not the "host," to extend the first greeting, this historical fragment effectively preserved Matyau precedence in the forest (vis-à-vis Watambiis), as well as the entitlements to land thus entailed.

First-Time also provided the "charter" for the most powerful ritual possessions of each clan, many of which dated back to that formative period. It was to these powers, and the First-Time ancestors associated with them, that knowledgeable Saamakas appealed in times of real crisis. Learning the details of their history provided an unmatched degree of personal security, for one need never be alone thereafter: the Old-Time

People and their enormous powers would be standing by one's side. Such specialized knowledge of the past, then, meant power in a very direct sense; it permitted some measure of control over the vagaries of the unpredictable present.

Saamaka collective identity is predicated on a single opposition: freedom versus slavery. The central role of First-Time in Saamaka life is ideological; preservation of its knowledge is their way of saying "never again." As I overheard one man reminding another, "If we forget the deeds of our ancestors, how can we hope to avoid being returned to Whitefolks' slavery?" Or, in the memorable words of Peleiki—a Matyau clan man then being groomed as a possible successor to Gaama Agbago—speaking to me, "This is the one thing Maroons really believe. It's stronger than anything else. . . . This is the greatest fear of all Maroons: that those times [slavery and the struggle for freedom] shall come again." The fear of group betrayal, forged in slavery and the decades of war, remained the cornerstone of the Saamaka moral system.

Meanwhile, Sally's dissertation research on art and gender followed seamlessly on her 1960s fieldwork, since women in Asindoopo were involved in the same range of social and artistic activities as those she'd worked with in Dangogo. She immersed herself in the world of women in this polygynous and strongly patriarchal society, where men were the uncontested authorities in everything from politics to religious life, focusing particularly on women's contributions to the visual and performing arts (recruiting Niko to help labeling calabash designs during the 1976 trip).

Sometimes there were serendipitous detours in Sally's conversations about art. A middle-aged woman we'd known in Dangogo, Akundumini, once mentioned to her that we weren't the first White people to come to Saamaka; a White man had come with his wife way back when she was barely an adolescent: "We called him Afiika Fandya [African Fringe]," she said. And her elderly mother filled in more details: "They had a woman who cooked for them named Coba. Their Creole man from the city made trouble with them and Gaama Dyankuso told them they had to leave." We realized from the details they provided that they were talking about Melville Herskovits, who reported in *Rebel Destiny* that Saamakas called him Ame'ika Fandya (American Fringe). We can only imagine that the shift to *African* Fringe was because he pressed Saamakas so hard about finding "Africanisms" among them. In any case, it was a revelation when they told us how the Herskovitses had been politely but firmly thrown out of Saamaka by the gaama, something we were able to confirm decades later when we read their previously private diaries.[9]

By the end of the 1976–77 school year, our third at Hopkins, during which I taught a high-powered seminar about Saamaka history with a terrific group of graduate students, I was more than ready for a break from departmental duties, and in 1978, we took off for a leave year at the Netherlands Institute for Advanced Study in Wassenaar, enrolling Niko and Leah in Dutch schools. Niko thrived in the new environment, soon speaking Dutch almost like a native. Leah, less taken with the change, often retreated into books, reading everything from the *Odyssey* and *Iliad* to Roald Dahl stories and Alex Haley's *Roots*, an early foreshadowing of her place in the world of literary criticism.

We enjoyed the Wassenaar ambience—family bike riding on the weekends to the nearby seaside dunes dotted with the ruins of German World War II concrete blockhouses (anticipating a D-Day that never happened), biking through tulip fields to the north or to Scheveningen beach to the south, as well as my brief, leafy ride to the institute each morning. After a few lunches with Dutch colleagues at the institute, I found the daily conversation embarrassing—complaints about immigrant Surinamers flooding the schools and concerns about their own daughters' safety amongst such people—so I began bringing sandwiches to eat in my office. And I took full advantage of being within biking distance of the Algemeen Rijksarchief in the Hague, with a seemingly infinite amount of Saamaka history hidden in its bowels.

---

9 The Herskovitses' books never mention their expulsion. Their diaries also reveal that they were accompanied on their trip to the gaama's village by a cook from the city ("Coba," Jacoba Abensitt, whom Frances described as "a literate young woman"), a "professional bush guide"/manservant (Marcus J. Schloss), and Alexander M. W. Wolff, the manager of the Suriname Balata Company warehouse, who had often dealt with the gaama on business matters. All members of this colonial entourage spoke English and all were effectively disappeared from the Herskovitses' published writings, leaving the false impression that the couple was alone "among the Bush Negroes of Dutch Guiana" and working in the Saamaka language. See Richard Price and Sally Price, *The Root of Roots: Or, How Afro-American Anthropology Got Its Start* (Chicago: Prickly Paradigm Press, 2003), available for download at www.richandsally.net.

Leah in Holland, absorbed in a book.

Meanwhile, Sally and I had agreed to serve as curators for a major exhibition of Suriname Maroon art, and Sally began drafting the book that would accompany it as it traveled from Los Angeles (UCLA's Fowler Museum) to Dallas (the museum of fine arts) to Baltimore (the Walters Art Gallery), and finally New York (the American Museum of Natural History).[10] During school vacations, we took family vacations in Paris, which we'd grown to love during our first year of marriage.[11]

At the archives in the Hague, I worked much as a traditional historian in copying out materials written by colonial administrators or soldiers who had led expeditions against the Saamakas, court proceedings, and

---

10 Sally Price and Richard Price, *Afro-American Arts from the Surinam Rain Forest* (Berkeley: University of California Press, 1980). The National Endowment for the Humanities' subsidy allowed the book, with its full-color illustrations, to sell for only eight dollars, which resulted in sales of many thousands of copies.

11 I have reason to believe that Sid deliberately waited till I was on leave that year to get Lévi-Strauss, who was flown over on the Concorde, invited to receive a much-mediatized honorary degree at Hopkins in February.

other eighteenth-century documents. I felt determined to juxtapose the written history I was discovering with the oral history I was learning from Saamakas. Feverishly, even in my dreams, I tried to imagine what Saamaka story about heroic ancestors matched with which events described by Dutch soldiers fighting against the rebels. And I found plenty.

Soon, I was composing a book but before long decided it was really two, the first to cover Saamaka history from its beginnings to the 1762 peace treaty with the Whites, the second to be devoted to the second half of the eighteenth century, as free Saamakas developed their society and culture. Excited, at last, to be working on First-Time—the knowledge most dear and ideologically central to my Saamaka hosts—I was enthusiastic about becoming what I began to call an ethnographic historian.

At that time, when I was beginning to write about Saamaka history, many—if not most—traditional Western historians (including colleagues in my own university) vehemently denied that oral history recounting events of the seventeenth or eighteenth centuries could be considered anything other than "myth" or "legend." Human memory, they argued, was simply too fallible.[12] I am proud that, along with historians of Africa and Oceania working during the same period, I was able to demonstrate in a series of books that these Western historians had grossly underestimated the capacity of humans in nonliterate societies around the world to transmit knowledge over the centuries and to help open up oral history to the same degree of historiographical attention that had traditionally been given to the written word.[13]

---

12 Such views persist among intellectuals today. "Let us imagine, in writing, how a world without writing might function. . . . What would it mean if nothing were written, if the pronouncement 'I give you my word' were sufficient as a contract, and if laws and liabilities were not codified as letters and words on a page? All language would be spoken text. . . . The great preserved works of our culture would have been doomed to extinction. . . . [Written language] is the *alpha* and *omega*, the *a* to *z* of what we learn from predecessors" (Delbanco, *Why Writing Matters*, 251–52).

13 See, for example, David William Cohen, *Womunafu's Bunafu: A Study of Authority in a Nineteenth-Century African Community* (Princeton, N.J.: Princeton University Press, 1977); Greg Dening, *Islands and Beaches. Discourse on a Silent Land: Marquesas 1774–1880* (Honolulu: University of Hawaii Press, 1980); R. Rosaldo, *Ilongot Headhunting.*

During fieldwork in the summer of 1978, we felt more fully welcome than ever before. Even Captain Kala, who had been something of an adversary in the 1960s, was happy about our return, greeting us with an esoteric proverb.[14]

> *Aso pipi mi sa dyoubi. Aso pipi mi sa dyoubi.* When you first came to Saamaka, people would say, "Abatili has brought a person to me, Dangasi [another of Kala's names], and all of Saamaka will be destroyed." How come they said that? Saamaka territory has a *tyina* [taboo] against Whitefolks. Well, they've brought him to the village they call Dangogo Hafupasi, a true slavery-time village. Outsiders do not come here! People said Abatili and I took him, brought him, put him here to kill every single living Saamaka. Then, on a day otherwise like any other, you [RP] come back, bearing all sorts of gifts for everyone. *Aso pipi mi sa dyoubi.* [He then explains the proverb:] Rice granary says that. When it's dry season and you begin to make a garden, you risk death at every turn. When you clear the underbrush, your machete can kill you, a snake can bite you, a tarantula can bite you; every sort of thing can kill you when you're clearing the underbrush! Then when you go to fell a tree, well, every single tree can kill you. The axe in your very hand can kill you. You do all those things, take all those risks, right through the time when you burn the field. And then the rice grows. You harvest it until you're all finished; you load it up in your granary. Until the granary is chock full! Then the granary says its praise name for you. *Aso pipi mi sa dyoubi.* Because the way you loaded up the granary until it was absolutely full, you can't possibly eat it all by yourself. When you cook it and eat it, until you can't eat more, you toss the leftovers to the fish. Let's say people come to visit you from another village. Well, you cook them some of it, even though they didn't do the work. You throw some to the chickens for them to eat. There are rats in the granary, tree squirrels too. They all eat it. It's available for everyone. *Aso pipi mi sa dyoubi.* The American came out from his country and arrived in Saamaka. People said Abatili and I put him here to destroy the world. But today: *aso pipi mi sa dyoubi.* They're all reaping the benefits. First-Time language! I, Dangasi, say so!

By this time, I possessed a considerable reputation as a historian among knowledgeable Saamakas. And an exchange of information became, for

---

14 I had a portable cassette recorder over my shoulder and switched it on as the captain greeted me. Kala later gave me permission to publish it.

some old men, the principal motive for "sitting down" with me. Not only did I know original Whitefolks' views on First-Time events, but I was fast building up a storehouse of Saamaka knowledge about the period that in its breadth exceeded the knowledge of any single Saamaka. Indeed, at a 1978 formal gathering in the gaama's reception hall, I was asked on behalf of the Matyau clan to write such a book for them; flattering me with a rhetorical declaration that I was now a Matyau, they asked me formally to be their chronicler.

It was this kind of official approval, which contrasted so strikingly with the explicit prohibitions of the 1960s on discussing First-Time at all, that permitted me to proceed. Much of my work with Saamaka historians that summer consisted of lengthy evening conversations, as I scribbled in notebooks and kept a tape recorder rolling. I also made a number of trips, usually accompanied by Abatili and sometimes by Sally, to villages upstream and down, to expand my First-Time knowledge with elders from other clans. Nonetheless, the gaama's permission did not really make any easier the act of eliciting First-Time knowledge from wary elders, as people very much kept their own counsel about how much, and exactly what, they wished to share with me. All of my discussions with Saamakas about First-Time must be firmly situated in their basic ideological context: "First-Time kills," "Never tell another more than half of what you know," and "Those times [the days of war, the days of Whitefolks' slavery] shall come again." Some of the strongest fears about divulging information were perspectival: the gaama was at first reluctant to have me traveling the river to speak with other clans about First-Time, as it might "confuse" Matyau priorities; and members of other clans were often afraid I would carry back what they might tell me to Matyaus or to other clans. The methods of work imposed by practical considerations ruled out most traditional modes of historical transmission; I could not, like a Saamaka, simply wait a lifetime and piece together what I had seen and heard. I had to seek people out, explain myself, and actively persuade them to share information, with little to offer except my own historical knowledge, compensation for their time (in money or, if they preferred, in gifts), and the excitement of joint discoveries—for some the most important inducement of all. I had to keep telling myself, as the Saamaka hunting proverb says, that "if you don't stir up a hole, you won't find out what's inside"; but I could never afford to forget its cautionary counterpart: "If you shake a dry tree, you'd better watch out for your head."

Sally's 1970s fieldwork produced some of the meat of the book that accompanied our traveling exhibition "Afro-American Arts from the Suriname Rain Forest" and also led to her book on art, gender, and polygyny.[15] In preparation for the exhibition, we devoted part of our time in Saamaka to inventorying (and in some cases collecting) Saamaka textiles—a form of Saamaka art that had been badly neglected by Westerners, who focused their interest in art almost exclusively on men's woodcarving. When we told Gaama Agbago about the upcoming event, he was delighted and offered to show us the textiles that women had given him over the years.

Together, we dragged seven massive trunks from his house to a shady spot where, with the help of his assistant Takite (Taki-tay), we could examine their contents. For us, the exercise promised to open up an ethnographic gold mine, rich in materials that would help flesh out Saamaka art history. For Agbago, it was to be an emotional journey into his personal past.

Takite helped open each carefully folded rectangle of cloth while Sally scribbled in her notebook, I manned the camera, and Agbago reminisced. This embroidered kerchief had been sewn by his mother, that cape was made by a late wife from Santigoon, that other was from his inauguration as gaama. For many of the cloths, however, these details weren't possible for him to retrieve. As with other men who'd opened their trunks for us, he'd lost track of specific origins for much of his collection, and the individual gifts had merged, weaving a generalized testimony to a lifetime of relationships.

When Agbago came to one small, round packet, his face lit up with a gentle smile. Turning his back to us, he tenderly undid the knot in the kerchief and set aside the small pieces of cloth it held, one by one, counting softly in a language he'd last heard in Guyane in the early years of the century. *Quinze!* Fifteen adolescent aprons that had been cut from their waist ties with his knife and slipped into his hunting sack. Fifteen young girls who'd become women in his hammock. He recounted the aprons to make sure he'd got the number right. "*Dee ogi di mi du*," he remarked with a grin: "My little mischiefs."

Many of those youthful lovers' faces were now forgotten, but Apumba

---

15 S. Price, *Co-Wives and Calabashes*, 1984 winner of the Alice and Edith Hamilton Prize in Women's Studies.

had been with him for more than seventy years. He had spoken for her even before her breasts were full, and when she died earlier in 1978, she had been the senior of his three wives, withered and frail, but still sharp-tongued and very much in charge.

When we told him about the exhibition that would introduce Americans to the arts of Saamakas, he announced that it would be only fitting for him, as gaama, to make a contribution and asked us to select four pieces to display. After a brief consultation, we put aside three patchwork capes sewn by Peepina, his wife from Totikampu who died in 1967 and with whom he'd had many children, plus a beautifully embroidered cape with appliquéd borders. Agbago had no problem giving up the first three, since Peepina had produced countless patchwork capes for him, but the fourth was special. It was sewn, he thought, by either his mother or, more likely, Apumba. The embroidered cape would embellish his coffin someday, so we were free to photograph it, but we would need to select an alternative for the exhibit.[16]

In the fall of 1978, returning to Hopkins from our year in Holland and our summer of fieldwork in Suriname, I continued chairing the department, spending my time with students and colleagues, and taking little time out for my own research and writing. I also presided over the forced move, decided by the university administration, from the department's home in its lovely old attic to a newer, modern building, with smaller and less idiosyncratic offices. But quite unexpectedly that fall, I got involved in a new project that would occupy me, and eventually Sally, for more than ten years.

---

16 Color images of these cloths, including the one we didn't take, are included in Sally Price and Richard Price, *Les Arts des Marrons* (La Roque d'Anthéron: Vents d'Ailleurs, 2005), 54, 90–91. The four cloths, all by Peepina, are now in the Richard and Sally Price Collection of the Schomburg Center in New York.

CHAPTER TEN

STUDYING TO BE SINGULAR
(1978–1992)

One October day in 1978, I got a phone call from Stuart Schwartz, a friend and leading historian of Brazil. Excitedly, he told me to hustle out to Minneapolis as soon as I could because he'd discovered a manuscript he knew would blow my mind. Already scheduled to attend the annual meeting of the American Anthropological Association in Los Angeles, I booked my flight with a two-day stopover in Minneapolis on the way home. Having breakfast in the convention hotel on Sunday, just before the flight to Minneapolis, I remember reading the screaming headlines in the *New York Times*. Jonestown had imploded. Jim Jones and nearly one thousand of his followers in Guyana were dead.

Stuart met me on a snowy Minnesota evening (I was woefully under-dressed in a thin raincoat), and the next day, he offered me a winter coat and brought me to the cozy James Ford Bell Library of rare books. There he showed me a recent acquisition from a Danish bookseller: a two-volume, 865-page manuscript copy of John Gabriel Stedman's *Narrative of a Five Years Expedition against the Revolted Negroes of Surinam*. It was dated 1790. The *Narrative*—the most famous book ever written about Suriname, illustrated with iconic engravings by William Blake, Francesco Bartolozzi, and others—had been published in London in 1796 and quickly translated into a half dozen languages while becoming one of the best-known works of antislavery campaigns. In the course of a few hours, I was able to determine that this was the original manuscript that Stedman had submitted to his publisher and had begun to realize that it differed substantially from all published versions. Thanking Stuart, who was as excited as I was, I flew back to Baltimore, facing a conundrum: Why was the published text—the one that everyone had always assumed Stedman had written—so different from this handwritten copy? What had happened between 1790, the date marked at the end of the manuscript in the Minnesota library, and the 1796 publication date of the first edition? To answer these questions, I began an adventure in literary sleuthing that was to take me to Germany, Holland, England, and Suriname, before returning to Minneapolis.

I had already read Stedman's published *Narrative* several times; Sally's father had given us a first edition as a gift in 1967. I considered it to be the most detailed outsider's description ever written of life in an eighteenth-century slave plantation society. Stedman's ongoing and intimate relations with members of all social classes, from enslaved Africans and Maroons to the governor of the colony, gave him special opportunities to describe the full panorama of Suriname life. And as a self-taught artist, he had made hundreds of watercolors and sketches on the spot, which had served as models for the famous engravings.

On return from Minneapolis, the most basic job was to produce a typescript of the handwritten text. I hired Scott Parris, one of our Hopkins graduate students, to do the job—he helped, also, in identifying differences with the published version. Another student, Rebecca Bateman, worked long hours in the library identifying Stedman's many literary allusions—a very laborious task that would have been a thousand times easier in the Internet era.

Through a colleague in literature, I had learned with excitement that an eccentric elderly descendant of Stedman lived in what was described to me as "a castle on the Rhine" and that she kept there a great deal of materials on his life and work. During the summer of 1980, when our family was in the Netherlands as guests of Harry and Ligia Hoetink, I was finally able to follow up. Taking the train to Koblenz am Rhein and then a taxi to Haus Besselich—a medieval abbey, part of which had been turned into a family archive—I met Hilda Von Barton-Stedman. Then ninety-two years old, she greeted me in overalls and mud-covered boots, explaining that she'd been working in her vineyards on the beautiful slope above the river. (What a view!—I could almost imagine the Rhinemaidens cavorting down below.) The impressive structure, she told me in French (or was it English?), had been bought in 1834 by her grandfather, himself the grandson of John Gabriel's brother. After changing her clothes, she offered me a glass of wine from her own vineyard, . . . and then another, and then a third . . . before she ushered me into her magnificent library, where an impressive portrait of John Gabriel Stedman, her father's father's father's brother, looked down from the wall.

Hilda, who frequently asked me, "Ein Glas Schnaps, Professor?" handing me one without waiting for a response (and joining me in downing one), made clear that she felt a special, almost spiritual affinity to the man she called John Gabriel. He had once written that "in all places I have been beloved by the inhabitants when known but at first cald mad in Scotland, mased [confused] in England, fou [crazy] by the namurois [Belgians], gek or dol [crazy or mad] by the Duch, and law [Sranan for insane] by the negros in Surinam, owing intirely to my studying to be singular in as much as can be so."[1]

And Hilda seemed to take this as her own motto as well. After showing me countless books relating to her hero and lamenting that occupying Allied troops had torn out some of their pages during World War II to use as toilet paper, she gave me a precious lead.

Not long after the end of the war, she said, she had visited a distant cousin in England who possessed a large stack of John Gabriel's papers and manuscripts. This woman strongly disliked the Stedman side of the family, however, calling John Gabriel "a terrible man," denying that the papers held any interest, and refusing to let Hilda see them except from across the room. Not only had John Gabriel married a "Black" woman, she explained, but his side of the family was much less distinguished than her own—"The Earl of Such and Such and Lady So and So" (as Hilda mimicked her). Hilda told me that this woman was "much older" than she and would be perhaps 110 years old if still alive. She knew she had her address somewhere, she said, and started over to a desk piled with papers and cards but, on the way, veered back toward a small table and offered me another schnapps. Her mind seemed to fade in and out, and she insisted on the glasses of schnapps—to the point that I eventually called it a day, knowing that before too long, when we returned for a sabbatical in the Netherlands, there would be another opportunity, if all went well.

Flash forward one year. We were in the Netherlands, spending the year in Oegstgeest, near Leiden—I working on *First-Time*, Sally on *Co-Wives and Calabashes*. I decided to introduce Sally to Hilda, made arrangements for a visit, and, accompanied by eleven-year-old Leah, we set out for Haus Besselich. This time, Hilda had her maid-servant Maria, who had lived with her for nearly ninety years, serve us lunch, accompanied by several bottles of wine from her vineyards. She spoke to Leah in German,

---

1   John Gabriel Stedman, Diary, November 29, 1785, James Ford Bell Library, University of Minnesota, Minneapolis. According to Samuel Johnson's *Dictionary of the English Language: In Which the Words Are Deduced from Their Original* (1785 edition, 1841), one of the meanings of singular is "having something not common to others." As Dustin Kennedy, referring to the late eighteenth century, writes, "Being singular, then, is a way to name a certain deviation from what is expected as normal." ("Going Viral: Stedman's *Narrative*, Textual Variation, and Life in Atlantic Studies," Romantic Circle, 2011, https://romantic-circles.org/praxis/circulations/HTML/praxis.2011.kennedy.html#back4.

apparently assuming that a child would not yet have learned a foreign tongue, and to us in a mixture of French and English. My goal was to have her find the address book in which, she said, she had her late British cousin's address. But after several hours, no avail. We left empty-handed, except for a crucial hint—Hilda had a niece, Hilda Emge-Von Barton Stedman, who lived in Bonn and who often drove over to check up on her. We took her address.

The younger Hilda, when I wrote, showed a keen interest in our quest and, to our relief, after a several month search through her aunt's belongings, found an old address book with the annotation: "Miss S. V. M. Pym, Orme Gardens (17 East Gate), Louth, Lincolnshire, England." Now, when a ninety-two-year-old reports a long-past encounter with someone who was "much older than I," one tends to entertain little hope of interviewing the person in question. So, on advice from anthropologist Adam Kuper, then teaching in Leiden, I wrote to the vicar of Louth to ascertain the date of her death and whether she had any descendants. By return mail, I received a letter from the manager of the Mabelthorpe Hall Old People's Home, near Louth, saying that Miss Pym ("Daisy"), who was ninety-eight years old, would be delighted to receive me. Not wishing to press my luck, I hurried out to buy a box of fancy Dutch chocolates and set out posthaste across the channel.

Although Daisy proved more charming than informative during our teatime visit due to declining mental faculties (mainly answering my questions with, "How very interesting, Professor!"), the manager put me in touch with her solicitor, who in turn introduced me to her close friends, an elderly couple who were her neighbors. They let me into the house that she had moved out of a decade earlier and in which everything was just as she had left it. In their presence, I went through desk drawers, hundreds of Christmas cards and scraps of memorabilia but nary a sign of John Gabriel. But when I explained more exactly what I was looking for, they offered that Daisy had a nephew (or was it some other male relative?) who also had keys to the place and who had, shortly after she moved into the old people's home, visited the house and removed "a chest of drawers and some other things." He lived, they said, in Brighton and liked to play the horses.

My attempts to contact the man proved fruitless. But I did find another trace. Poking around London, I made an appointment to visit "Maggs Brothers Ltd.: Rare Books and Manuscripts, since 1853," on Bedford

Square in Bloomsbury, having been tipped off that Mr. Maggs was the most knowledgeable of all London antiquarians. After I'd explained my quest, the very formal John Maggs smiled, pivoted his chair, and opened a safe, bringing out a stack of Stedman's handwritten diaries and papers, some written while he was a soldier in eighteenth-century Suriname. Not surprisingly, he wasn't inclined to discuss their provenience. But I assured him I had a buyer and arranged, by phone, for the James Ford Bell Library to negotiate their purchase.

Mr. Maggs was as puzzled as I about the origin of the Stedman manuscript already at Minnesota. I told him it had come from Rosenkilde & Bagger, Bookseller, in Copenhagen, who claimed to have bought it in London. It certainly didn't come from him, he assured me. But he had an idea. "Why don't you try Such-and-Such Second-Hand Books, over in Such-and-Such? [I don't remember the names]. But be careful, it's not a very nice part of the city."

So, I took a taxi and entered a large room, filled with tables of dusty books. Getting up my courage, I tried to chat with the sales assistant, having picked up a copy of Orwell's *Coming Up for Air* (which by chance I had recently read) and saying something about how well that book captured the joys of fishing—a word the author actually used. The bookseller's assistant, condescendingly, remarked, "You mean 'angling'! Fishing is an American word." Having gotten off to a bad start, I nonetheless told him about my quest for the origins of the Minnesota Stedman manuscript and of Mr. Maggs's suggestion that I ask at his store. He brightened up. "Wait a minute. Yes, I remember it well. In '65 or '66 the manuscript came in, two volumes it was, and I was thinking it was very interesting but before I could really go through it, the Gov'nor [his boss] sold it to a Danish bookseller who was passing through." "Who sold it to you?" I asked. "Two Brighton knockers, very disagreeable chaps. You know, Brighton knockers are the worst of the lot." (That evening, I learned that in British parlance, knockers are sharp-eyed fellows who, getting a foot in the front door by one fast-talking means or another, offer to buy a painting, book, or other unsuspected valuable for a pittance from an innocent, often elderly, person in need of cash, and then unload it quickly in another town, no questions asked.)

The circle closed. Daisy's Brighton-dwelling relative had sold the papers to a Brighton knocker who unloaded it in London, whence it traveled to Denmark and thence to Minneapolis. And we were able to construct a genealogy showing the transmission of the manuscript from Stedman to his daughter (Maria Joanna) to her daughter (Louisa Mary Amelia) and, when she died, to her husband's daughter with his second wife, Daisy Pym.

I was able to discover that Miss Pym's connection to the Stedman family was solely through her father's first marriage, to John Gabriel's granddaughter, who had died, presumably with considerable disgrace to the family, a certified lunatic. It was upon the early death of her parents (about 1890), that Daisy had become the grudging keeper of John Gabriel's papers, including his manuscript of the "Narrative."

The papers and diaries that Mr. Maggs sold to the James Ford Bell Library allowed me to put the final pieces of the puzzle in place. Not only did they include the fieldnotes Stedman had written on the spot in Suriname (which served as the basis for the "Narrative"), they also included the daily journal entries between 1791—when he submitted his manuscript and watercolors to his publisher—and 1796, when the *Narrative* was finally published. And they went a long way toward explaining why, when Stedman saw what his publisher had printed in early 1796, he claimed to have burned two thousand copies of the book in a rage. They reveal that Joseph Johnson, the publisher, had engaged a writer named William Thomson to serve as "literary dry-nurse" to the "Narrative"; that he rewrote the text, sentence by sentence; and that, when Stedman saw the result, he said that his book had been "mard intirely" and wrote of "My Spoilt M. Script . . . printed full of lies and nonsense."[2]

After a few years, Sally came on board, and we worked through Stedman's diaries, made countless annotations to the 1790 manuscript itself, and wrote a lengthy introduction analyzing the differences between what Stedman wrote in 1790 and what appeared in the 1796 publication. There was a substantial alteration of Stedman's views on race, slavery, and social justice; many sexual allusions, including descriptions of relations between European men and enslaved African women, were deleted; Stedman's relationship with his lover, the enslaved Joanna, was modified; and much else. We were able to restore early deletions and modifications

---

2   John Gabriel Stedman, Diary, June 24, 1795, and June 5, 1795; Letter, January 17, 1796; see John Gabriel Stedman, *Narrative of a Five Years Expedition against the Revolted Negroes of Surinam.* Newly Transcribed from the Original 1790 Manuscript, ed. Richard Price and Sally Price (Baltimore: Johns Hopkins University Press, 1988), L.

involving Stedman's horror at the Dutch planters' use of casual torture to discipline their slaves; his love and admiration for Joanna; his strong belief in racial equality; and his outrage that "in 20 Years two millions of People are murdered to Provide us with Coffee & Sugar."[3]

In 1988, the Johns Hopkins University Press finally brought out our critical edition.[4] David Brion Davis, the doyen of American slavery studies, reviewing it in the *New York Review of Books*, noted: "After the passage of two centuries, we now have a superbly edited critical edition of the book Stedman actually wrote. . . . The 1790 *Narrative* rivals the most radical abolitionist literature in its scathing portrayal of a slave society[,] . . . [and Blake's] engravings included scenes of slave life that helped form the core of international abolitionist iconography for generations to come."[5]

Even more pleasing was a letter we received from Claude Lévi-Strauss, to whom we had sent a copy of the book. Dated August 16, 1988, it reads (in French):

> Dear Friends,
>
> I received your *Stedman* in the countryside, where I spent the summer, and having opened it, I could not put it aside until I had finished it. This original version, rediscovered by you, is a marvel, as much for what it reveals about the personality of the author as for his style full of verve, to which the orthographic fantasies add even more spice. One thinks of a Cervantes narrating true adventures instead of imaginary ones.
>
> The freshness and vivacity of the sentiment, the half-intentional humor of the expression, make this *Journal* a prodigious literary success. I found pleasure reading it at every moment. . . . Your passionate introduction, your erudite notes, nurtured by your knowledge of the

---

3 Stedman, *Narrative of a Five Years Expedition*, 533.

4 See footnote 2. A couple of years after it was published, the Johns Hopkins University Press asked us to produce an abridged, modernized version, especially for classroom use: John Gabriel Stedman, *Stedman's Surinam: Life in an Eighteenth-Century Slave Society. An Abridged, Modernized Edition of "Narrative of a Five Years Expedition against the Revolted Negroes of Surinam,"* ed. Richard Price and Sally Price (Baltimore: Johns Hopkins University Press, 1992).

5 David Brion Davis, "The Ends of Slavery," *New York Review of Books* 36, no. 5 (1989): 29–34.

local terrain, add even more to the interest of a work that will seduce innumerable readers beyond the small circle of specialists. Finally, I don't need to tell you how much I was touched by your kind words on pages xi and 199.[6] . . .

Again, I congratulate you in having succeeded in this *chef d'oeuvre*. Dear friends, please accept my most cordial sentiments.

[signed] Claude Lévi-Strauss

---

6   We had written that "we would like to acknowledge the kindness of Claude Lévi-Strauss, who continues to represent for us the epitome of Old World erudition" and had cited a letter he wrote us in 1986 that elucidated Stedman's allusion to hanging his hammock in the jungle like "Mahomet betwixt the two Load Stones" (Stedman, *Narrative of a Five Years Expedition*, xi, 199, 642).

JOHNS HOPKINS II
(1979–1983)

CHAPTER ELEVEN

Sally and I spent the summer of 1979 in Suriname, collecting for our upcoming exhibit. As part of its educational program, the UCLA museum wanted objects that could be handled, by both the blind and school children, and we did our best to comply. Some of our days were spent in Paramaribo's Fort Zeelandia, which had been a prison earlier in the century but was now home to the Surinaams Museum, working in both the storerooms and its excellent historical library (the former Koloniale Bibliotheek). One memorable Sunday afternoon, Museum Director Jimmy Douglas, the former chief of police, invited us to join him and his wife in the fort's courtyard for a private luncheon of a special Suriname delicacy—*pindasoep* (peanut soup)—that he'd cooked himself. As we ate, he regaled us with stories of criminals he'd hanged in that very space, describing how he'd learned the proper formula for length-of-rope to weight-of-victim from his counterpart in Georgetown, Guyana. Two years after our luncheon, after the army-led coup d'état, the museum was hastily cleared out, and the fort became the headquarters for the military. And in 1982, it was the site of the infamous December Murders, when Desi Bouterse, then commander-in-chief (later two-term elected president of Suriname), tortured and killed fifteen prominent citizens—newspaper editors, lawyers, labor union leaders, and others.

The following summer, Niko, Leah, Sally, and I returned to the Netherlands, spending the first half at the gracious home of Harry and Ligia Hoetink in Bussum, while they were in the Dominican Republic. While there, we slogged through the laborious task of making the index for *Afro-American Arts*, writing out hundreds of index cards and organizing them in piles in an attempt to follow the museum's instructions. Then we all took off for several weeks on the campus of UCLA, where we worked on the layout and proofs of the book and the final installation of the ambitious exhibit itself. The exhibit designer, who customized Los Angeles cars in his spare time, painted some of the walls Pepto-Bismol pink—the exhibit's later incarnations, in Dallas, Baltimore, and New York, were considerably more muted, jungle greens and earth tones. We ended the summer with a two-week family vacation exploring mainland Yucatan and Isla Mujeres.

I then continued my teaching and departmental duties, working long days consulting with students and colleagues. Several times, I participated in NEH museum panels in Washington, getting to know interesting colleagues in other disciplines such as Svetlana Alpers, a brilliant art historian from Berkeley. That year, we also became friends with Toño Díaz-Royo, a psychologist and art critic from Puerto Rico to whom we gave a courtesy affiliation while his wife, Cruz, finished a doctorate in the School of Public Health. It was a friendship that continued to grow over the years.

In 1981–82, we returned to the Netherlands, where I had a second leave year, supported by the Fulbright Foundation, and Sally had a NATO postdoctoral fellowship for work in Dutch museum collections. I gave an occasional seminar or lecture at Leiden or Utrecht (where our old friend Bonno Thoden van Velzen was a professor) but was otherwise free. In October, we had a shocking phone call from George Collier at Stanford, breaking the news that Shelly Rosaldo, who was just beginning fieldwork with Renato among the Ifugao, had suffered a fatal fall into a riverbed, while walking with village women along a cliffside path. We were devastated.[1]

Living in a standard Dutch house in Oegstgeest, next door to Leiden, I was finally able to complete the first of my ethnographic histories, *First-Time*. (When we returned to Baltimore, Sally and I designed the complex page layouts by cutting pieces of typewritten text with an X-Acto knife and affixing them to boards.) During that year, we became friends with Diane Vernon, a former American actress who had done PhD research with the Okanisi Maroons and was living in a *chaumière* in Normandy— we exchanged visits a couple of times, and she helped me settle on the experimental form of *First-Time*. We spent many weekend days with anthropologists Adam and Jessica Kuper, who were teaching in Leiden. We also enjoyed socializing with Gary and Loekie Schwartz, often at their stately home on a canal in Maarsen; he was a lively Rembrandt scholar and she later translated Sally's "primitive art" book into Dutch. Niko loved his academic Dutch high school, studying several languages, ice-skating with his friends on the frozen canals, and in the spring, working in the tu-

---

1   Years later, Renato—who was left with two young children after Shelly's death—wrote a moving series of remembrance poems, *The Day of Shelly's Death: The Poetry and Ethnography of Grief* (Durham, N.C.: Duke University Press, 2013). After Shelly's death and Renato's remarriage, our relationship with him somehow faded—not because of any wish on our part.

lip fields; Leah, stuck in a "Christelijke" school (the only option available to us), was understandably less enthusiastic and turned again to serious reading. We often bicycled along a branch of the Rhine, much-diminished (if still storied in my imagination) by the time it reached this part of the Netherlands on its way to the sea.

During Easter vacation, while Leah visited Diane in Normandy, and Niko accompanied my mother on a trip to London, Sally and I traveled to Barcelona to visit Amparo, our friend from Los Olivos, and her husband, Francisco. In the 1970s, they had moved with members of their family and a number of others into apartments in the working-class Prat de Llobregat, making the transition from village fountain to washing machines for the women, from gardens and pig farming to factory work for the men (and some of the women). On Sundays, the whole family would leave their apartments and gather in their *huerta*, a rectangular plot that the mayor had given to each of the immigrant Andalusian families on unused land just under the flight path of the Barcelona International Airport. Arriving Sunday morning with jugs of wine, bottles of oil and vinegar, sausages and chunks of cheese, and loaves of bread, the families would harvest their own tomatoes, garlic, cucumbers, and green peppers, the women would make gazpacho, and everyone would settle in for a quiet afternoon of gossip and relaxation.

Monday morning, after a quick coffee in the apartment, Francisco told me his head hurt and could I accompany him to the pharmacy. I was concerned that he might be late for his job—he was by then foreman of one of the crews that cleaned out the planes of Iberia Airlines between flights. But we headed across the street to a bar, where he asked for "*dos aspirinas*" and, when the glasses of Rioja were set in front of us, I realized that this was simply a morning ritual (which he told me he repeated multiple times during his working day).

We also visited Conce—the oldest daughter in our Los Olivos host family—and her husband, Luis, who had instead moved to nearby Nerva, part of the Minas de Rio Tinto complex with one of the oldest and largest (and most polluting) copper mines on Earth, a desolate moonscape of a place where Luis proudly served as a mailman. (Luis died soon after of a heart attack, and Conce returned to Los Olivos.)

Back in Baltimore for the fall of 1982, our exhibition had already traveled from Los Angeles to Dallas and was soon due to appear at the Walters

Art Gallery, not far from where we were living. We accepted an invitation to bring a group of Saamaka drummers, dancers, and singers to put on performances there as well as in Washington, D.C., and New York City, the exhibit's next venue, over a ten-day period. Knowing how foreign the experience would be for the nine men and women who were chosen, some of whom had never been outside of Suriname, and how reluctant they would be to eat in restaurants for fear of menstrual pollution from cooks in the kitchen, we had them stay in our house, sleeping on mattresses on the floor, and cooking communal meals in our kitchen. We were especially pleased that Abatili was in the group, allowing us to reciprocate the hospitality he had shown us in Dangogo so many years earlier. The men quickly learned to navigate the neighborhood and enjoyed "going hunting" to buy things in local stores, while the women phrased the same outings as going to their gardens. One unanticipated pleasure during the group's stay was the involvement of a Baltimore troupe of African American dancers (as well as African American artist Joyce Scott) who, undeterred by the language barrier, befriended the Saamakas, coming to our house almost every evening, and often staying late into the night, for music and dancing, joined by some of our graduate students, who served as DJs.

Soon after we participated in the opening of the exhibition in New York, we took a collection of our Maroon calabashes to the Dominican Republic, where we gave lectures and curated an exhibition at the Museo del Hombre Dominicano. Manuel García-Arévalo, who owned a beautiful private museum chock full of Taíno objects in a penthouse atop the 7UP factory, lent us a jeep, which allowed us a several-day tour of that fascinating country.

We spent the summer of 1983 with Niko and Leah in Petite Anse, in the home of Emilien's recently deceased mother. That's when Emilien for the first time gently scolded me about something I had done. A couple of years earlier in Baltimore, Rolph Trouillot had told me he was flying to Martinique for a conference and wanted advice about getting over to neighboring Dominica to begin his dissertation fieldwork. I urged him to go to Petite Anse, introduce himself to Emilien and Merlande, and ask Emilien to arrange passage across the northern channel by fisherman's *canot*, since I knew that Emilien had fishing acquaintances in the north and that Rolph, as a creolophone, would have no trouble communicating with them. He later told me he'd spent the night and that they'd helped him on his way. But Emilien said that he and Merlande hadn't shut their eyes the whole night out of fear of the "voodoo" Rolph might be doing to them. How, he asked, could I have been so thoughtless as to have sent a Haitian to stay in their home? In retrospect, I should have known that for an anthropologist, mixing worlds is often fraught.

That summer, Niko helped Emilien in his café, often manning the cash register. Leah spent time with her friend Véronique, the granddaughter of the local canoe carpenter I'd known in the 1960s. It was an idyllic moment, and I began working seriously on the research about a self-taught artist and folk hero named Médard that would lead, fifteen years later, to *The Convict and the Colonel*. Sally and I spent a good deal of that summer daydreaming about living permanently in this place. Would it be possible to keep up our research and writing, without becoming the proverbial beach bums or rummies? We would talk exhaustively through the logistics. Could we manage financially on half of my relatively high salary plus research grants, if we were to spend only half of each year at Hopkins? Ever since Yale, we had socked away a significant portion of my salary into savings. . . . Then we would return to reality.

CHAPTER TWELVE

THINGS FALL APART
(1983–1985)

In the fall of 1983, *First-Time* was published and won a national prize.[1] Katherine Verdery organized a party at her apartment to celebrate, which was lovely, though we were unsure how to understand Sid's absence. Around the same time, Jackie let me know that Sid would really appreciate a large surprise party for his sixtieth birthday at the annual meetings of the American Anthropological Association in Washington, D.C., and gave me an extensive list of colleagues and friends from around the country (and the world) to invite. I set about renting Washington's Textile Museum for the evening, sending out invitations, arranging hors d'oeuvres (a Jamaican caterer? or was it Haitian?), a band (same question), and a microphone. There must have been more than a hundred guests (including Sid's sister, who flew in, I think, from California). I served as emcee and introduced guests who wanted to speak. Maurice Godelier was there and read an homage from Lévi-Strauss. By the time it was over, I felt happy that it had gone so well. A few days later, however, Jackie let me know, through an intermediary, that Sid was disappointed . . . that although I'd done what was necessary, he believed that my heart was not really in it. I felt hurt.

Over the course of the year, Sally and I had conversations about the fact that we enjoyed field research and writing more than university life, and we started thinking about how we could arrange to take more time off. The very real satisfaction of putting together a successful anthropology department was transitioning to a more routine life of teaching (which I continued to enjoy) and administrative duties, which, even in the relatively "lite" form that existed at Hopkins, gave me far less pleasure. In one of my meetings with the dean, I mentioned the discussions that Sally and I were having about going on half time, at half pay, explaining that it would be at some future date, most logically when our children had left for college. He laughed. "That's silly! Most of my senior professors only

---

1   Richard Price, *First-Time: The Historical Vision of an Afro-American People* (Baltimore: Johns Hopkins University Press, 1983), was awarded the Elsie Clews Parsons Prize of the American Folklore Society for "the best book on folklore published during the past two years."

work half time and they still take their full salaries." But I insisted that I was serious and that I wanted his acceptance of the plan in writing so we could make concrete plans. The idea was that several years hence, in the year of my choice, I would be present only one semester a year, receiving half of my salary, with the other half being used to appoint a junior person with similar specialties.[2] He reluctantly said he'd ask the president of the university if such an arrangement was possible. And some months later, he handed me a letter outlining the arrangement, signed by the president. In the meantime, he said, he'd try to persuade me not to implement it. I filed away the letter and felt good about having an option to move into greater freedom at some future time.[3]

We spent the summer of 1984 in Baltimore, working on the Stedman volume, while Leah was with Sally's sister, Becky Sato, in Tokyo, helping her take care of her newborn son, and Niko spent the summer in Martinique with a fisherman's family he had become friendly with the previous summer.

By the fall, Sally and I were gradually becoming aware of more general tensions lurking below the surface of the department that had seemed, for a decade, so solidary. There were unsettling incidents popping up here and there in our daily interactions that suggested problems might be brewing in the very close relationship I'd had with Sid for twenty years. Some occurred while Sid and Sally worked together on a coedited book, *Caribbean Contours*.[4] Others occurred in our daily interactions—Sid once stopped by Sally's office to announce, out of the blue, that "Rich may be a good scholar but he's not a nice human being," before walk-

---

2   I was thinking at the time of trying to attract Rolph Trouillot, who had just become an assistant professor at Duke, back to Hopkins as a faculty member.

3   I was shocked to hear, years later, that department rumor had it that I could request a half-salary arrangement because we (or my parents) were super-rich. In fact, we were financially independent of my (middle-class) parents and had from the first been able to save money from my salary. Sally and I always lived more modestly than our faculty peers—we never had a "cleaning woman" or a second car and spent very little on clothes or other personal items. And we had always been successful in obtaining research grants and fellowships. Before I presented my proposal to the dean, we had made careful financial projections and determined that we would be able to make it on half of my relatively high salary.

4   Sidney W. Mintz and Sally Price, eds., *Caribbean Contours* (Baltimore: Johns Hopkins University Press, 1985).

ing out with no further explanation. And one involved a perplexing visit that Jackie made to our house while Sid was traveling. Sid also presented a handwritten bill to Sally after his cooperative Christmas Eve dinner party designed, he told her, to correct a disparity between the cost of ingredients borne by different participants (her pasta putenesca versus his suckling pig as well as different brands of French champagne). We tried to brush these encounters off, but clearly, something was amiss.

One evening, we went to the movies to see *Amadeus*, a story about the relationship between Mozart and Antonio Salieri. Coming out of the theater, I saw that Sally was trembling. When I asked what was wrong, she said, her voice shaking, "That movie . . . it's about us. . . ." Sometime later, while at a colloquium in Puerto Rico, we told our psychologist friend Toño Díaz about some of the things Sid had been doing, hoping for useful advice from a person who was close to both Sid and us. "Forget it," he said. "Just because Sid has a father complex doesn't mean you have to have a son complex. Pay no attention and just get on with your lives." When we returned to Baltimore, that's what we tried to do. But then an opportunity came up for Sally, which led to further tensions.

The Anthropology and Art History Departments had received an NEH grant to develop an interdisciplinary PhD program in art and anthropology, and an international search was launched for a new faculty member to direct it. I excused myself from all involvement, given that Sally was planning to apply, and Sid agreed to be chair of the search committee, though he later excused himself in favor of Bill Sturtevant. By the time the distinguished committee of senior scholars—Sturtevant, Bill Holm (University of Washington), William Davenport (University of Pennsylvania and Sid's former PhD student at Yale), and from Hopkins, Assistant Professor Ashraf Ghani[5] in anthropology and Professors Yves-Alain Bois and Charles Dempsey in art history—weighed in on the candidates, Sally (who had received her PhD under Sturtevant's direction in 1981) was the unanimous choice and was invited to meet with the dean. By that time, it was already May. I was about to go on leave for a year, Sally had won a research grant from NEH that was about to start, and we were about to

---

5   Yes, this is Ashraf Ghani, future president of Afghanistan. I used to urge him to finish his book manuscript on the history of Afghanistan so I could recommend him for tenure, but he would always reply that he couldn't "because the history of Afghanistan isn't finished yet."

embark on a long-planned year in France, so she asked the dean whether she could use the first year for planning and not accept students until the following year. He agreed that this made sense. On the day she received the official contract, we were invited to dinner at Ashraf's. (We enjoyed socializing with Ashraf and his wife, Rula, and Niko and Leah occasionally babysat for their two children, Mariam and Tarek.) Sally was excited about the dean's agreement to give her the first year off and shared the news at dinner. No one congratulated her or said they were pleased; instead there was an eerie silence around the table. Another unsettling moment, but after we got home, we decided to pay attention to Toño's advice and put it out of our minds.

I was looking forward to a year of teaching at the École des Hautes Études en Sciences Sociales, the premier graduate school for anthropologists in France. I'd been invited by François Furet, distinguished historian of the French Revolution and president of the EHESS, during a visit he had made to Hopkins for a lecture. He had told me that he loved *First-Time* and wanted me to spend the year as visiting professor at his institution—and he in fact set up all the necessary paperwork for my visit.

DOWN AND OUT IN PARIS
1985–1987

We spent the summer in the family cottage of our old friend Patrick Menget (a former graduate school classmate) in Port Blanc, Bretagne, waiting for our rental apartment in Paris to be free. Then we rented a car for a drive to Los Olivos for a visit and continued up to Barcelona, where Amparo had moved some years earlier. There, Amparo's newly urbanized nephews and nieces told Niko and Leah they would take them downtown to see a true *maravilla* and off they went to El Corte Ingles (Spain's largest department store) to show them escalators. In the evening, the four of us got dressed up and were taken by Amparo and her sister to the second marvel, the Magic Fountain of Montjuïc, with its sound and light show. They'd come a long way from Los Olivos.

Soon after we arrived in Paris, where I was to serve as Directeur d'Études Associé at the École des Hautes Études en Sciences Sociales, the Hopkins dean wrote to me, saying that the university was instigating five-year plans for all its departments. It would be a good time, he said, to inform Emily Martin, the new chair of anthropology, about my intent to go on half time at some future date. So I wrote to her, making clear that the plan was an option to be considered later, presumably when our children were in college.

That letter turned my declining relationship with Sid into a veritable meltdown. The letter I got back from the department was angry. It was accusatory. It argued that my "secret" arrangement with the dean was immoral—"a violation of trust, . . . leaving on the shoulders of two what should have been carried by three." I replied, explaining that I had of course intended to discuss this with them in person before deciding to implement the plan. But the damage had been done.

There followed more letters and a slew of international phone calls— several with the dean, who said that he couldn't make heads or tails of what the department was arguing. Calls from friends in other departments, however sympathetic and supportive, were unanimous—the air at Hopkins, for reasons that remained mysterious to them, had been poisoned against us, with the result that there was no way that we or our children could ever again be happy in Baltimore. Several called it "a coup." They urged us to explore options at other universities. We felt deeply wronged, hurt, and sad, but after months of painful discussions, some with Niko and Leah, we took the decision to cut ties completely with Johns Hopkins. (I was reminded of the decision made with my parents, after my high school truck accident, to defy conventional opinion and to opt for a hoped-for better future.) In February, we both simply resigned, and I wrote a personal letter to each graduate student, briefly explaining.[1]

This was still the pre-Internet era and we were living abroad, so it took several months before we began hearing the scuttlebutt about our break. Patrick Menget, who had recently been lecturing in the States, said the three explanations he heard were exactly what he would have expected from American colleagues—that I had committed offenses involving either money, sex, or nepotism. Over time, other friends told us what they'd heard—that my homosexual relationship with the dean had finally been exposed or that the large-scale sex orgies held in our home had become a general embarrassment. Rolph Trouillot and Brackette Williams, who'd been in the department when the problems were brewing, may have seen it most clearly: "You were just too happy," quipped Rolph. Brackette chided us, "You were so naïve!" Eric Wolf, who'd once been Sid's closest friend, wrote me a sweet letter of support, reminding me that, "we all hurt each other in small ways, and sometimes in big ones."[2] Afro-Americanist Roger Abrahams, who knew both Sid and me well, wrote, "You could have knocked me over with a leaf. But you've had twenty really good years together—that's much longer than most such academic friendships survive." In retrospect, the greatest wound caused

---

1   The dean asked us to sign letters promising we would not sue the university, which we did—we had never sued anybody for anything in our lives—and the university sent us a severance check of $5,000 plus a letter from the president thanking me for my years of service. (After Sid's death in 2015, Katherine Verdery, who had been on leave in Romania during the year of our conflict, told us that Sid always refused to say anything about his reasons for wanting us to leave, though she asked him repeatedly over the years. And others also told us that throughout his life, he consistently refused to speak about it, even when pressed.)

2   Indeed, it did feel to me like Wotan-Brünnhilde (in Act 3 of *Die Walküre*), with the possible addition of the biblical story of Potiphar's wife, which I'd learned from Stedman.

by the break was that it deprived me of having close mentorship relations, and friendships, with gifted graduate students.

Once we arrived in Paris, Sally worked on getting Niko and Leah enrolled in a prestigious public lycée (in the equivalent of tenth and eleventh grades), which eventually produced some interesting insights into
the French system of education.[3] Leah's best friend was Aklil, the daughter of the Ethiopian ambassador to France; it was a considerable embarrassment to their teachers that by the end of the year, the two best students in the class were the two foreigners.[4] Niko had several close friends
who helped him learn how French teenagers goofed off and hung out. In
terms of schoolwork, we were surprised by how unfazed he was by taking
math and physics in a foreign language. In the spring, he applied for early
admission to Harvard and, with the help of letters from his Baltimore
teachers, was accepted, after the equivalent of his junior year.

Understandably less happy and carefree than usual, I didn't get a lot
of work done that year. I also did no teaching. When I showed up at the
École des Hautes Études en Sciences Sociales in the fall, I was told that
François Furet was no longer president and that the new president, anthropologist Marc Augé (an acquaintance of my colleagues at Hopkins),
had programmed no courses for me to teach that year—though I would,
of course, continue to draw my salary.

I nevertheless kept plugging along on *Alabi's World*, trying to figure
out the proper "voice," the appropriate literary form for the mass of oral
and archival data, in several languages. Sally, despite frequent nightmares
about Hopkins, kept working on her NEH grant—exploring perceptions
of "primitive art" by interviewing collectors, museum curators, and others, from Pierre Bourdieu to Alban Bensa and of course our old friend
Lévi-Strauss. And we made an effort to keep busy, attending seminars at
the Laboratoire d'anthropologie sociale, meeting often with French col-

---

3   See the description of Leah's microscope experience in Sally's *Primitive Art in Civilized Places* (Chicago: University of Chicago Press, 1989), 15–16.
4   The next fall, to Leah's disappointment, Aklil didn't show up at school. We later
learned that, in the wake of political changes in Ethiopia, her family had fled Paris and
received asylum in the United States. Aklil is now a physician in Maryland.

leagues, and maintaining an active dinner-party social life. We gave lectures in France, England, Denmark, and Sweden.[5] We also kept up with news from Martinique via visits with Emilien's sister Liliane—one of the first people from Petite Anse to pass the bac, she'd gone on to become a tax inspector in Paris. Liliane also initiated us into the life of Antilleans in Paris. When I asked, for example, where the Antillean neighborhoods were, she said, "We're all over, spread across the sixth [attic] floors of every walkup, in many parts of the city." Our relationship with Antilleans in Paris grew significantly over the years.

Martinique came up in another way as well. In April, Sally was meeting with Michel Leiris in his office in the basement of the Musée de l'Homme, interviewing him about the world of primitive art dealers in Paris. Aware of his interest in Martinique, she mentioned my ongoing research and told him about our interest in living more of the time in Martinique. Visibly excited, he picked up the phone and dialed Aimé Césaire to share the story of Médard. Fortunately, he couldn't get through—it was 4:00 a.m. in Fort-de-France—but Leiris did write Césaire about us, asking him to welcome us when we arrived.

In our once-elegant apartment on the posh Avenue de Breteuil, rented from a psychoanalyst, we were reminded of how much we enjoyed being in Paris. And thanks to Maurice Godelier (a friend of Sid's, but not at all surprised, he told us, by what had happened between us), I received a position for the next year as a visiting professor at the University of Paris, one semester at Nanterre and the other (arranged in part by sociologist Kristin Couper) at Saint-Denis, at full salary.[6] At times, Paris opened its quirky charms to us: Sally reconnected with Paris-based textile artist Sheila Hicks (whom we'd met in Baltimore through Sturtevant), and

---

5 After our lectures in Lund, our hosts, anthropologists Jonathan Friedman and Kajsa Ekholm Friedman, invited us for a weekend at their second home on the Baltic, where, after finishing off chunks of smoked eel and a bottle of akvavit, we strolled on the beach, taking deep breaths of the wonderful sea air. Next morning we heard on Swedish radio that Chernobyl had exploded the previous day, blowing a giant radioactive cloud over that very beach.

6 Maurice continued to be supportive of our activities throughout our years in Paris. Among other things, he wrote a long foreword to the French edition of Sally's "primitive art" book and presented it at the Salon du Livre when it was published. Kristin attended every one of my classes and became a fast friend; the previous year, she had arranged a similar position at Saint-Denis for Cornel West.

Leah began hanging around her atelier, providing occasional services as an errand-runner, once being asked, for example, to return a delicate tea-cup to the elderly Juliette Man Ray in her apartment on the other side of the Jardin de Luxembourg, who insisted on offering her a plate of rather spoiled plums.

One day, we received a phone call from the parents of Chris Steiner, who'd taken a couple of undergraduate classes with me at Hopkins (one was called "Being an Anthropologist"). They gushed that their son had once been an indifferent student but, inspired by these classes, was now on his way to grad school at Harvard. On vacation in Paris, they wanted to thank me. They took us to an elegant restaurant and during dinner, when Chris's father mentioned that he'd been an Air France pilot, we told him that Niko had been playing with a flight simulator game on my computer. "Oh my, would you mind if we went back to your apartment after dessert? I'd love to see it," he said. Once we got back and woke Niko up, the two of them shared their enthusiasm, landing a plane, if memory serves, at Chicago's O'Hare field.[7]

When summer came, we had yet another life-changing experience. A telegram from Paramaribo told us that our old friend Gaama Agbago was gravely ill in the hospital and wanted to see us before he died. We arranged for art historian Irene Winter, visiting Paris from the University of Pennsylvania, to stay in our apartment with Leah, Niko went to stay at a friend's house, and we booked tickets for the next day, flying to Martinique on Air France, on to Trinidad on LIAT, and thence to Paramaribo on Surinam Airways, arriving after midnight. In the morning at the hospital, we were informed that Agbago had been flown back to the Saamaka capital, after the doctors had decided they could do no more for him. We hurried to the municipal airport, where light planes flew to the interior, and paid a pilot to fly us in three days later, the first date we could arrange. We then spent two days wandering the streets, buying quantities of cloth and tobacco, and a few cases of rum as gifts for Saamakas and visiting with city acquaintances to assess the political situation since Desi Bouterse's 1980 coup d'état and the notorious December Murders of 1982. One evening, we had dinner in a Chinese restaurant with the owner

---

7 Chris Steiner went on to become a leading scholar of African art.

of the Jeruzalem Bazaar, where Saamakas shopped, who whispered to us that we were surrounded at other tables by undercover policemen, listening to our conversation.

Sunday at midnight, two heavily armed military police banged on the door of our hotel room and charged in, announcing that we were being deported. They let us pull on some clothes and shoved us into a police Volkswagen, leaving behind all the presents we'd bought for Saamakas. Through forest and savannas, we were tailed all the way by another MP car, never being given any explanation for what was happening. We felt sure that at any moment they were going to stop and do us in—but the ride ended at Albina, in eastern Suriname, where we were locked in a barracks room till dawn. At the dock, our passports were stamped all over *ONGELDIG* (invalid), and we were hustled onto a ferry to Guyane with a warning never to return.

By chance, and unbeknownst to us, the civil war between Ronnie Brunswijk's Jungle Commando and the government was about to break out, and, as stalwart friends of the Maroons, we had apparently been designated personae non gratae. When the U.S. Embassy asked for clarification about our expulsion, the Suriname government responded that it had been "an administrative error." Numerous friends in Paramaribo—people with political street smarts—suggested that such warnings from the military were meaningful and that it would be wise for us to keep our distance. (Gaama Agbago clung to life until 1989, when he died quietly at the age of 102. I was badly torn between my wish to attend his funeral and Sally's cautionary stance. In the end, I didn't take the risk and we had to content ourselves with videos and personal reports of the spectacular ceremony.)

Suddenly, we found ourselves in Guyane, feeling shaken, with just the clothes on our backs, our wallets, and our passports, so we took a road taxi to the European space center at Kourou, where Saamakas we'd known in Suriname were working as manual laborers.

Such was our introduction to Guyane, where we have spent a significant portion of our lives ever since.

On the way back to Paris, we made a stopover in Martinique to see Emilien and Merlande.

Then, having picked up Niko and Leah, we set out for Baltimore, where

Behind the counter at Le Rayon, 1986.

we emptied our house with the help of a yard sale organized by Niko and a friend of his, and said goodbye to our home of ten years. (Kathy Ryan, our one-time colleague at Hopkins, stopped by with a six-pack during our yard sale, and we sat on the front steps, reminiscing about the department's halcyon years.)

With Niko ready to start Harvard, Sally, Leah, and I returned to Paris and moved into a beautiful apartment on the rue des Écoles belonging to Marie-France Vigneras, a professor of mathematics who was on leave at Berkeley. That year, Leah finished eleventh grade at her lycée and then, like her brother, went directly to Harvard, having scored high on her SATs and written an imaginative application essay about the kitchen maid in *The Joy of Cooking*. I remained personally if not clinically depressed for the only time of my life during much of that year, slowly adjusting to life without the students that had been so important to my life and without a university identity. But I taught my French university classes and kept plugging away on my green-screen Seequa Chameleon luggable computer, running WordPerfect software, drafting *Alabi's World*, the second of my books about Saamaka history. Meanwhile, Sally alternated between two projects—conducting interviews with members of the Paris "primitive art" world and working over transcriptions of the folktales we'd recorded at wakes in Saamaka in the 1960s.[8] At the same time, she dealt with the feelings of betrayal by Hopkins colleagues (Sid in particular) that refused to go away by pouring them into a diary and beginning a pseudonymous novel provisionally called "Diary of a Faculty Wife."

We occasionally talked about settling more permanently in Paris, which continued to charm us on various levels. There were dinner parties at the homes of French friends and others that we hosted (which often included visitors from the States, from Paul Rabinow, Rebecca Scott, and Jack Greene to Renato Rosaldo, Katherine Verdery, Ken Bilby, and Scott Guggenheim, as well as French colleagues—Françoise Héritier, Marc Augé, Denise Paulme, Maria Pia Di Bella, Patrick Menget, Michael Houseman, and François Roustang.)

The year's activities took place against a background of bureaucratic encounters with the French State, for which a little background may help contextualize. During my final undergraduate year, Sally and I had taken a seminar with Laurence Wylie on French civilization. Larry (as he asked us to call him) was an unassuming Quaker who had taught for years at Haverford and then, soon after he published *Village in the Vaucluse* (1957), which chronicled his family's sabbatical in the south of France, was tapped to be the first C. Douglas Dillon Professor of the Civilization of France at Harvard. As his *NYT* obituary said, he "spent decades in pursuit of the essence of the French soul." Besides showing us various French New Wave films, he argued that "Le Système D" (from *se débrouiller*) was the key to understanding France. "As a child grows up he learns that this duality characterizes life. There is on the one hand the paralyzing network of official laws and regulations. Beneath this is the area of human relationships where with resourcefulness one may move freely to accomplish what may be legally unattainable. . . . Generally speaking the people of [the village] believe that effective action is accomplished not officially through legal channels but unofficially through personal contacts."[9]

---

8 The entire corpus of field recordings that we made in the 1960s (which included folktales, riddles, religious and secular songs, drumming of many varieties, oracle sessions, prayers, council meetings, children's games, and speech in esoteric languages) is on permanent deposit at the Archives of Traditional Music, Folklore Institute, Indiana University. That collection includes 117 5-inch reels, 1,030 pages of typed transcriptions, and a brief introductory essay.

9 Laurence Wylie, *Village in the Vaucluse* (Cambridge, Mass.: Harvard University Press, 1957), 335–36.

This turned out to be a good description of the various battles that we have fought with French bureaucracy over the years. For the most part, our own occasional small victories took place far from metropolitan France. Once we had become locally "famous" through books about Guyane, and the radio and TV appearances they brought with them, we were several times able to help Saamaka migrants obtain crucial residence papers by visiting the prefect and making a special plea for our nonliterate friends. And our intervention, during a dinner at the home of Guyane's district attorney, played a central role in getting our friend Tooy freed from prison.

But in the spring of 1986, in Paris, when Chirac's anti-immigration minister of the interior Charles Pasqua took charge—he once boasted "we will terrorize the terrorists"—we found ourselves in trouble. Before Pasqua, our visits to the *prefecture de police* (the central police station), which routinely meant three or four hours of waiting for a five-minute argument through a small, grated window, ended with a two- or three-month reprieve to our residence and work permits. But during 1986, when he was regnant, we spent many days at the prefecture—one memorable time with Leah and me finally getting two-month extensions but Sally not. For three or four weeks, Sally could not leave our apartment, for fear of being "controlled" on the street and deported. (She was at the time conducting interviews with Michel Leiris for the international journal *Current Anthropology*, and it was only because she was accompanied by her fellow interviewer Jean Jamin who, as a state official, had a *bleu-blanc-rouge* identity card, that it was safe for her to take the twenty-minute walk from our apartment to Leiris's.[10])

My own experience that spring was even worse. One day out of the blue, the secretary to the president of the University of Paris VIII, where I was teaching, phoned to tell me that I was not to meet my class the next day and that my salary would no longer be paid. "I'm not authorized to tell you why," she said, "but it has something to do with the DST [the directorate of the French National Police that served as domestic intelli-

---

10 Sally Price and Jean Jamin, "A Conversation with Michel Leiris," *Current Anthropology* 29 (1988): 157–74. That article reproduced portraits of Leiris by Picasso, Giacometti, Francis Bacon, and André Masson. Sally had suggested including a collage portrait by Lou-Laurin Lam (widow of Wifredo Lam), and Leiris viewed it tenderly: "You see? It's a portrait of me in the form of a monkey who's masturbating." But for the article, he said, he wanted artwork by his friends, not their wives.

gence agency]. You have been ordered to remain in your apartment until further notice."

For a day or two, we discussed the situation with friends over the phone, all of whom commiserated and emphasized the seriousness of the matter, though none could offer an explanation or think of a way out. But when we spoke with Aurore Monod, a colleague from Nanterre, she said she could help. "Just stay where you are. I'll be over to your place after I teach my seminar today. Don't worry about a thing." When she arrived at our apartment, she said, "Give me your passport and then go to a movie and relax. I'll be back to you tomorrow." It turned out that her brother, the head of one of France's largest multinationals, was a close friend and tennis partner of President Chirac. Fortunately, he was in Paris when she went to see him after her class, he called the president (or his chief of staff), and I got a call from the university early the next morning that I was fully reinstated.[11] We took my rescue as a practical demonstration of Wylie's Système D in full bloom.

I hadn't been making applications for a new job, but one came up serendipitously during the fall. An acquaintance at George Mason University, who had written an admiring review of *First-Time*, asked me to send him my CV and permit him to submit my name for a new distinguished professorship, just announced, which I did. Some weeks later, I got a phone call from the provost to discuss a range of issues from salary and title to starting date and course loads. He said a final offer would follow soon. We were pleased we'd be able to move on. But not long after, our acquaintance, quite distraught, called to say that the offer was off, that he was very angry, and that he had decided to leave the university for good (which he did, getting a professorship at an Ivy League university the following year). What had happened, he told me, was that "there had been a phone call"—he wasn't sure from whom—that contained sufficient warning bells for the provost to drop the appointment. We were shocked and disappointed but didn't dwell on it, expecting other possibilities to open up before long.

In November, we had another life-changing surprise. Our old friend from Petite Anse, Emilien, rang us up. "Richard, listen closely," he said.

---

11 Our best guess was that our expulsion from Suriname to Guyane had been picked up on my secret service file, which my Nanterre friend told me had a pencil mark on its cover, saying *connu* (known), suggesting that I was a potential terrorist.

"I'm in the phone booth [Petite Anse's only one] and have just one coin, so I can't talk long. I've found a house that you're going to buy." The next day there were back and forth phone calls about holding it until I could see it. Sally also spoke on the phone with Aimé Césaire, who promised to call the town's mayor to ask him to welcome us warmly. A week later, told by Emilien that I had to come the very next day to sign, I explained that I couldn't because I had a class to teach the next day at Nanterre. "Let Sally teach it," he said, and so she did.

Arriving at the site with the real estate agent as dusk settled in, I found a simple house that had been built by the owner. The agent pointed out that, among its attractive features, it had "a pigsty with three apartments" and said it wouldn't be complicated to install municipal water to replace the garden hose then connected to a roadside cistern. Because there was no electricity, the details were hard to make out, but the moonlight allowed me to see a beautiful view of the sea. It was clear to me that this could be our future home. So, after phoning Sally, I signed some preliminary papers and flew back to Paris. Several months later, we became Martiniquan homeowners.

The rest of the spring was devoted to setting up visiting appointments for 1987–88. Sally applied for a Mellon postdoc at Penn, I applied for a fellowship at the Wesleyan Humanities Center.[12] And we called on Stuart Schwartz, who had helped so much on our Stedman edition, at the University of Minnesota, to see if he might be able to set up visiting positions for us there. We had begun a new life as freelance academics, without a university affiliation, based in the rural Caribbean.

---

12 We were accepted at each but eventually declined them.

CHAPTER FOURTEEN

FREELANCING
(1987–1995)

Being tropical people by preference, we suffered during our year-long stay in Minnesota, where it sometimes reached minus forty degrees (centigrade *and* Fahrenheit). While our friends at the university went jogging or ice-fishing on weekends, we preferred to turn up the heat, put on Caribbean music, and work at home. We learned about headbolt heaters, which turned cars on and off while they were parked at downtown parking meters, but they were not something we were ready to attach to the red pickup truck that we had driven from the East Coast.

At the university, I taught a class on Caribbean history and a seminar on history and anthropology that attracted several students from Africa who were studying with Allen Isaacman. In addition to a course on non-Western art, Sally agreed to give a course on gender through the recently founded Center for Advanced Feminist Studies (a title that gave me pause). The academic ambience was pleasant, we renewed our friendship with Stuart Schwartz, and we enjoyed getting to know new colleagues, including linguist Genevieve Escure, who helped us explore Minneapolis, and John Wright, professor of English who had founded the African American Studies program and who taught us a lot about the realities of being Black in Minnesota.

At the same time, we were each finishing a book—*Alabi's World* for me, and *Primitive Art in Civilized Places* for Sally. *Alabi's World* was, in a way, my first deep dive into ethnographic history. Like *First-Time*, it concerned the initial century of the Saamakas. Early in that work, I argue that ethnographic history

> must be animated by a constant attentiveness to meaning (teasing out the significance of experience and actions to the actors—a kind of ethnological hermeneutics), to the process of producing histories (the relations of power in creating and suppressing historical discourse, the social negotiation of historical knowledge, the relationship between the author and the historical observers upon whose records he depends), to relationships between the author and his historical subjects, to processes of knowing (maintaining the distance of others' categories), and to problems of form and "catching experience whole." To paraphrase Greg Dening, ethnographic history, shaped by the ironic

trope in which things are never what they seem to be, would at its best be a thoroughly demystifying art (contrasting with "guilded history," which Dening reminds us tends also to be "gilded history").[1]

Because I was determined to underscore perspectivity in the telling of history, I wanted to devise some way to keep the voices in the book separate, rather than melding them together the way historians usually did, and settled on a typographical solution. Saamaka voices, I decided, would be printed in an italic, unjustified font; German missionary voices in a heavy, Gothic font; Dutch administrator voices in bold italics; and my own voice in a standard font. With its many photos and engravings and its multiple fonts, the book followed typographic experiments I'd initiated in *First-Time*, where Saamakas' descriptions of historical events ran along the tops of the pages and my commentary on them along the bottoms of the same pages. Some critics dubbed all this "postmodern," but for me, it was simply a way to present Native voices as seriously as those of Western ones.

Since the late 1960s and 1970s, I had been reading a good bit of Latin American literature (Borges, Carpentier, Cortázar, García Márquez) and was particularly attracted to Vargas Llosa's narrative experiments with time (for example, in *The Green House*) and with voice (for example, in *Conversation in the Cathedral*). A lifetime of movie going had also undoubtedly imprinted numerous nonlinear narrative techniques on my mind. And, feeling the freedom that came with being part of the last academic generation to have achieved tenure early and relatively effortlessly, by the mid-1970s it seemed quite natural to begin experimenting with narrative, matching theoretical concerns about the politics of representation with practical solutions involving the poetics of representation. I had begun to argue that different historical or ethnographic situations lent themselves to different literary forms (and vice versa) and that the ethnographer or historian should face each society or period—or for that matter each potential book—in a new and newly problematized way, searching out or even inventing a literary form that did not come preselected or ready-made. At about the same time, my old friend Renato Rosaldo gave his own assessment of "the discipline's new project," arguing

---

1   Richard Price, *Alabi's World* (Baltimore: Johns Hopkins University Press, 1990), xvi–xvii.

that it clearly demanded "a wider array of rhetorical forms than had been used during the classic period."[2]

One of the highlights of that year at Minnesota was a trip I took with Stuart Schwartz to São Paulo for the commemoration of the one hundredth anniversary of the abolition of slavery. Two years earlier, we had flown to Brazil together to participate in a planning meeting for the event. There were one hundred historians at that session, almost all from Brazil. At one point, I stood up and asked, as politely as I could, why there was only one visibly Black historian in the room. That evening, at a reception in a fancy penthouse, with many Black servants passing the hors d'oeuvres, I was approached by the only dark-skinned man who was wearing a suit and tie, who said he had heard my remark and wanted to shake my hand. He was, he said, the newly appointed head of affirmative action for all of Brazil, named at the end of the dictatorship, with a small office, a chair, a desk, and a typewriter, but no secretary. We exchanged letters and newspaper clippings for several years.

As the spring semester drew to a close in Minneapolis, I was asked by some colleagues whether we would be interested in accepting permanent positions as professors. In spite of my feelings about the climate, I said yes and even had a couple of encouraging meetings with the dean, but then . . . nothing. Anthropologist Mischa Penn, Morse Distinguished Teaching Professor of Social Science, reported to us: "The dean handed the department the keys to two new Jaguars, free of charge, and the chair told him we're not interested."

We had decided to spend 1988–89 in Martinique, setting up our new life there. (Niko was taking his junior year at the University of São Paulo, and Leah, after a summer interning at PEN in New York, was a Harvard sophomore.) Settling into our little house by the sea—installing electricity, getting a telephone, buying a (Soviet-made) refrigerator, building

---

2   Renato Rosaldo, *Culture and Truth: The Remaking of Social Analysis* (Boston: Beacon, 1989), 231. As Clifford Geertz, looking backward, later wrote: "There *is* apparently something to the idea of Zeitgeist, or at least to that of mental contagion. One thinks one is setting bravely off in an unprecedented direction and then looks up to find all sorts of people one has never even heard of headed the same way" (*Available Light: Anthropological Reflections on Philosophical Topics* [Princeton, N.J.: Princeton University Press, 2000], 16).

bookcases, and installing running water—went fairly smoothly, but we ran into roadblocks when we tried to get our Nissan pickup, which we'd shipped from New York, off the docks. The problem was that to get a Martinique (French) license plate a car needed to be *homologué*, properly certified to French standards, which its catalytic converter and certain other features didn't allow. After trying every dodge we knew for two frustrating months, during which we had no choice but to rent a car, we reluctantly paid a visit to Aimé Césaire and asked if he could help. Of course, he said, and two days later we drove it off the dock. (Since our pickup wasn't on the official French list of what qualified as a vehicle, Césaire had persuaded the authorities to classify it legally as an "antique," which they did—it was fifteen months old.) Another successful implementation of the Système D.

Before we left New York for Martinique, we'd gotten rid of our Seequa Chameleon luggables and each bought a Zenith 183, one of the first (still quite bulky) laptops to be equipped with a hard disk, running WordPerfect word-processing software. Sally's diary for the year is filled with repeated computer breakdowns, from electrical short circuits to hard-drive failures. Twice, we had to ask a visitor from the United States to carry a computer back to the States for repairs and then lean on the goodwill of my uncle Bobby, in Manhattan, to have it fixed and pass it on to someone on their way to Martinique, since there was no one on the island with the necessary know-how for the repair. (During those times, Sally and I would take turns on the other machine, once for more than two months.) When we had the manuscript of *Two Evenings in Saramaka* ready for submission, neither our home printer nor any of the ten or so commercial print shops on the island was able to produce the necessary diacritical marks, so I had to fly to Guadeloupe for a day, where a friend had located a firm that, for a hefty fee, produced the eight-hundred-plus double-spaced pages while I waited.

Keeping up with the international academic world—correspondence with colleagues, production of manuscripts, negotiations with publishers, applying for grants, arranging lecture trips, and more—posed constant challenges. Our telephone operated intermittently and mail sporadically. (Modems, the Internet, and email were still almost a decade away.) We spent a lot of time writing letters and made at least weekly trips to Fort-de-France, more than an hour away, to send or receive bundles of mail via Bic Pac (the local precursor of FedEx)—we asked people to send mail to my mother or sister in the States, who would then forward it to us in a package; Ma or Joanie also generously took care of rerouting our outgoing mail, which we sent in a Bic Pac bundle from Martinique each week, through the U.S. Postal Service. Everything involved with publishing books and articles, from manuscript submission and contract negotiations to copyediting and proofreading, happened on paper—reams of it—so there was a constant flow of heavy mail back and forth between our rural island home and the States. And then, on a more mundane level, frequent strikes meant that electricity and water disappeared for days at a time.

Our small black and white TV showed only a couple of local channels, since there were mountains between our house and the capital. For U.S. news, we relied mainly on a shortwave radio station from Puerto Rico, but a couple of times a week, I would also drive to a village half an hour away where there was a hotel that sold the previous day's *International Herald Tribune*.

In November, we flew up to New York, where Sally stayed with my mother while I went to Spain for a week-long conference. Arriving back on a wintry evening—it happened to be my birthday—I took a taxi straight to the Waldorf Astoria, where I knew that Sally had been invited to dinner by David Brent, anthropology editor at the University of Chicago Press, to sign the contract for her book, *Primitive Art in Civilized Places*. David looked shocked when I showed up unexpectedly and pulled up a chair. There was still some meat left on the rack of lamb they'd been sharing, but the bottle of champagne was nearly empty, so another was ordered. Eventually David pulled out the book contract, which specified an advance of $2,500 and a royalty rate (after the first five thousand copies at 10 percent) of 12 1/2 percent. Assuming the role of Sally's agent, I told him about her rival offer, from Penguin in England (which was, in truth, still being negotiated), for a $16,000 advance and a 15 percent royalty rate. After a certain amount of hemming and hawing, he said that he really wanted this book, replaced the $2,500 with a handwritten $10,000, corrected the royalty rate to 15 percent, and initialed the changes. After he and Sally signed, we finished the champagne.

Not long after, someone sent us a cartoon that had just been published in the *New Yorker*.[3] We wondered if it had somehow been inspired by our move.

---

3 Jack Ziegler, *New Yorker*, March 20, 1989.

"Hey, what can I say? It's not Baltimore, but then what is?"

Our writing in Anse Chaudière that year centered on the Saamaka folktale project (listening over and over to the 1968 reel-to-reel tape recordings), making a modernized abridgment of Stedman's *Narrative*, and continuing research with fishermen and others in Martinique about the ever-mysterious Médard—trying to find his remaining artworks, interviewing people who had known him. Most days, after a morning of work, we drove over the hill to Petite Anse to eat our midday meal with Emilien and Merlande. She always said she enjoyed cooking for the four of us and that meals were more fun than when she was alone with Emilien. So, a cucumber and tomato salad, a *court-bouillon de poisson* (*poisson rouge, dorade, tazard, requin,* or *raye*) or, if Emilien was cooking, a *blaff* (fish cooked in a clear peppery broth) accompanied by a fresh baguette and glass of red wine and some local fruit for dessert. Then, back to our house for a quick nap in a hammock.

Emilien and Merlande, in front of Le Rayon.

And during that year in Martinique, we set up our next academic gig, a full year as visitors at Stanford—me as a senior fellow at the Stanford Humanities Center, and Sally as a visiting professor in the Anthropology Department.

In August 1989, we flew up to New York, visited my mother and her second husband (my father having run off with his dental hygienist in the 1970s), and picked up the old Toyota station wagon that she'd been keeping for us ever since we left Johns Hopkins, for the cross-country drive to California.

The Humanities Center was in Mariposa House, a rambling Victorian structure. As visiting scholars, we were installed in commodious offices overlooking well-watered lawns, bright-eyed students, earnest professors, and the campus bike shop. Everyone was friendly, the weather was pleasant, and we saw hot tubs for the first time (some of which had been converted into herb planters after the wilder 1960s). But overall, our sampling of the California lifestyle made us realize we were more East Coast people. We visited San Francisco; gave lectures at Berkeley, Santa Cruz, and the San Francisco Museum of Art; and taught a joint course on African American folktales that culminated in a raucous public performance of a Saamaka folktale by the class.[4] I offered a graduate seminar on history and anthropology in which I met Peter Redfield and Catherine Benoît (then students at Berkeley who drove over to Stanford each week), who became lifelong friends; we enjoyed stimulating weekly dinners with former Hopkins graduate student Brackette Williams, teaching that year at Berkeley, often with some of her adoring students in tow. And we enjoyed the company of literary scholars Marge Garber and Barbara Johnson (and their dog Wagner), folklorist Bill Ferris, linguist and opera singer Bill Beeman, and intellectual historian Bernardo Subercaseaux (who later hosted Leah in Chile for a summer).

One day, the secretary at the Center knocked on my door with a fax. The director of Guyane's nascent "national museum" (in quotation marks because Guyane was not really a nation but a far-flung *département* of France in South America) had asked us to be members of the "scientific committee" that would decide on the collecting and exhibition policies of the museum, slated to have its grand opening in time for the 1992 Columbian quincentenary. The fax read (in French), "I append to this fax several photos representing a set of musical instruments which have been proposed for sale, and ask that you be so kind as to let me know your sentiments on the subject. *A priori*, the instruments appear to be authentic antiquities."

I called Sally in from the neighboring office, and we held the glossy paper in front of a window to try to make out the details. Two of the instruments—a side-blown wooden trumpet and a banjo—looked like dead ringers for instruments that Stedman had depicted in his plate on "Musical Instruments of the African Negroes." What a coup they would be for the new museum! The horn Stedman sketched in the 1770s had long been thought lost, and his banjo had been tucked away in a storeroom of the Leiden museum, mislabeled and unnoticed for over a century, until we rediscovered it in the 1970s.[5] Till now, there were no other

---

4   Grad student John McWhorter, who was the interlocutor in the performance, became a professor at Columbia, wrote a grammar of the Saamaka language, and now comments frequently in the media—see, for example, John McWhorter, "How the N-Word Became Unsayable," *New York Times*, April 30, 2021.

5   Richard Price and Sally Price, "John Gabriel Stedman's collection of 18th-century artifacts from Suriname," *Nieuwe West-Indische Gids* 53 (1979): 121–40.

instruments of this vintage anywhere in world collections. But were they authentic?

We faxed the museum director back: "Your photocopies suggest that these instruments, were they to prove genuine, would be of considerable ethnological interest not only for Guyane but for the history of Afro-America more generally." And we informed her that we had made plane reservations that would bring us to Guyane for the summer's collecting expedition among the Maroons of the Maroni and Lawa Rivers. After we arrived in Guyane and viewed the musical instruments, we cautioned the director about their purchase, saying that we needed to investigate further.

Thus began an adventure that would stretch over five years. Critics were quick to label the two books we wrote about these experiences "postmodern." *Equatoria* has diary entries from our collecting expeditions on the recto pages and ironical snippets from other people's writings plus Sally's pen-and-ink sketches of artifacts on the versos, and *Enigma Variations* is a novel that has images, some "authentic," others photoshopped as digital "forgeries," on each page (without saying which are which). Since those books tell the story both of our "scientific" collecting expeditions (our interrogations about whether the enterprise of ethnographic collecting, of museums, and of exhibiting cultures, has any lasting worth or is morally doomed) and our private-eye-like experiences unveiling an exquisitely skilled forger of primitive art, I won't say more here.[6]

During that year, we also got involved in an initiative of National Public Radio, which had launched an effort to make its programming more multicultural, sponsoring a series of lavish meetings in San Francisco—we attended four, I think, over the next several years. Called the Working Group on a New American Sensibility, it was intended to include voices from every segment of the country's population, prominent members of the African American, Native American, Asian American, Caribbean American, and Chicano communities, joined by a token White minority.[7]

----

6   Richard Price and Sally Price, *Equatoria* (New York: Routledge, 1992); *Enigma Variations: A Novel* (Cambridge, Mass.: Harvard University Press, 1995), also available in German and French translations.

7   Besides ourselves, participants included: Marie Acosta-Colon, Henry Louis Gates Jr., Suzan Harjo, Steven Lavine, Lawrence Levine, Mari Matsuda, Raymund Paredes, Bernice Johnson Reagon, Jack (John Kuo Wei) Tchen, Marta Vega, Jim West, Tomás

Two other memorable events of that year in California: the devastating Loma Prieto earthquake that damaged a number of Stanford buildings and kept us sleeping on a mattress next to the door of our ground-floor apartment for months; and the better part of a day spent with photographers from *Newsweek*, who arrived with a carful of camera equipment to produce a shot of Sally for an article on her just-published *Primitive Art in Civilized Places*.[8]

Fall 1990: After a full year away from our Martinique home, we were glad to settle back in. In October, I applied for a fellowship at Princeton for spring '92, first giving us a year and a half in Martinique, so we could work on the book about ethnographic collecting, inspired by our summer in Guyane. My spirits rose when *Alabi's World*, which I'd struggled with for so many discouraging years, was finally published and Johns Hopkins University Press sent me a long review by Eric Hobsbawm in the *New York Review of Books* that called it "a splendid effort to recover the past."[9]

In December, we enjoyed a several-day visit from historian Natalie Zemon Davis and her husband, Chan, a mathematician and poet. (I had warned her that we didn't have hot water, but she said that wouldn't be a problem.) Natalie was working on *Women in the Margins*, which included a chapter on naturalist-artist Maria Sibylla Merian and her Suriname adventures at the turn of the seventeenth century, and she had phoned to ask if she could spend some time in our personal library and get hints about how to negotiate their planned stay in Paramaribo—they would be going there right from our house. ("I need to breathe the same air she did," Natalie said.) We had a good time together; I shared with Chan my love of Walcott's recently published *Omeros*, which he hadn't yet read, and there was lots of time for discussion with Natalie about Suriname, including our cautions about the delicate political situation—the

Ybarra-Frausto, and Trinh Minh-ha (who, with her husband, Jean-Paul Bourdier, has remained a friend over the years).

8   Peter Plagens, "All the Way from Darkest . . . You Guys in the Pith Helmets: Clean Up Your Act," *Newsweek*, December 18, 1989, 76. A journalist later remarked that the book "rattled glass cases throughout the art world"—Jennifer Schuessler, "Inside Publishing," *Lingua Franca*, September/October 1995, 26.

9   E. J. Hobsbawm, "Escaped Slaves of the Forest," *New York Review of Books* 6 (December 1990): 46–48.

civil war was still raging at the time. Natalie hinted that I would be named a fellow at Princeton for 1992 and encouraged Sally to seek a visiting professorship in the Department of Art and Archaeology.

Soon after, Leah and Niko arrived on vacation—she from Harvard, he from Stanford, where he was doing an MA in Latin American Studies. During that visit, they both encouraged me to work more systematically on the story of Médard, to be less hesitant about writing a book that was, in part, about our Martiniquan neighbors.

The rest of the year was busy: our main preoccupation remained writing our book on ethnographic collecting (though, as usual, we were also writing diverse articles and book reviews). Meanwhile, Princeton said yes to both of us for the following spring; we began to think about a comparative museums project (in Guyane, Madrid, and Belize); we worked over the copyediting and sample pages of the Stedman abridgment; I collaborated (gingerly) by airmail with Sid on the preface to the Beacon edition of *The Birth of African American Culture* and negotiated with bureaucrats in Guyane about getting a subsidy for a French edition of *First-Time*; we flew to San Francisco for one of those NPR multicultural meetings; and Sally and I became book review editors for the leading Caribbeanist journal, *New West Indian Guide*—a post that, as I write, continues to occupy much of our time.[10]

During the summer of 1991, we conducted our second *mission scientifique* in Guyane, this time collecting artifacts up the Maroni and Tapanahoni Rivers, among Okanisi and Pamaka Maroons. We were also actively following leads about art forgery that had intrigued us the previous summer in Guyane and that eventually led to *Enigma Variations*.

Fall '91, in addition to continuing fieldwork on the Médard project,

---

10 That journal had been published from 1919 to 1959 as the *West-Indische Gids* (at first exclusively in Dutch) and then as the *Nieuwe West-Indische Gids*—with contributions in its heyday by a range of important Caribbean scholars, from Melville Herskovits and Jan Voorhoeve to Irving Rouse and Sidney Mintz. But by the 1970s, there was really no fully functioning pan-Caribbean journal in English, so a meeting was organized at Harry Hoetink's house, with Sid, Harry, Sally, and me. After Sid dropped out, two further meetings in Utrecht, with additional scholars, led to the *New West Indian Guide*, an English language continuation of the venerable journal, which in its latest (open-source) incarnation publishes articles, review articles, and book reviews (fifty per issue) in all disciplines. See https://brill.com/nwig.

I read proofs of *The Birth of African American Culture* and, with Sally, proofs of the Stedman abridgment. Sally wrote a preface for the second edition of *Co-Wives*, and we each put in a proposal to the Guggenheim Foundation for our comparative museums project. Then, just before we left for Princeton, we were delighted to hear that Bill Germano at Routledge had accepted *Equatoria* for publication. (Meanwhile, Leah spent the year at the École Normale Supérieure in Paris, while Niko was in Beijing working three jobs as a beginning journalist.)

After New Year's, we headed to Princeton, where Natalie had arranged an apartment for us. Sally taught two courses (African and African American Art and a seminar on museums) in the Art and Archaeology Department, which she found a bit stuffy—a colleague told her that hiring a PhD from Berkeley (as opposed to Harvard or Princeton) counted as "diversity"—and I worked on the Médard project. In addition to Natalie, we enjoyed getting to know others on the faculty, including Jim Boon, Jorge Klor de Alva, and Bob Darnton. Together, we presented a seminar paper in the History Department that drew on (the not-yet-published) *Equatoria*, and we learned that we had each won a Guggenheim fellowship for the following year. Freelancing was continuing to work for us, though of course our income was considerably less than it had been at Hopkins.

We also had an invitation to participate in the coming summer's Festival of American Folklife, the Smithsonian Institution's annual several-week fête on the National Mall. My former student Ken Bilby and a Smithsonian colleague, Diana N'Diaye, were organizing a get-together of Maroons from throughout the hemisphere—Saamakas and Okanisis from Suriname, Alukus from Guyane, Jamaicans from Moore Town and Accompong, Black Seminoles from Texas and Mexico, Palenqueros from Colombia, and others. Worried about the prospect of participating in some sort of human zoo, we had a talk with Roger Abrahams, then at Penn, who understood our concerns but said that "public folklore" would benefit from our critique and that we should accept the challenge. In the end, we agreed to be what the Smithsonian called "presenters" (and full-time chaperones) for the Suriname and Guyane delegations on condition that we would be free to write about the experience. It was a wild ride, but it also allowed us to think through important questions about Western presentations of non-Western Others.[11] In addition to seeing old friends from Saamaka, including Gaama Songo, who had been installed as Agbago's successor, we also had a chance to renew our acquaintance with Colonel Harris of the Moore Town Maroons of Jamaica, with whom we had stayed for a few memorable days a decade earlier, in the Blue Mountains.

While we were in Princeton, Natalie said she had something important to tell us, so we invited her for dinner in our apartment. She began with a backstory, recounting how her husband, Chan, had lost his professorship at Michigan during the McCarthy years, was jailed (I think), and was forced into permanent exile in Canada. Then she got to the main thing she wanted us to know. While she was directing the Davis Center and my application for a one-semester fellowship came up, she had received a phone call from a colleague in the Princeton Anthropology Department, a close friend of one of my former JHU colleagues (not Sid), whom I had never met. He advised her, she said, that under no circumstances should she bring me to the Princeton campus, as it would present "a grave embarrassment to the institution." When she asked him why, he said he could not disclose that information. On what basis was he making this claim? He said he couldn't say. "You should be ashamed of yourself," she said and hung up. But she decided to follow up. Her first call was to her fellow historian Stuart Schwartz at Minnesota, to ask how our year there had gone. Just fine, he said. But then he added that before we were hired, someone had phoned, warning him not to take us on. Natalie then called the director of the Stanford Humanities Center and asked how our year there had gone. Swimmingly, he said. But he also said there'd been a phone call, warning him that we shouldn't be invited. "You need to know," Natalie told us, "that you will always have a cloud over your heads because of Hopkins. My advice is just to do your work and get on with it. But I wanted you to know."

The several last-minute job rejections we'd suffered began to make sense.

---

11   Richard Price and Sally Price, *On the Mall: Presenting Maroon Tradition-Bearers at the 1992 Festival of American Folklife* (Bloomington: Folklore Institute, Indiana University, 1994).

Back home in Martinique after our summer at the Folklife Festival, we had a double celebration, with the arrival of first copies of *Equatoria* and *The Birth of African American Culture*. Now that we no longer had "normal" university identities (and realized that we might never have any), the publication of books was becoming more important to us personally— the face of our public identity. So it was a special pleasure to learn that *Alabi's World* had won both the 1991 Albert J. Beveridge Award in American History, given by the American Historical Association for "the best work on American history from 1492 to the present," and the Gordon K. Lewis Memorial Award for Caribbean Scholarship, for the best book of the year, given by the Caribbean Studies Association.[12]

In December, we flew up to the annual meetings of the American Anthropological Association in San Francisco and, on the way home, stopped for a conference at Brigham Young University, where Rolph, Brackette, Sally, and I, as well as several other Caribbeanists had been invited to present lectures. I was bowled over by the lecture Rolph gave about race to a class of aspiring Mormon missionaries to Haiti, delivered spontaneously after the laptop with his prepared paper had been stolen en route. Over the course of an hour, as he spoke passionately about the history of the country, he intermittently called their attention to his expensive shoes, his suit and tie, his watch, eyeglasses, moustache, baldness, and his university titles and erudition until, by the end of the hour, he stood before them . . . "absolutely White." It was a breathtaking *"leçon"* on the Haitian construction of race.

Supported by our Guggenheims, we devoted much of the year to our comparative museums project, doing extensive travel in Guyane, Spain, Belize, and Puerto Rico.[13] We ended up with a lengthy museological autopsy, tacking back and forth between questions of exhibition content/presentation and the interactions of museums with larger historical/political realities.

---

12 Meanwhile, Leah began her first year of graduate studies in comp lit at Yale, and Niko was hired by the Associated Press and assigned to cover the state legislature in Carson City, Nevada.

13 Toño Díaz generously showed us around several interesting new museum projects in Ponce, Puerto Rico, but we ended up treating them only in a long footnote.

Three countries, three languages, three major museums slated to open in the early 1990s— . . . all three are kaput.

The Musée Régional in Cayenne, part of a larger program of modernization and development for the French Overseas *département* of Guyane, was to be an ultra-modern state-of-the-art ethnological museum in the French mode. The Museo de América in Madrid, a from-scratch rehabilitation of a Franco-era monument, was drawing on the latest postmodern museological theory to portray Spain's historical legacy in the New World. And the Museum of Belize, in the new capital of Belmopan, was constructing the largest single building in the country and equipping it with the very latest hi-tech devices, to project a dynamic image of this young Central American nation. Our plan was to observe the development of each institution, to attend each opening, and to assess public reaction through interviews with visitors and analysis of press coverage.

Madrid, February 1991. The building has been renovated and the exhibition plans completed in detail. In the wake of a public letter protesting Spain's entry into the Gulf War, the museum's powerful patron in the ministry of culture is fired and the museum project abandoned.

Cayenne, September 1991. The collections have been constituted and the site is being terraced by bulldozers. A corruption scandal rocks the Conseil Régional of French Guiana and all government funds for construction projects are frozen for the next five years.

Belmopan, June 1993. Exhibition plans have been worked out and ground is being broken for the building itself. Suddenly, national elections are called, the opposition unexpectedly wins, and the museum project is shelved.[14]

R.I.P.

The most intellectually intriguing of these museum projects concerned the Museo de América.[15] In 1989, Manuel Gutiérrez Estévez, Spain's leading Mesoamericanist anthropologist, was asked by Jaime Bri-

---

14 These are the opening lines from Richard Price and Sally Price, "Executing Culture: Musée, Museo, Museum," *American Anthropologist* 97 (1995): 97–109.

15 Its twenty thousand-plus objects include some of the greatest treasures of American art: the Tro-Cortesiano ("Madrid") Codex; the gold of the Quimbayas; Moche, Nazca, and Inka ceramics of Peru; an extensive collection of pre-Columbian Peruvian textiles; a magnificent collection of colonial Mexican ceramics; important colonial paintings including the famous "Castas" series from Mexico and Adrián Sánchez Galque's depiction of Zambo kings visiting Quito in 1599; the contact-era Malaspina collection of Northwest Coast Indian art; and much more.

huega, a professor of contemporary art then serving as subminister of culture, to develop a radical renovation of the Franco-era monument. "But I hate museums," Gutiérrez protested, "They bore me to death!" "That's exactly why," said Brihuega, "I want to persuade you to take it on." Gutiérrez formed a stellar international committee charged with creating an antimuseum—militantly nonauthoritarian and nondidactic, designed to inspire doubt and to encourage multiple readings—a dream museum: provocative, interactive, antipedagogic, and contestational. For example, in the plan for the lowland South America section devoted to the stimulants and hallucinogens that shuttle users on ecstatic journeys across cosmic thresholds, the baroque volumes of the museo were to be converted into a series of psychedelic spaces. The *ayahuasca* exhibit was to have "soft walls and broad hanging bands both of fluorescent cloth . . . [across which move] in slow motion projections of sixty color representations of ayahuasca visions. The projections sweep over the walls, the bands, the exhibited objects, and the visitor." There were to be plumed cosmic serpents rising up through house interiors, four-headed anacondas pointing in the cardinal directions, shamanic voices chanting softly as visitors move through the exhibit, and much else. But international politics—the Gulf War—turned this, like our other two museum projects, into a *musée imaginaire*.

I had gotten to know Gutiérrez ("Manolo") through a series of week-long intellectual encounters he had organized in the late 1980s and 1990s, three in a picturesque former convent called La Coria, in Trujillo, Estremadura (birthplace of the conquistador Francisco Pizarro—as I stood on the ramparts of the convent, looking west over the magnificent countryside, I imagined I could see all the way to Peru), and one in Olivenza, also in Estremadura but on the border with Portugal. (Sally also took part in two of these.) Each such meeting brought together a stimulating group of scholars—Mick Taussig, Barbara and Dennis Tedlock, Miguel León-Portilla, Jorge Klor de Alva, Carlos Rodrigues Brandâo, Rolena Adorno, David Maybury-Lewis, and others—along with some of Manolo's students from Madrid.[16] I remember these get-togethers as among the most pleasurable of all "conferences" I've attended. And they prepared Sally and me for the investigation/autopsy of the Museo de América that we undertook, with Manolo's help, during our Guggenheim year.

---

16 Four volumes of these papers were published by Siglo XXI under the general title of *De Palabra y Obra en el Nuevo Mundo*.

Sometime during the winter of 1993–94, we got a call from a reporter at the *Chronicle of Higher Education* who wanted to interview us about our life as successful academics who had departed the academy. We hosted her in Martinique for a couple of days and agreed to write a piece about our experience. Once she'd left, we debated how explicit we should be about our departure from Hopkins and drafted a rather full version of the story, which we titled "Anthropologists Go Home." It began by quoting a recent obituary of Ruth Landes, author of the landmark *The City of Women* (1947), about her research in Bahia among adherents of the Afro-Brazilian religion known as Candomblé.

> "Ruth Schlossberg Landes, 82 . . . died at her home in Hamilton, Ontario. . . . Introduced to Franz Boas and Ruth Benedict, she began at Columbia in anthropology . . . and received her PhD in 1935. . . . Allegedly, a joint letter from Arthur Ramos, a psychological anthropologist purportedly jealous of Landes, and Melville Herskovits to Gunnar Myrdal, for whom Landes worked in 1939, slandered her modus operandi in fieldwork and torpedoed her career in Brazilian research as well as making her persona non grata for full academic employment. She taught at Brooklyn, Fisk, Claremont, Los Angeles State, and Tulane on 1–2 year or summer appointments."
>
> Why did this obituary stop us in our tracks? Because of a letter that arrived in our mailbox on the morning of Sally's birthday in 1985, while we were spending a sabbatical year in Paris. . . . [The text then described our decision to leave Hopkins and our assumption that we would quickly find employment, perhaps at our half-time ideal, at a comparable U.S. institution.]
>
> We were wrong. Since that moment, a half dozen potential appointments—in the mid-West, on the West Coast, in the Ivy League—have been aborted, often by a discreet phone call or two at the very final stage, according to reliable reports. In Ruth Landes's case, a forty-page letter is said to have been quietly circulated by Ramos/Herskovits; we were recently told by Landes's literary executor that the real motive seems to have been sexual jealousy on the part of Ramos because of Landes's affair in Bahia with Edison Carneiro, an Afro-Brazilian anthropologist. With today's technology, of course, no such traces need be left. "You'll be interested to know that they left Hopkins under unsavory circumstances" seems to suffice to deans or department chairs.
>
> Because it is not customary for visible academics simply to walk out of their jobs, our decision sparked speculation. During the past seven years, friends and casual acquaintances (from the U.S., Europe, South

America, and Australia) have passed on to us stories they have heard—often told in tandem—explaining our departure from Hopkins and accounting for our wherewithal to live as independent scholars in the Caribbean: (1) Rich stole large sums of money from the Johns Hopkins University Press [or in some versions, from the Department], (2) The Prices held sexual orgies for graduate students in their home, (3) Rich was carrying on a homosexual relationship with the dean, (4) Rich was addicted to [choose your drug], (5) Rich pocketed student fellowships, (6) Sally got her job thanks to Rich's behind-the-scenes manipulations, (7) the NEH forced Hopkins to ask for Rich's resignation because of #6, (8) The Prices were paid $300,000 in an out-of-court agreement not to sue the university for [it's not clear what].

Like Landes, we have been successful at finding temporary appointments, at institutions of our choice. . . . One of our senior colleagues had insisted that no one could function as a serious anthropologist without a university base; the tropical climate, he assured anyone who would listen, would lead to inevitable decline, lubricated by the local distillates of the sugar cane. Or, as Clifford Geertz observes, "That there is some sort of chair or other under every anthropologist, Collège de France to All Souls, University College to Morningside Heights, seems by now part of the natural order of things. There are [a] few more completely academized professions, perhaps—paleography and the study of lichens—but not many." So, our stepping outside of this pervasive pattern of academic anthropological culture, and settling as residents in a Martiniquan community where we had first done fieldwork twenty-five years before, presented both special challenges and special opportunities for something we love—committing what Geertz has called "the ethnographical act." . . .

Despite our largely successful resolve to relegate our [Hopkins] experience to a forgettable past, its haunting presence tends to creep into our published work as well, creating an occasional subtext for people who've heard this or heard that. A scene of two anthropologists gossiping in *Equatoria*, for example, is accompanied by a passage from Gabriel García Marquez's *In Evil Hour*: "It was said of him that in that same bedroom he'd murdered a man he found sleeping with his wife, that he'd buried him secretly in the courtyard. The truth was different: Adalberto Asís had, with a shotgun blast, killed a monkey he'd caught masturbating on the bedroom beam with his eyes fixed on his wife while she was changing her clothes. He'd died forty years later without having been able to rectify the legend." So, apparently, did Ruth Landes.

We sent the complete draft of this article to two trusted friends, Brackette, who was a recent PhD in the department at the time of our leaving, and Natalie, whose opinion we highly valued. Brackette said we should publish it unchanged. But Natalie held up a warning flag. "You have a choice: Do you want to be talked about and remembered in terms of the scandal, whatever it was, at Johns Hopkins, or do you want to be remembered for your work? If you publish this, everyone (in the small world of academia) will be talking about it and it will never end."

In the end, we took Natalie's advice and published a considerably softer version in the *Chronicle*.[17] Right or wrong, we tried not to look back.

In the spring, we had cause for a celebration. I learned that *Alabi's World* had been selected for the most prestigious book award in anthropology, the J. I. Staley Prize of the School of American Research.[18] Sally and I were flown up, first class, for the ceremony in Santa Fe, and my father came from his home in Chapel Hill.[19] My brief acceptance speech (keyed to the New Mexico locale) expressed how I was feeling at the time.

> Three days ago, sitting under a calabash tree looking out at the blue-green Caribbean, I was thinking how much anthropology has become like a big corporation. There are tremendous pressures within the academy to conform, intellectually and otherwise. The privileges of success, of course, are considerable, and those who make it spend most of their time at 31,000 feet—much like successful businessmen.[20]

---

17 "Anthropologists Go Home: Tropical Reflections on the Academy," *Chronicle of Higher Education*, August 11, 1993, B3–B4 (retitled without permission by the *Chronicle* as: "'Based Where We Ought to Be': 2 Anthropologists Abandon the Comforts of an Academic Home for a Fisherman's Cottage in Martinique"). Years later, another reporter for the *Chronicle* visited Martinique and wrote a very sympathetic, full-page article about us, our work, our house, and our cooking—Carolyn J. Mooney, "On Martinique, 2 Scholars Explore the Permeability of Cultural Boundaries," *Chronicle of Higher Education*, April 7, 2000, B2.

18 It was the last time that J. I. Staley himself presented the award; he died in 1995.

19 My father had always shown support for my efforts—when I was in high school, he took off from work to attend many of my soccer games and track meets, often being the only father there.

20 Had I been better able to see into the future, I could have added that growing inequality, leading to tremendous precarity for many PhDs, was already rearing its head in universities. And that the days of getting academic employment and achieving tenure relatively easily, receiving substantial advances for academic books, and being paid

Thirty some years ago, when I decided to become an anthropologist, I imagined it as a highly individualistic, solitary, romantic endeavor. The Southwest figured in too. Though a New Yorker, I'd spent some weeks, while in high school, on the Navaho and Hopi reservations, and I jumped at the chance to participate in a freshman seminar at Harvard taught by Clyde Kluckhohn—who spent twenty or thirty summers near Ramah, New Mexico, on Navaho lands. And when he died prematurely—in a cabin on the Pecos River, if I remember, it was Evon Vogt—a Ramah native—who kind of took me over and encouraged my anthropological interests. The vision of anthropology I received from these men was adventuresome, iconoclastic, and risk-taking, as well as morally and ethically involved.

I put in my time, eventually founding a department at Johns Hopkins, and serving three terms as chair. And then, seven years ago, there was a much-publicized break with my colleagues. I resigned, as did Sally, lucrative life positions at a prestigious university, ultimately in order to have more time and freedom to pursue our work. We now have no jobs, we have no tenure. We're materially poorer and have no security. But we have our independence—and the freedom to write and think and experiment as we wish.

Corporate anthropology is a closed little community, giving the illusion of being far-flung geographically but it's in fact a close-knit world where news and opinions travel with the speed of e-mail. Since leaving Hopkins, I've been somewhat marginalized within that world—a plunge in conference invitations, a plunge in citations. When we've spent a semester or a year visiting back in the States, it's always been because colleagues in other disciplines—never anthropology—have invited us: historians, Afro-Americanists, Latin Americanists for me, art historians and women's studies people for Sally.

Though *Alabi's World* was researched for more than a decade, the bulk of it was written during the hardest period of my life—right after the break with what I'm calling corporate anthropology. It was not an easy time to force myself to continue, but I did so doggedly, often saying to Sally that here is a book that perhaps three people will read but I'm going to write it anyway.

Now, the book has won three prizes, the first from the American Historical Association (which really pleased me, since the book was

---

enviable salaries (all of which had been true in my case) would soon be gone, except for a minority of elite practitioners. For many new PhDs, a life of serving as a long-term adjunct professor was already looming.

*In Santa Fe with my father,
who flew out for the ceremony.*

in a way openly critical of traditional history), the second from the Caribbean Studies Association (which pleased me even more, since the jury were scholars from the Caribbean), and now the present honor. Coming as it does from a distinguished panel of anthropologists and following in the footsteps of books that represent the very best that our discipline produces [Sid's close friend Eric Wolf had recently won the first year's award for his *Europe and the People without History*], you can perhaps now understand why the Staley Prize means so much to me personally. It is a kind of vindication of the choices Sally and I have made, a recognition that the kind of work we do—however iconoclastic—still carries resonances for people in our discipline. In a way, then, this prize is a homecoming for me, a kind of public coming back to anthropology. I'm very grateful.

And in an interview I gave in Santa Fe at the same event, I talked about how the world of anthropology was changing.

A discipline dies if it doesn't grow. In the 1950s and 1960s we were given very narrow models. . . . The traditional monographic form had become stifling. Somehow, our generation has succeeded in breaking some of those bounds, and it's made things very exciting. It's a wonderful time for ethnography. We have opportunities to collaborate in new ways with people who, twenty or thirty years ago, we used to call our informants. And we have freedom as ethnographers to think about form in writing, to try to match form to content in interesting ways.[21]

⮌

In the fall of 1993, after another summer in Guyane, we decided to present the story of our art-sleuthing experiences in the form of a novel (even though it hewed fairly closely to reality), in order to protect the reputation and livelihood of certain characters, as well as for our own safety.[22] Once we had a draft, our friend George Lamming read it during a visit from Barbados and offered advice as a novelist. "You need to let your imaginations roam yet more freely," he argued. We realized he was right and composed a different, more creative, conclusion to the story.[23]

Our work on *Enigma* made clear that our laptops would not be up to the task of producing the photoshopped images (some "authentic," some "forged") that we planned to include, one on each page, throughout the book. We needed more sophisticated equipment. So we applied for fellowships for spring '94 at the University of Florida, where we would have access to the university's computer lab.

Living in a rented faculty house in suburban Gainesville, we were confirmed that a decision made in the late 1970s had been wise. I had been flown down from Hopkins twice as a candidate for a cushy research professorship. The first time, Charles Wagley, the retiring holder of the chair, met me at the airport, took me to an oyster shack for a dozen of Apa-

---

21 This interview was published in full in the *1993 Annual Report of the School of American Research*, Santa Fe, N.Mex., 22–25.

22 When we shared what we were up to with art historian Gary Schwartz, a specialist on Rembrandt we'd gotten to know during our years in Holland, he warned us in a letter, "You need to be concerned about your safety. This is a very dangerous world, where murders happen."

23 The *Wall Street Journal* reviewer wrote of the published ending, "It's a wow finish, but I'm not going to let the ocelot out of the bag" (Raymond Sokolow, "Faking It in the Green Hell," *Wall Street Journal*, August 17, 1995, A9).

lachicola's finest, and introduced me to the department where I gave a lecture and met with the dean. Soon invited back, this time with Sally and set up by the department with a real estate agent who showed us possible neighborhoods, we again met with the dean. But, in the end, the strong-man of the department, cultural materialist Marvin Harris, argued that I was a poet rather than an anthropologist (he told me that to my face) and, according to a friend in the department, announced that he would resign if I was given the chair. The dean simply pocketed the position.[24]

Soon after we settled into Gainesville, Sally was invited to a confer-ence on originals and copies in art by the chair of the Princeton Art and Archaeology Department, where she'd spent a semester as a visiting assistant professor. She prepared a paper based on the forgery case we had in press at Harvard and flew up to New Jersey, where the chair had arranged for her and a speaker from Germany, as a friendly gesture, to stay as guests in his home rather than in the hotel where the other partic-ipants were put up. But shortly after her arrival, the German's uninvited visit to her room quickly clarified the plan that lay behind that "friendly gesture."

Remembering that Rolena Adorno, whom we'd met at one of Manolo's conferences in Spain, taught at Princeton, Sally phoned her and arranged to get invited for dinner; after stretching the visit as long as she could, she quietly snuck back to her room, braced the door shut with a chair, and had a fitful sleep. After getting through the one-day conference without mishap, she flew back to Gainesville, feeling dirty and humiliated. Her experience reminded me of the time at Hopkins when a woman walked into my office smiling broadly, announced that she had been sent by her graduate advisor (a recent guest speaker in the department seminar from New York), and spread her legs, exposing herself to me. The #MeToo movement was decades away, but the use of women in male bonding was already well developed in academia.

One day while in Gainesville, we attended a performance by Teatro Lo'il Maxil (Monkey Business Theatre), which had developed out of Sna Jtz'ibajom (House of the Writer), a Tzotzil-Tzeltal writers cooperative formed in the 1980s in southern Mexico under the aegis of our old friend from Harvard and Chiapas Bob Laughlin (then curator of Mesoamerican

---

24 We would not, in the end, have accepted, being at the time quite happy at Hopkins and not being able to imagine Leah stuck at Gainesville High, amongst the cheerleaders. College-town Gainesville somehow wasn't our style.

ethnology at the Smithsonian).[25] (We bought a Zapatista Subcomandante Marcos doll there that now stands at attention on a bookcase in our bedroom.) The group then went on to perform in Immokalee, in the Everglades, where five thousand Maya (including a hundred Tzeltal-speaking Chamulas) and Haitian workers picked tomatoes, chile peppers, and oranges. After the armed Chicano foremen judged the performance—which spoke to the abuses inflicted on the immigrant laborers—incendiary, the Indigenous troupers had to flee for their lives in the middle of the night to the Miami airport.[26]

At that performance, we ran into Barbara and Dennis Tedlock, anthropologists whom we had known since we overlapped for a year at Yale in the early 1970s and whose work (on Zunis and on Quiche Mayas) we admired. The next day, we drove together to Cedar Key to eat oysters on the Gulf, passing through Rosewood, the site of Florida's most infamous race massacre (1923). And all the time discussing the fate of anthropology, which was very much on our minds. Humanities (and the postmodern turn) and Science seemed inexorably pitted against each other (Marvin Harris and Kim Romney, two of my nemeses, led the Science brigades), and the Tedlocks, who were literary and artistic, had just been appointed editors of anthropology's flagship journal, promising to encourage "new forms of field research and new forms of representation."[27] As Sally later wrote in some reflections about the state of anthropology at this time, "All this caused outrage among anthropologists working in more traditional 'scientific' modes, from componential analysis to ethnoscience, who nearly came to blows with the 'postmodernists' during a fiery confrontation in the plenary meeting of the American Anthropological Association of 1995."[28] And, if memory serves, the Tedlocks told us that they were already receiving anonymous death threats and that the FBI was monitoring their telephones. They encouraged us to submit our long article on museums (the aforementioned "Executing Culture") to their journal, and it was published in the first issue under their editorship.

---

25 See Robert M. Laughlin and Sna Jtz'ibajom, *Monkey Business Theatre* (Austin: University of Texas Press, 2008).

26 "An Interview with Robert M. Laughlin," *American Anthropologist* 97 (1995): 445–48.

27 Barbara Tedlock and Dennis Tedlock, "From the Editors," *American Anthropologist* 97 (1995): 8–9.

28 Sally Price, "Art, Anthropology, and Museums: Post-Colonial Directions in the United States," *Afrikadaa* 9 (April 2015): 102–15, quote on p. 109.

Some of our other friends suffered severely from these 1990s culture wars that, in the words of the *Chronicle of Higher Education*, "pitted positivism and empiricism against a relativistic and humanistic vision."[29] In 1996, tensions between the factions of the Stanford Anthropology Department had become such that Provost Condoleezza Rice appointed a nonanthropologist as interim chair after Renato, who had been chair, suffered a stroke, "which people on both sides blamed at least partly on stress from the feud."[30] The battle for control was fierce—"an anthropological Antietam," according to the *Chronicle*—and in 1998, the department formally split in two. *Stanford Magazine*'s version laconically reported that "two senior professors on the cultural side grew so exasperated that they chose early retirement." That was George and Jane Collier who, like Renato, had been intellectual, as well as institutional, leaders of the department. (George later quipped to me, "If I hadn't retired, I'd have had a heart attack.") What a loss for the discipline!

During that spring at Gainesville, while producing our computerized images, we received a call from Tomoko Hamada, the chair of the Anthropology Department at the College of William & Mary, inviting us to give lectures. During that visit, we were ushered into the office of Provost Gillian Cell, a British historian, who was interested in establishing a PhD program in anthropology and wanted to know how she could interest us in joining the faculty. At that point, we'd had enough of almost-hirings and whispered backstabbings, so we decided to let her know that we had left Hopkins after a personal conflict with Sid Mintz and that if she tried to hire us she could expect to receive some hostile views of us. We realized that as a historian, she would take seriously the advice of Jack Greene, eminent Hopkins historian of colonial America and a regular visitor in the halls of William & Mary, so we told her to get advice from Jack. He'd been close to both us and Sid and was in a good position to let them know about the breakup. Apparently, he did, since we received what we'd asked for—two full (named) professorships and a one-semester-per-year teaching obligation at half-pay. The idea was to allow us to spend something more than eight months a year in Martinique. We agreed to begin in 1995.

---

29 Christopher Shea, "Tribal Skirmishes in Anthropology," *Chronicle of Higher Education*, September 11, 1998.

30 Mitchell Leslie, "Divided They Stand," *Stanford Magazine*, January/February 2000.

We spent the summer of '94 in Martinique, finishing *Enigma Variations*. In the fall, we were invited for a six-week stay at the University of Illinois, where historian Dan Littlefield and anthropologist Norm Whitten had organized a semester-long seminar devoted to our books and wanted the students to hear us talk about them, one each week. We were given a room in a motel surrounded by cornfields and couldn't help thinking of the description we'd heard of Urbana-Champaign as "the twice-misnamed city." One of the memorable moments of that visit came when I mentioned, in the course of a public lecture, the political December Murders of 1982 in Suriname. A student approached us afterward and told us, tearfully, that her father, a prominent journalist, had been one of the fifteen victims. Desi Bouterse, the dictator at the time, had held the telephone to his face as he was being tortured, she said, so that her mother, whom he had rung up in the middle of the night, could hear his desperate cries.

In November, we flew to São Paulo, where I presented a paper at a conference, "Palmares: 300 Anos," and then on to Bahia, our first introduction to that most seductive of Brazilian cities, where we became friendly with historian João Reis. Back in Martinique, we prepared for our first semester of teaching in Williamsburg but also continued a heavy traveling schedule; Sally's diary mentions ten lectures by each of us in various cities of Spain, Brazil, and the United States. Just before leaving, we were delighted to get copies of *Enigma Variations* (the first novel ever published by Harvard) and a review in the *Wall Street Journal*:

> A fabulous and unique artifact, an art-historical whodunit told with great flair, intelligence and sensitivity. . . . A hybrid work that keeps tempting you to read it as fact although it is officially labeled fiction. . . . Puzzling out which is which is part of the enigmatic charm of the Prices' book—a novel based on the authors' anthropological experiences. The Prices certainly have the great novelist's ability to breathe life into the people they invent—and also, it appears, to breathe life into the living.[31]

---

31 Sokolow, "Faking It," A9. Sid Mintz, anonymized, makes a cameo appearance on page 75.

CHAPTER FIFTEEN

THE COLLEGE OF WILLIAM & MARY (1995–2011)

During our semester-long visits at the venerable College of William & Mary in Virginia, we enjoyed comfortable (one might say very privileged) positions, earning (half of) salaries that were among the highest at the college. Our teaching obligations were not particularly demanding—I generally taught authors I enjoyed reading: Mick Taussig, Barbara Tedlock, Paul Rabinow, Nancy Scheper-Hughes, Anna Tsing, Renato Rosaldo, Rolph Trouillot, Jim Clifford, Jill Lepore, Natalie Davis . . . ; we attended faculty meetings in multiple departments (anthropology and American studies for both of us, plus history for me), which was not overly arduous; and the bureaucratic demands on our time were not terribly burdensome, especially after our colleagues in cultural anthropology effectively ditched efforts to establish a serious PhD program, apparently feeling it would entail too much extra work.

Sally enjoyed working with students in her museums class (sometimes on weekends) to mount creative exhibitions in the Anthropology Department's hall cases, which she got the university to renovate for these projects, and I launched relationships with a number of interesting colleagues and graduate students, mainly in the History Department. Social life tended to be relatively low key but we enjoyed making new (and ongoing) friendships, for example with Phil Morgan, Ron Hoffman, and Kris Lane, who were then in the History Department; Chris Bongie, who directed Literary and Cultural Studies; Bob Gross, who directed American Studies; Joanne Braxton, who was director of Africana House; and visitors such as anthropologist Manuel Ferreira Lima Filho from Goiânia (who later brought us to Brazil twice for lectures), anthropologist and creator of artist books Dan Rose, and novelist David Bradley, whose books we had long admired.

Over the sixteen years of our tenure, however, our enthusiasm gradually waned. The Anthropology Department's focus on archaeology, the ever-growing bureaucratic demands (voluminous and time-consuming tenure reviews, annual reports, teaching evaluations, ad infinitum), the rise in concerns about various aspects of political correctitude, and our increasing awareness of (perfectly understandable) resentment on the part of a number of colleagues who were putting in full-time but earning salaries that were half of ours . . . all this fueled our eagerness to return full-time to Martinique, Paris, and our various research sites. In 2011, when I reached the age of seventy, we retired, emeriti.

"The Burg," as some called it, was for us a peculiar place. W&M, the country's second-oldest institution of higher education—attended by three future presidents including Thomas Jefferson—stands at one end of Duke of Gloucester ("DOG") Street, with the impressive colonial capitol of Virginia at the other. (We walked its length for exercise almost every day.) In between these landmarks sprawls the Republican Disneyland of Colonial Williamsburg, the living museum set up by the Rockefellers in the 1920s and still going strong. (During our time at W&M, we participated in endless debates about whether the living museum should have a separate department of African American interpretation, given that more than half of the population in 1776 consisted of enslaved Africans.) Beyond its colonial core, the town features scores of motels and chain restaurants, designed to make visitors feel at home. Walking to campus in the early morning, we would see buses filled with Black service workers (janitors, gardeners, cleaning women . . .) unloading their passengers; at the end of the day, they would return on this same public transportation to their homes in more rural, predominantly Black areas. Local high schools and other institutions had been segregated until the late 1960s, and we always felt that the aura still lingered.

CHAPTER SIXTEEN

GUYANE
(1986–2020)

After our 1986 expulsion from Suriname, Guyane became our primary "field site," the place where we met with Saamakas and other Maroons and worked on deepening our understanding of their lives. Over the years, we have visited too many times to count. From Martinique, it was just a two-hour flight away, and Air France made the run at least twice a day.

Our first trip from Martinique came in the summer of 1987, while Leah was visiting Sally's sister again, this time in Iowa City, and Niko (an anthropology major) was doing fieldwork in Chiapas.[1] We were working on our long-standing folktale project, fortunate to have located several Saamaka men who had been present at the very wakes we had recorded in Dangogo twenty years earlier, and who now worked at the missile base. Each afternoon and evening, after they had put in their full workdays, we visited with them, eating watermelon, drinking beer, and listening and relistening to the tapes on our reel-to-reel Uher recorder, to refine our transcriptions. They also offered further information, from alternative versions of songs to background on esoteric allusions, all of which fed into the final book.[2]

But we also spent time that summer in Saint-Laurent-du-Maroni. Once the center of Guyane's infamous penal colony, Saint-Laurent had only some two thousand Maroons in 1985—half the town's population—but the civil war in Suriname brought a sudden influx of ten thousand Maroon refugees streaming across the border, many forcibly housed in hastily set up camps surrounded by barbed wire and guarded by French Foreign Legionnaires. While we stayed with our friend Diane Vernon, who by then had moved from Normandy to the old colonial hospital, serving as a cultural mediator between the French-speaking doctors and

---

1   George Collier, who was running Vogtie's Chiapas project that summer, placed Niko with the same family we had lived with in the 1960s—the man who, as a boy, had slept above us in the corn bin—see Niko Price with Richard Price and Sally Price, "Indian Summers," in *Ethnographic Encounters in Southern Mesoamerica: Essays in Honor of Evon Zartman Vogt, Jr.*, ed. Victoria R. Bricker and Gary H. Gossen (Albany: Institute for Mesoamerican Studies, 1989), 125–32.

2   Richard Price and Sally Price, *Two Evenings in Saramaka* (Chicago: University of Chicago Press, 1991).

The Kourou crew: RP, Lodi, Sineli, Kasolu, Antonisi, Amoida, SP.

nurses and the overwhelmingly Maroon population of patients, we got our first look at the horrors of that war.

During this visit, we spent time with my Hopkins student advisee, Ken Bilby, who was finishing up his PhD research in Saint-Laurent. Ken helped us grasp what was happening in the war.

> The turning point came in November and December 1986, when a
> military campaign in eastern Suriname resulted in more than 150
> civilian deaths. In a number of Cottica River Ndjuka [Okanisi] villages,
> unarmed Maroons—including pregnant women and children—were
> rounded up and massacred. . . . Within a few weeks, more than 10,000
> of these Maroon refugees had arrived in French Guiana. Witnesses
> narrated horrific accounts of defenseless villagers being lined up and
> mowed down with automatic weapons while they pleaded for their
> lives. I was there when the refugees began to pour into Saint-Laurent,
> and I spoke to several of these eyewitnesses, only days after the
> massacres took place. Of the many atrocities related, one in particular
> seemed to stand out for its brutality. In the settlement of Moiwana, not
> far from Albina, a soldier had torn an infant from its mother's arms,
> placed the barrel of his gun in its mouth, and pulled the trigger.[3]

3   Kenneth M. Bilby, "The Remaking of the Aluku: Culture, Politics, and Maroon Ethnicity in French South America" (PhD diss., Johns Hopkins University, 1990), 505–6.

One day, the chief psychiatrist at the hospital where Diane worked asked our assistance in communicating with a fourteen-year-old Saamaka patient incarcerated in one of the refugee camps. According to the doctor, young "Baala" had been brought to the hospital by an older brother a few months earlier, having suffered a nervous crisis. The doctor tranquilized him and, after several days, interviewed him, eliciting a story about a broken calabash that had been made by his mother. The doctor told us the boy's condition was due to his relationship with his mother, symbolized by the broken calabash, and he spun out for us various Freudian implications. "What's it like to conduct a psychiatric interview when you don't speak the patient's language?" we asked. "Thank goodness for the universal language of symbols," the good doctor replied.

After several days of chemical treatment, Baala was placed in Camp A, the refugee camp next to the Saint-Laurent airstrip. The psychiatrist ended his summary of Baala's pathology by saying that the boy stopped speaking as soon as he arrived in the camp. (I remarked to Sally, sotto voce, that this case reminded me of the incident described by Stedman in which a fourteen-year-old enslaved youth had been deliberately deprived of speech and driven mad by a sadistic overseer. Sally replied: "*Ou malin!*"—in Martiniquan Creole, roughly: "Don't be such a smartass!")

Since Baala had been abandoned by his relatives, the psychiatrist hoped we would be able to give an opinion and help him figure out what to do with the boy. With the doctor at the wheel, the car was waved through the military checkpoint at the entrance to Camp A. Baala's behavior confirmed the psychiatrist's summary; he seemed disturbed and said nothing. We asked the doctor, in French, to leave us alone with him and greeted Baala in Saamakatongo. Suddenly, a broad grin, a normal fourteen-year-old. We introduced ourselves and said we were interested in what had happened to him.

He'd been held against his will for many weeks, he said, surrounded by Okanisis who spoke a language he could barely understand. His words came tumbling out. The White doctor scared him; the White nurses scared him; the soldiers scared him. His brother, he said, had been secretly visiting him every three or four days during the night, sneaking in across the barbed wire fence because he, too, was scared of the soldiers and the nurses and the doctors, had no French papers, and, like many Saamakas in Guyane, lived in constant fear of discovery and deportation back to Suriname. Now, Baala said, he simply wanted to get out of this awful place. We told him we'd see what we could do and went off with the psychiatrist, who agreed that we should visit the family to confirm that they were prepared to receive him back.

Off we drove to a Saamaka settlement some ten kilometers away, just past the largest of the Maroon refugee camps. Baala's friends and relatives were delighted that he could be released. Nothing would please them more, they said, than to be able to have him back, but they'd been too frightened of the soldiers and the doctor to try to arrange his release themselves. We took one of Baala's brothers with us and drove down the road to the giant refugee camp where the psychiatrist was consulting. There was a menacing aspect to this place, where White crew-cut legionnaires lived on a central hill surrounded by a heavy barbed wire barrier hung with a large skull-and-crossbones warning sign. We persuaded the psychiatrist to release Baala into his brother's custody that very day, and he wrote a note for us to take, along with Baala's brother, back to Camp A.

Before leaving, we couldn't resist a comment or two on why Baala had been silent—no one spoke his language, he was terribly frightened of the soldiers and the doctor, he was incarcerated in a squalid camp—and we tried to give him some sense of what French colonialism, backed by automatic weapons, looked like from the perspective of a fourteen-year-old boy who'd grown up in a Saamaka village in the rainforest. The psychiatrist appeared not to comprehend, protesting that he'd never been anything but kind toward the boy (which was certainly true). We drove back to Camp A, and Baala was soon on his way home, where we visited him a few weeks later, happily fishing in a creek with his friends.

On subsequent visits to Guyane over the next thirty years, we frequently stayed with Diane in Saint-Laurent, learning about the fast-changing town and meeting her health worker colleagues and schoolteacher friends, who helped us get a handle on what by 2020 has become a city of sixty thousand, with a Maroon population of forty-six thousand—the largest majority Maroon city in the world.

In 1989, we were invited (like Diane) to present lectures at a conference in Cayenne devoted to the characteristically Guyanais package of "Identity, Culture, and Development." Compared to Martinique, Guyane is a remarkably cosmopolitan place—immigrants from Suriname, Brazil, Haiti, China, Vietnam, France, and elsewhere—with three-quarters of the adult population born outside the territory. Guyane is also the most

profoundly colonial place we know. At the conference, we tried to say
something about the inequalities we were growing used to seeing.

Not long ago, we had the occasion to visit some old friends in the
so-called "Village Saramaka" at Kourou. Living in mean little con-
structions almost in the shadow of the Ariane rocket, these immigrant
workers continue to supply much of the manual labor at the missile
base. We accompanied a woman (who had been our neighbor twenty
years earlier in Dangogo [Suriname]) on what she called "a little trip to
her provision-ground"; entering the small supermarket nearby, barefoot and bare-breasted, she selected her groceries—a frozen chicken
from Brittany (with labels in French and Arabic), a tin of sardines
from Nantes, some Parisian candies for the kids. The next day, back
in Cayenne, we were invited by colleagues from ORSTOM [now IRD],
the major French scientific research organization in Guyane] to a posh
restaurant where, under a set-piece "tropical" thatch roof, we drank
fine wines from the metropole and ate delicious stews of monkey,
armadillo, and tapir—all everyday foods of Saamakas back home in
Suriname.

The old "Village Saramaka" in Kourou.

It was during that visit that we were formally asked to supervise the planning of the Maroon section of the *département*'s nascent museum. The director, a Creole woman with a PhD in folklore, was to take charge of the section on Creoles, and anthropologists Pierre and Françoise Grenand and Gérard Collomb were to handle the Amerindian sections. The yet-to-be-built institution was explicitly envisioned as a *musée de l'homme guyanais*. We felt ambivalent, having serious doubts about whether ethnographic collecting could ever be done without violence and whether the whole concept of an ethnological museum made sense at the end of the twentieth century. But, as with the Folklife Festival, we decided to become engaged, with the idea that we would someday write about our experiences.

We undertook collecting expeditions for the museum along the inland rivers in the summers of 1990 (accompanied by Ken, who had done much of his dissertation research with the Aluku) and 1991 (accompanied by Diane, who had long worked with Okanisis). At the same time, we continued our increasingly obsessive sleuthing about art forgery, culminating in success during the summer of 1993, when we finally figured out what was going on in the high-stakes local art and museum world. In a nutshell: a French lycée teacher, teaming up with a Saamaka woodcarver as an innocent assistant, had produced the remarkable musical instrument "antiquities" that the director of the museum had purchased (despite our warnings) three years earlier, claiming that they had been acquired from a Suriname planter who had inherited them from an eighteenth-century ancestor, who had a new instrument added to his "slave orchestra" each time he sired a child on the plantation.[4]

During our visits to Guyane in the mid-'90s, we became increasingly concerned about disparaging views of Maroons, expressed by people of all classes and ethnicities and from the capital to the most far-flung rural areas. After the massive immigration of Suriname Maroons as a result of the civil war, they were appearing in schools, hospitals, and the central prison as never before, fueling stereotypes and resentments in the population at large. So we decided to work on a book designed to help Guyanais understand some basic truths—for example, that the Maroons they encountered in their daily lives are not a single people but four dis-

4   For details, see Price and Price, *Equatoria* and *Enigma Variations*.

As detectives in Bahia, where
Enigma Variations *ends.*

tinct groups, speaking different languages and with their own customs, identities, and histories of immigration; that the ancestors of all these people escaped from plantations in Suriname, not Guyane; that Maroons in Guyane were numerous and would, collectively, soon be the largest population group in this multiethnic society; and that Maroons, far from being ignorant "primitives," are known worldwide for the richness of their cultures and their deep historical knowledge.

With the financial support of the Direction des Affaires Culturelles (the local branch of the French ministry of culture), we drove a dilapidated government-owned 2CV and spent several months visiting Maroons who lived in diverse circumstances, from Saamaka migrant families who were considered "illegals" to Guyanais-born Alukus who worked for the local government and from old friends whom we had first known in Dangogo in the 1960s to new acquaintances we met along the roads and rivers that we traveled. Our goal was to provide local journalists, schoolteachers, physicians, nurses, prison guards, store owners, and the general public accurate information—historical, cultural, demographic—about the Maroons they were now dealing with on a daily basis. We wrote the book directly in French, and it was published with numerous color illustrations. *Les Marrons*,[5] a low-priced "general public" book, sold nearly six thousand copies in the Cayenne airport, in supermarkets, and in the few bookstores of a territory where much of the population had never read a book.

Those visits around the millennium, gathering material for *Les Marrons*, were memorable. Days with our Dangogo friends in their jerry-built shacks in the "Village Saramaka" in Kourou—watching Paris's Bastille Day parade on a TV in a one-room house whose bare board walls were covered with discarded blueprints of the inside of Ariane rocket engines that our friends, who had jobs as janitors, had fished out of wastebaskets at the missile base, enjoying Ronaldo's double as Brazil beat Germany in the final of World Cup 2002 in a Brazilian bar in Kourou jammed with German rocket scientists and their families, their cheeks striped black, red, and gold, and more.

But our deepest involvement with Guyane began in 2000 when we met Tooy Alexander, a Saamaka some fifteen years my senior. He had been flown from his home in Cayenne to Martinique by a local businessman who was hoping that Saamakas' famous ritual powers could solve some personal and financial problems that were turning his life upside down.

Clifford Geertz once called anthropologists "merchants of astonishment."[6] But for me, it was Tooy who played that role. I met him some thirty-five years into my Saamaka research, and it wasn't long before he took me through the looking glass and down the rabbit hole. He guided me into a world of gods and demons, of wonders, delights, and magical cures that rivaled that of Wagner's ring. He shared with me the hidden worlds that, for him, made life worth living and, for me, continue to amaze and fascinate. *Travels with Tooy*, in unbridgeably different ways, was his book as much as mine—his gift to me, my gift to him.[7]

At first glance, the rough shantytowns that ring Cayenne, where Haitian, Brazilian, Guyanese, and Suriname migrants live cheek by jowl,

---

5   Richard Price and Sally Price, *Les Marrons* (Châteauneuf-le-Rouge: Vents d'ailleurs, 2003).

6   Geertz, *Available Light*, 64.

7   Richard Price, *Travels with Tooy: History, Memory, and the African American Imagination* (Chicago: University of Chicago Press, 2008). The following paragraphs are adapted from that book.

With Tooy in his consulting room.

might seem the least likely of places to meet a fellow intellectual. And yet . . . the poverty that threatens to crush the spirit of both the hard-working and the unemployed can leave largely untouched the richness of the imagination. Amid the mud and stench and random violence, Tooy—captain of the Saamakas of Cayenne—ran a household in which spiritual and rhetorical gifts abounded. I felt privileged to play a part in it for fifteen years.

Tooy, who died in 2015, belonged to a long and distinctive tradition of emigration by Saamaka men to Guyane. For a century and a half, the migrants clustered together in sites spread across that French territory. Though often working for outsiders to earn money, they spent the great bulk of their social lives with other Saamakas. Meanwhile, their *imaginaire*—their thoughts, their dreams, their hopes—was forever grounded in their homeland in the neighboring country of Suriname. In Guyane, even if they had come there voluntarily, they were always in exile. Their central point of reference remained their home village and its spiritual possessions, the stretch of river and forest that surrounds it, the places they had hunted and gardened in, the world that their heroic ancestors first carved out in the Suriname rainforest more than three hundred years earlier.

Tooy was an inveterate time traveler. Like other Saamaka men, he spent a great deal of time thinking about his distant ancestors, some of whose lives he knew intimately, as well as other normally invisible beings. Neither nostalgia nor intellectual exercise, these voyages helped him understand who he was—his forebears' specific powers, wrapped up in their individual histories, gave him much of the energy he had to confront the world. Tooy spent a lifetime putting together his knowledge of them, as he participated in countless rites, political gatherings, and family councils. Over the years that I knew him, he generously shared fragments of what he knew with me, in part in the hope of learning more from my own stock of stories, built up over years as an ethnographer of the Saamaka past.

Tooy loved crossing boundaries—between centuries and continents, between the worlds of the living and the dead, between the visible and the invisible, between villages on land and under the sea. Whoosh! we're in eighteenth-century Suriname, surrounded by African arrivants who are as familiar as our current friends and neighbors. Whoosh! we're talking about migrant Saamakas who built a new world in French Guiana at the end of the nineteenth century. Whoosh, we're speaking with the sea-gods who control the world's money supply.

Tooy had a unique vision of Africa—a land of men's men, where those who prepared themselves properly could take off and soar like eagles, where others could dive into the river in the morning and commune with the spirits underwater till nightfall, where men had gods and *obias* who could cure any disease that ailed their fellows—a land of warriors impenetrable to spears or bullets, men who had never eaten salt nor ever shaken hands with a White man. And he could speak many fragments of the languages they had used.

In his Nobel lecture, *The Antilles: Fragments of Epic Memory*,

Tooy.

Derek Walcott spoke of what these captive Africans brought to the New World:

> Deprived of their original language, the captured . . . tribes create their own, accreting and secreting fragments of an old, an epic vocabulary . . . from Africa, but to an ancestral, an ecstatic rhythm in the blood that cannot be subdued by slavery. . . . The original language dissolves from the exhaustion of distance like fog trying to cross an ocean. . . . The stripped man is driven back to that self-astonishing, elemental force, his mind. That is the basis of the Antillean experience, this shipwreck of fragments, these echoes, these shards of a huge tribal vocabulary, these partially remembered customs, and they are not decayed but strong. They survived the Middle Passage.[8]

One day in 2005, quite spontaneously, Tooy gave me his own version: "When the Old Ones came out from Africa, they couldn't bring their obia pots and stools—but they knew how to summon their gods and have them make new ones on this side. They no longer had the original pots or stools, but they carried the knowledge in their hearts."

Tooy's remark evokes both some of what was lost in the Middle Passage and some of what his captive African ancestors successfully carried to the Americas. Along with the rest of what he taught me, it suggests as well that it may be time to lay to rest the hoary academic debate between those who stress African continuities in the Americas (including the ongoing importance of African "ethnicities") and those who stress the Africans' creation of institutions in the New World. He taught me the importance of what we call creolization.

Occasionally, we participated in the process.

When we first met Tooy in 2000, hosting him during his stay in Martinique, Sally and I showed him a wooden sculpture of the Brazilian sea goddess Iemanjá, which we'd bought in Cachoeira (Bahia) a couple of years earlier when we were teaching in Brazil. Tooy looked at her lovingly, saying, "What a great thing that would be to put in my obia house!" And, over the following days, he often asked me to say her name for him. He liked to pronounce it as "Yemanzaa."[9]

Two years later, after his (distressingly wrongful) conviction on a charge

---

8   https://www.nobelprize.org/prizes/literature/1992/walcott/lecture/.

9   The figure is fourteen inches high, dated 1998, and signed by Mimo.

of rape,[10] Tooy is flown to the high-security prison wing of the hospital in Martinique for emergency open-heart surgery. When I arrive for my daily half-hour visit, the gendarmes are rougher than usual when they pat me down— the pen and folded-up sheet of paper in my pocket don't sneak by today though the apple I bring as a gift is permitted. Keys turn and the steel door clanks open. Tooy is sitting on his bed looking alone and frightened, in an isolation cell hundreds of miles from home, treated like the dangerous criminal he isn't and about to undergo the dreaded knife. I take the only chair and try some comforting small talk. He sings me a song he'd heard in a dream: *Mama, mi mama Yemanzaa / Mi ta haika i, yooo / Yei mi mama yaaa?* (Mother, my mother Yemanzaa, I'm waiting for you. Do you hear, my mother?) "I walked north in the dream," he explains, "and went down a big hill and then turned east on an old path up a hill where I saw a very large jaguar, sound asleep." "Do you think that's a bad omen?" he asks. "No, it's good!" he laughs. And he sings the song to Yemanzaa again.

The sculpture of Iemanjá that we gave Tooy.

In 2003, on our way home from another trip to Brazil, we stop in Cayenne after Tooy has been liberated and he mentions that he's thinking about making an altar to Yemanzaa. And then finally, on our first visit in 2005, we present Tooy with our statue of the goddess for him to keep, and he sings us a new song to her: *Ma Yema-e, Mama Yema, gaan tangi mi ta begi unu fu di suti odi f'i, Ma Yemazala, mi ta meni i-o, mi mama, Mama Yema, mi ta begi i yeti fu di suti odi f'i yei mama-e, Ma Yema . . . zaa!* (Mother Yemanzaa, I offer thanks for your sweet greetings, I keep thinking of you, I continue asking you for those sweet greetings of yours, Mother Yemanzaa). He's overjoyed but decides to keep the goddess in her wrapping until his wife, Yaai, gets back from her stay in Saint-

---

10 See R. Price, *Travels with Tooy*, 177–205.

Laurent, so she and the sea-god that possesses her can participate in placing her on his Wenti (sea-god) altar.

When Saamakas first came to the Oyapock River in Guyane, as canoemen in the gold rush around 1900, they realized they had truly arrived in the heart of Wenti country. One man was possessed by a Wenti-god named Wananzai, who would dive into the river in the morning and come back in the evening with remarkable tales of the underwater world. The men learned from Wananzai that at Gaama Lajan (The Mother of All Money)—a rock formation several kilometers downriver from their village—under the water was what might best be described as the Central Bank of the World. There, Wenti maidens—not at all unlike Wagner's Rhinemaidens (Woglinde, Wellgunde, and Flosshilde)—stand watch over barrels and barrels of golden coins, which they sometimes roll out into the sun to dry, singing beautiful songs all the while. (Tooy knew many of the songs and sang them for me.) They also learned that Wentis have strong affinities with Whitefolks and that Wentis abhor death and blood, nor do they like rum or other strong drink, nor do they like sun or heat, nor do they mix with evil. Rather, they love white, bright, shiny, clean things, sugary, bubbly things, and all things cool from the sea.

One of the first Wenti-gods that Saamakas learned about was Tata Yembuamba, "The Big Man of Oloni" (the great underwater city in which he lived). Once, Tooy told me, Yembuamba took Tooy's brother's possessing spirit, Flibanti, for a visit to this magical place, and later, Flibanti told him about it—how, for example, if you don't know the password they won't even let you step ashore—they'll turn you into ashes! (Tooy confided that to enter the realm of the Wenti-gods the password is *senoo, senoo* plus the name of the Wenti-god you're coming to see.) Flibanti also told Tooy about a special pool they have down there called *kibamba-wata* (Whitefolks' water). If you're a man of sixty and they throw you in, you emerge a youth of seventeen. Once in Cayenne, Flibanti himself (possessing Tooy's brother) told me, almost dreamily, that "Tata Yembuamba is the whitest of white. He walks on the Earth till he's finished and then he travels undersea." His brothers and sisters in Oloni include Todje, the tutelary spirit of the late Gaama Agbago, and three beautiful sea-god sisters with musical names: Yowentina, Korantina, and Amentina. Tooy's relations with sea-gods are multiplex: Yowentina is married to Flibanti, the god in Tooy's brother's head; and Tooy's Okanisi wife is the master of a particularly powerful Wenti named Basi Yontini, who is their son. (Are we back in *The Ring of the Nibelungen*?)

During one of the visits of Tooy's own possession god in 2005, he instructs me to make a Wenti altar at our home in Martinique. "Here's what to do to make sure you have no problems, to make your life the way it ought to be. When you get home, on the lowest terrace facing the sea, where you'd go if you were going to get into a boat, find a short little table and place it there. Cover it with whatever pretty cloth you wish. But be sure it's a Thursday, the Wentis' day! Then you and Madame [Tooy's god's term of reference for Sally] should sit down there; you and those people will eat together. Go sit down and drink with them. Call on Ma Yema to come and join you! You and she should work together." And then he adds, "But do watch out on the west side there. There's an Adatu [a toad-spirit Komanti] who has designs on your wife. He's not evil. Let him come to the altar too. Beer should never be lacking there for the Wentis, sugar-cane syrup for the earthmother, a bit of honey for the Adatu. In the evenings go sit down there, in the mornings go sit down there. Drink a little with them!"

Back home, Sally and I built the altar facing the sea. In the subsequent years, we often shared a drink with the Wentis, watching for the green flash as the sun slipped below the horizon. I always made sure there was a dollop of honey in a little jar for that Adatu. Contemporary creolization in action!

Or again, while we were in Bahia, we spent time in the home—which was in the process of becoming a museum—of Pierre Fatumbi Verger, photographer and self-taught ethnographer of the Atlantic world, born in France, resident of Salvador, and incessant traveler, who had died two years earlier. In 2002, during Tooy's time in the prison wing of the hospital in Martinique, he slept with a book under his mattress. I had managed to persuade the frighteningly tough gendarmes who guarded him that this book—Verger's *Orixás*, with photos of Yoruba gods in Africa and the New World, which we'd given him as a present—was the equivalent of the Bible for him and was therefore permitted in his cell by French law. During our daily half-hour visits, we often turned the pages together and he'd ask me to read the captions. Some pictures of Ogoun in possession in Nigeria inspired him to reveal that his brother's Saamaka possession spirit, Flibanti, too, likes to eat dog—as well as jaguar! He also relishes an animal I'd never heard of called *zanau*, which has but one eye. "It's as tall as a room," Tooy tells me, "and it lives on a mountain that has six peaks which you can see from Montagne Tortue on the Approuague River. It picks people up in its claws and devours them! There's a cave where it keeps the bones." He adds, "No man's ever gone hunting in that place and returned alive!" When I later consult a map, I see, uneasily, that it's right near where they're building the new highway between the towns of Régina and Saint-Georges-de-l'Oyapock.

In 2020, I was asked to write a chapter for the catalog of a photo exhibit in Berlin about a brief visit that Verger made in 1948 to an Okanisi Maroon village in Suriname, accompanied by anthropologist Alfred Métraux (with whom I was slated to study in 1963!). I wrote it using a combination of Métraux's published diaries, Verger's written comments on the visit, and his own vivid photos.[11]

Tooy was at once my closest friend—even closer than Sid had been during our days at Hopkins—and my greatest teacher.[12] Once, on the eve of our flight back to Martinique, Tooy launched into one of his philosophical games: "Someday, you'll forget a person you love," he tells me, testing. I say it's not possible. But he insists: "I'm sure that if someone says something bad about me to you, you'll want to fight him. And if someone says something bad about you to me, I'll rip him apart. If someone comes to kill you with a gun, I'd say shoot me first. All that's clear. But something could still happen so that I would no longer want to take your bullet." I begin to understand where he's going. "It's called betrayal!" he says. (I think of Johns Hopkins!) "We could fight about something, but that wouldn't change the way we feel about each other. There's a god in [the Saamaka village of] Kayana called Miteenzu Banangoma. When it possesses someone it says, 'Hee! I'm Magwenu from Ayowe. I'm Your-friend-who-deceives-you-till-you-find-evil!' If a true friend betrays you, do you think you'll ever cross his doorstep again?" Tooy pauses, then continues. "There are three kinds of false friends. There's the friend who loves you because of something you're doing that he wishes he could do too. Or the friend who loves you because he wants your wife. Or the friend who loves you because you have lots of money. In each case, when he's finished getting what he wants, he's gone. But a true friend loves your breath, your sweat, the way you are." "You know why I love you?" he asks.

---

11   Richard Price, "Pierre Verger among the Aukans: Suriname 1948," in *Pierre Verger in Suriname*, ed. Willem de Rooij (Berlin: Walther König, 2020), 283–86.

12   In 2021, after reading a draft of this book, Toño Díaz-Royo wrote me that Sid made clear, during visits to Puerto Rico in the final years of his life, that he was "resentful" of my relationship with Tooy.

Gathering medicinal leaves.

A bit embarrassed, I joke that it's because he's after my wife, which makes him laugh. "I love your sweat," he says, "your very blood. The way you sit down here, sweating." He waves Sally and me into the room adjoining the Dungulali [ritual] chamber, where he has prepared an obia-canoe filled with leaves for us to bathe in. It's been a week since the leaves were left to soak and the liquid is not only black but smells something awful. Tooy tells us cheerfully that he knows we can't bathe in it the next day since we're leaving, and we'd stink so much they wouldn't allow us onto Air France. Now's the time. We bathe.

Walcott spoke about the concurrent joy, solemnity, and obligation of bearing witness to what we may call, with Michel-Rolph Trouillot, the miracle of creolization.

> There is a force of exultation, a celebration of luck, when a writer finds himself a witness to the early morning of a culture that is defining itself, branch by branch, leaf by leaf, in that self-defining dawn, which is why, especially at the edge of the sea, it is good to make a ritual of the sunrise. Then the noun the "Antilles" ripples like brightening water, and the sounds of leaves, palm fronds, and birds are the sounds of a fresh dialect, the native tongue. The personal vocabulary, the individ-

ual melody whose metre is one's biography, joins in that sound, with any luck, and the body moves like a walking, a waking island.

This is the benediction that is celebrated, a fresh language and a fresh people, and this is the frightening duty owed.[13]

Tooy taught me that exultation and inspired that frightening duty.[14] In 2015, after a lingering illness, he passed into the land of the ancestors.

During the years we shared with Tooy, we made frequent visits to Guyane, staying in the room he had built expressly for us on top of his modest house, in a shantytown neighborhood of Brazilian migrants at the edge of Cayenne. Tooy made his living as a curer, and his door was open to all Guyanais. In the course of a day with him, we would hear conversations in Saamaka, Okanisi, Aluku, Guyanais Creole, Haitian Creole, Sranantongo, Portuguese, and French. After the American version of *Travels with Tooy* was published, I spent several days going through it with him to make sure that the French translation, then in preparation, would meet his wishes. (Tooy had never been to Western school and was not literate, but he understood that many of the people he knew in Guyane would read the book.) At the request of his daughter, I removed all mention of his trial and conviction on a (spurious) charge of rape and the special means we used to set him free. And Tooy accompanied me to the book launchings at the university and at bookstores when *Voyages avec Tooy* came out, enjoying every moment.[15]

Often enough, we had obligations in Guyane that lay outside of Tooy's world—a six-week-long lecture series at the University in Cayenne, book signings, a linguistics conference, speaking to high school or junior high school classes, or appearances on the nightly TV news. We were always

---

13 Walcott, "Antilles."

14 I wish he'd been able to more fully understand the pleasure I got from *Travels* winning three major book prizes: the Clifford Geertz Prize in the Anthropology of Religion, the Victor Turner Prize in Ethnographic Writing, and the Gordon K. and Sybil Lewis Memorial Award for Caribbean Scholarship.

15 For detailed reflections on the ways my relationship with Tooy compared with the 1960s relationship between anthropologist Carlos Castaneda and Don Juan and related reflections on how anthropology and the study of religion have changed in the interim, see Richard Price, "From *The Teachings of Don Juan* to *Travels with Tooy*: One Anthropologist's Trip," *Journal of the Anthropology of Consciousness* 22 (2011): 138–60 (also available at www.richandsally.net).

struck by the contrasts between his circle and those that dominated Guyane, which we interacted with regularly. We occasionally dined at the homes of government leaders—the prefect, the attorney general, the president of the Collectivité Térritoriale (who in 2018 presented us with the Medal of Guyane), and the director of cultural affairs.

One evening, for example, we attended a dinner party that thrust us back to the late nineteenth century and across the sea to, say, French West Africa. At a table laden with fine wine and French food, we were surrounded by White French couples who'd all arrived from the metropole during the past one to four years (and were soon to depart)—including a *sous-préfet* (subprefect), a representative of France's Ministry of Culture, another from the Ministry of Education, and one from the Ministry of Justice, engaged in conversations about the locals that, at best, reeked of the *mission civilisatrice*. When they asked which hotel we were staying in and we replied that we were guests of our Saamaka friend Tooy in the Brazilian ghetto of Les Paletuviers (The Mangroves), there was alarm, consternation, and disbelief. "But White people can't go there at night!" And we've had similar experiences with upper-class Creole society, which, while largely excluded from colonial White society, does a lot of downward gazing of its own. The shrinking Creole elite, with its low, bourgeois birthrate, feels increasingly overwhelmed by the rising tide of migrants and their many babies and embattled, despite their control of local political institutions.

In 2005, we flew to Guyane to launch two new books—*Les Marrons* and *Les Arts des Marrons*—and were invited by Léon Bertrand, mayor of Saint-Laurent-du-Maroni and Jacques Chirac's minister of tourism, to present *Les arts des Marrons* in the town hall. *"Le tout Saint-Laurent,"* he said, would be present. And, indeed, the prefect and other dignitaries made the three-hour trip from Cayenne, dressed in their formal white uniforms, some with their fashionably attired wives. Although the hall was filled almost exclusively with Whites and Creoles, it made sense for the mayor to be promoting a book that celebrated Maroon art in this majority-Maroon town. And not only did he gratefully accept the copy we signed for him but he promised to bring another copy with our dedication to President Chirac, whom he said he would see in a cabinet meeting in Paris later that week. (Several weeks later, in Martinique, we received a note of thanks from the president.) Unfortunately, the evening did not end smoothly. After the champagne and hors d'oeuvres had been passed around, the mayor had made his speech, and we had completed our own brief presentation of the book, the head of a local cultural association, a Frenchman who had a habit of attacking our historical understandings of Maroon arts, launched a violent verbal assault. When I responded, he rushed me with fists flying. After the gendarmes were called and escorted him out of the hall, peace was restored, and we drove back to Tooy's.[16]

After Tooy's death, we visited Guyane less frequently, keeping up with his widow and family mainly by phone. But in 2016, we made one memorable trip across the face of the territory when we had three new books to share (two in French and one in the Saamaka language), presenting them in bookstores, town halls, and schools in many of Guyane's towns.[17] Whenever we spoke in schools in western Guyane—whether in Saint-Laurent or Mana—students' faces lit right up when we would switch from French to Saamakatongo. The great majority of students were Maroons and being shown even that small token of respect made a very big difference.

And then in 2018, we drove across Guyane, and traveled up its largest river, with financial help from the Department of Cultural Affairs, conducting research for a radical updating of the original (2003) edition of *Les Marrons*. By the time that new edition appears in 2022 (in both French and English[18]), Maroons will constitute 36 percent of Guyane, making them its largest single ethnic group, and there will have been tremendous changes in almost every aspect of Maroon life, from education, to language, to religion, to increased participation in the drug trade.

---

16 This was neither the first nor last time this man attacked us. In 2013, before an audience of several hundred attending an international conference on Maroons in Saint-Laurent-du-Maroni, he stood up to shout out (in French), after Sally had presented a paper on Maroon art, "Sally: It is obvious that you are not only blind but also deaf and dumb. You need to find another profession." He then stalked out. (In the 1980s, he had boasted to a travel writer, "'I am host of a radio program in Cayenne. You might say I am the Johnny Carson of French Guiana. Since French Guiana is absolutely the asshole of the whole world, I am keeping busy on my program, sifting the *merde*'"—Thurston Clarke, *Equator: A Journey* [New York: Morrow, 1988], 82).

17 Richard Price, *Les premiers temps: La conception de l'histoire des Marrons saramaka* (La Roque d'Anthéron: Vents d'ailleurs, 2013); Richard Price and Sally Price, *Deux soirées de contes saamaka* (La Roque d'Anthéron: Vents d'ailleurs, 2016); Richard Price and Sally Price, *Boo Go a Kontukonde* (La Roque d'Anthéron: Vents d'ailleurs, 2016).

18 Richard Price and Sally Price, *Maroons in Guyane: Past, Present, Future* (Athens: University of Georgia Press, 2022); Richard Price and Sally Price, *Les Marrons en Guyane* (Matoury, Guyane: Ibis Rouge, 2022).

CHAPTER SEVENTEEN

BECOMING A
PART-TIME ACTIVIST
(1990–2020)

Around 1990, while we were continuing our careers as freelancing anthropologists in Martinique, I was contacted by David Padilla, assistant executive secretary of the Inter-American Commission on Human Rights. He asked for my help with an ongoing case known as *Aloeboetoe v. Suriname*. I gladly accepted, pleased at the idea of being able to give something concrete back to the Saamaka People. After all, anthropologists of my generation, trained during the 1960s, children of the civil rights movement and the Vietnam War, had always carried a modicum of guilt. How could we give something of value back to those peoples who had welcomed us into their lives? They were, however unwittingly, making our careers, allowing us to live comfortably in the richest country in the world, while they, in many cases at least, subsisted in precarious economic and political circumstances. We could rationalize that we were educating movers and shakers, including people in their own nation-states, about their lived realities, helping to humanize them in the eyes of those who often saw them as primitive or otherwise unworthy. But our agemates often felt relatively powerless to do much of direct value for the people we wrote our books about.

The details of the *Aloeboetoe* case need not detain us here.[1] Suffice it to say that my four-hour testimony before the Inter-American Court of Human Rights in San Jose, Costa Rica, centered on First-Time history and that the Saamaka People won their case, receiving nearly half a million U.S. dollars in compensation for the torture and murder of seven unarmed youths by members of the national army of Suriname.

When the Court adjourned and everyone stood while the black-robed justices filed out, Suriname's highest-ranking witness at the trial, Judge Advocate General Ramon de Freitas, strolled over to me and extended his hand. "You know," he said in Dutch with a sly smile, "since the Revolution [the coup d'état of 1980], Maroons no longer live as separate peoples. Since you were last in Suriname, they've all moved to the city, they all go

---

1 See Richard Price, "Executing Ethnicity: The Killings in Suriname," *Cultural Anthropology* 10 (1995): 437–71.

to school, they all read and write, and there's no more polygamy. In fact, President Venetiaan considers them his brothers." And then, he added a more personal message, a thinly veiled death threat. "My colleagues and I [in the military] are well-aware of your many writings, and we hope you will come back to Suriname soon. Indeed, we will be preparing *a very special welcome for you*, whenever you arrive."

By publishing details of that court case and in various other writings about the civil war, about Suriname's subsequent transformation from dictatorship to narcocracy, and about that nation's historical neglect and oppression of its Maroon and Indigenous peoples, I was making a safe return to Suriname even less imaginable for us. Nevertheless, the shift to a publicly militant stance against a government that most Saamakas and other Maroons saw as oppressive felt completely natural. Morally (and in terms of "professional ethics"), it was a no-brainer, however painful the personal consequences.[2]

Several years later, I was given an opportunity to act in the same vein. I was contacted by human rights attorney Fergus MacKay, who had been asked by the Saamakas to help them defend their territory against the State of Suriname, which had begun leasing large tracts of their forest to multinational logging companies from China, Malaysia, and Indonesia, as well as Canadian goldmining companies. As the newly formed VSG (Association of Saamaka Authorities), composed of traditional leaders from villages all along the river, began submitting their filings to the Inter-American Commission of Human Rights in Washington, D.C., Fergus asked me to write supportive documents (sometimes sworn affidavits) that he submitted to the Commission as annexes. Ethnographic and historical (and professorial) authority had become, in the eyes of the Inter-American Commission, an important complement to the local knowledge standing behind the VSG's submissions to the Commission.

The VSG's initial petition in 2000 was accompanied by a ten-page report that I provided at Fergus's request. In addition, relevant parts of my

---

2   Our continued reluctance to set foot in Suriname is strengthened by the threat that local laws pose for such writings. Freedom House, in its 2015 report, noted that "Suriname . . . has some of the most severe criminal defamation laws in the Caribbean. These include prison sentences of up to seven years for 'public expression of enmity, hatred, or contempt' toward the government, and up to five years' imprisonment for insulting the head of state."

oral testimony about Saamaka society and history from the 1992 hearing before the Court were cited in the body of the document. Fergus had asked me to address the issue of Saamaka territory, land ownership, and land use. I then added a note on sovereignty, stressing the strength of Saamaka notions of territorial control and its historical origins.

Not long after, when the VSG—alarmed by further Chinese logging incursions into their territory—petitioned the Commission to impose precautionary measures, I agreed to write a supportive report to the Commission, arguing that "the destruction of the Saamakas' forest would mean the end of Saamaka culture" and that, without protective measures, "ethnocide—the destruction of a culture that is widely regarded as being one of the most creative and vibrant in the entire African diaspora—seems the most likely outcome."

The largely heroic story of the Saamaka struggle to gain permanent control over their traditional territory is told in *Rainforest Warriors*, as are the details of what transpired before the Inter-American Court for Human Rights in 2007.[3] For present purposes, I would highlight both the importance of "expert" ethnographic and historical testimony in determining the outcome before the Court and the tensions between human rights discourse and ethnographic realities. While these latter tensions would not have been evident to the distinguished justices, whose assumptions about human nature and law were thoroughly "Western," they were on my mind throughout my testimony and cross-examination by Suriname's attorneys, and they have lingered with me since.

Anthropology and human rights law have experienced tensions ever since Melville Herskovits's controversial 1947 memo written on behalf of the American Anthropological Association to Eleanor Roosevelt, chair of the nascent United Nations Commission on Human Rights, which argued for "the right of men to live in terms of their own traditions."[4] The Universal Declaration of Human Rights proclaimed a series of universal values (concerning, for example, racial, gender, and religious equality)

---

3 My *Rainforest Warriors: Human Rights on Trial* (Philadelphia: University of Pennsylvania Press, 2011) was the winner of the Senior Book Prize of the American Ethological Society and the Best Book Prize, American Political Science Association, Human Rights Program. See also the five-minute video on YouTube narrated by Robert Redford at https://www.youtube.com/watch?v=gEoMn32MSDs.

4 Melville J. Herskovits, "Statement on Human Rights," *American Anthropologist* 49 (1947): 539–43.

that Herskovits, a staunch cultural relativist and anti-imperialist, did not believe were appropriate to impose cross-culturally. North American anthropologists in the immediate post–World War II era, looking over their shoulders at Nazism, were divided on these issues.[5]

International human rights law is built on such categories as "culture," and "tribal people"/"Indigenous people" (which, from another perspective, might seem little more than a successor label for the once-prominent category of "primitive people"). These terms carry heavy cultural baggage for many educated Westerners, including judges, lawyers, and politicians. That baggage begins with the very idea that these peoples (these Others) share certain characteristics that make them different from "us." For example, it is often said that they are bound by "tradition," that their lives are fraught with myth and symbolism, that their societies are resistant to change and governed by "custom," that they live outside of history, ruled by the changing seasons and in perfect harmony with nature—you add the rest.

But since the beginning of the final quarter of the twentieth century, anthropologists and historians have been criticizing such commonsense Western ideas that essentialize "culture" (and "cultures") and that put a prime on "tradition" as the central diacritic of cultural authenticity. Anthropologists, who until well into the twentieth century focused on custom and tradition in small-scale societies, have for several decades routinely emphasized these same societies' openness and historical interactions as well as the importance of change and development in them—as in all societies. No longer do anthropologists (or most historians) work within an "us/them" binary, within the ideological framework that created the West and its Others, or in what Michel-Rolph Trouillot famously called the "savage slot." As he put it, "There is no Other, but multitudes of others who are all others for different reasons."[6]

---

5 See, for discussion, Jerry Gershenhorn, *Melville J. Herskovits and the Racial Politics of Knowledge* (Lincoln: University of Nebraska Press, 2004), 207–14. For more general discussion of the tension between human rights discourse and cultural relativism, see, for example, Jane K. Cowan, Marie-Bénédicte Dembour, and Richard A. Wilson, eds., *Culture and Rights: Anthropological Perspectives* (Cambridge: Cambridge University Press, 2001); and Lynda S. Bell, Andrew J. Nathan, and Ilan Peleg, eds., *Negotiating Culture and Human Rights* (New York: Columbia University Press, 2001).

6 Michel-Rolph Trouillot, "Anthropology and the Savage Slot: The Poetics and Politics of Otherness," in *Recapturing Anthropology: Working in the Present*, ed. Richard Fox (Santa Fe, N.Mex.: SAR Press 1992), 17–44, quote from p. 39.

This tension over the nature of "primitive" societies puts special burdens on an ethnographer or a human rights lawyer arguing on behalf of the Saamaka before the Inter-American Court. It sometimes becomes necessary, for purposes of argument, to accept the multiple fictions that created the category of "tribal peoples."[7] At the same time, it becomes necessary to engage in a teaching effort—aimed at the judges and representatives of the state, who are likely to share certain stereotypes about "tribal peoples"—stressing that such peoples live (and have always lived) fully in history, exercise their own agency, adopt (and have always adopted) changes, and possess a degree of historical consciousness that permits them to make sophisticated choices about directions for their society's future. In short, it becomes necessary to insist that "they" are, in every way, as modern as "we." The testimony that took place before the Court makes clear that the practical need to support the idea of there being such a thing as "tribal peoples" and simultaneously to criticize the cultural baggage that undergirds it creates tensions that are not always easily resolved either for the sympathetic lawyer or for the anthropologist who serves as expert witness.

My testimony stressed the importance of the Saamakas' conception of history in the definition of their peoplehood and identity. I spoke a good deal about the ways in which Saamakas were different from other Surinamers—language, religion, legal system, clothing, houses, relationship to the land, their conception of history, and so on. For strategic reasons, I shortchanged modernization and change in favor of enduring ideologies and practices. But I did not need to compromise my anthropological integrity by speaking directly about "tradition" or "tribal peoples"—the justices (and lawyers) made what seemed to them a natural translation from my ethnographic comments into these kinds of categories. One can get some sense of the reasons behind my strategy in the courtroom by examining the way that the Court framed its final judgment, which in many respects depended on an essentializing gaze, the kind of anthropology that was already on the wane by the 1960s. Note the justices' dependence on such terms as *culture, tradition, custom,* and *tribal peoples.*

The Court ruled that "the members of the Saamaka people make up a

---

7   One might, perhaps, make this worldwide category more intellectually defensible by emphasizing colonialism and other historical and present-day similarities of unequal power—that is, these peoples' similar structural position within nation-states, rather than any cultural similarities or proclivities that they are alleged to share.

tribal community . . . not indigenous to the region, but that share similar characteristics with indigenous peoples . . . whose social, cultural and economic characteristics are different from other sections of the national community, particularly because of their special relationship with their ancestral territories, and because they regulate themselves, at least partially, by their own norms, customs, and/or traditions."[8]

And in considering "whether and to what extent the members of the Saamaka people have a right to use and enjoy the natural resources that lie on and within their alleged traditionally owned territory," the Court argued that the natural resources of the forest and the river, as outlined in the detailed map made by Saamakas that I used as part of my testimony, are indeed essential to their continued physical and cultural survival as a people, that these resources fall under the protection of the American Convention, and that these resources form part of the Saamakas' corporate ownership rights.

Among its other rulings in the case, the Court wrote that, "regarding large-scale development or investment projects that would have a major impact within Saamaka territory, the State has a duty, not only to consult with the Saamakas, but also to obtain their free, prior, and informed consent, according to their customs and traditions."

After deliberations about the value of the timber extracted and the environmental damages caused by the invading multinationals, the Court determined a substantial monetary award (roughly U.S.$675,000) to go to the Saamaka People. And it also declared that Suriname must rewrite its laws, including the constitution, if necessary, to recognize Indigenous and Maroon groups as legal personalities, to permit such groups to own and effectively control property communally, and to give them title to the territories that they define as their own, including considerable rights of sovereignty within these territories.

It should be clear that the right to define *culture* (and such related terms as *tribal* and *tradition*) has long since flown the anthropological coop and that, like it or not, we must deal with the myriad manifestations of these terms out there in the real, not just theorized, world. These terms and concepts, however much contested in current anthropology, formed

---

8   The full text of the judgment, from which my quotations are taken, is available at https://www.forestpeoples.org/sites/default/files/publication/2010/09 /surinameiachrsaramakajudgmentaug08eng.pdf.

the core of the landmark judgment in the case of the *Saramaka People v. Suriname.*

I want to return, for a moment, to the 2007 trial and its immediate aftermath. At the end of the long second day, after the justices had filed out, I walked over to where the large Suriname delegation was gathered and stuck my hand out to Suriname's attorney general, Subhas Punwasi, one of my main adversaries during the contentious cross-examination. (In retrospect, I'm not sure why I made this gesture but suppose it was an attempt to break a tense situation and to do it from what I suddenly felt was a position of strength.) He declined the handshake and began berating me, "You called us dogs. You said that Surinamers are dogs! After all Suriname has done for you . . ." I interrupted, trying to explain that I was merely repeating the words of the two Saamaka witnesses the day before who said that they often felt as if the government of Suriname treated *them* like dogs. "I never called Surinamers dogs." "Yes, you did!" he said very deliberately. "And if I have anything to do with it, you will never again set foot in my country." At this point Hans Lim a Po, Suriname's lead lawyer, through clenched teeth, turned to me, "Tomorrow night, as soon as we get back to Suriname, I will be meeting with President Venetiaan, and the first thing I intend to tell him is that you called Surinamers dogs. . . . I can assure you he will see that you never come to Suriname again." Meanwhile, Fergus, having seen me walk over to the Surinamers, told Sally to get over there fast and pull me away before a fistfight erupted. In the event, since things were already getting heated, both Fergus and Sally rushed over and got between me and the other men and pulled me over to the other side of the room.

So that was my last direct encounter with Suriname officialdom. Since the trial, matters in Suriname have gone from bad to worse, from both Saamakas' perspectives and our own. In 2010, ex-dictator Bouterse (who in 1999 had been convicted of international drug trafficking in absentia by a Dutch court and sentenced to sixteen years in prison and a fine of $2.3 million and whose conviction for the 1982 murder of fifteen leading citizens—lawyers, journalists, professors—was pronounced only in 2019) was elected president of the country. In 2015, he was reelected. Other than paying the compensation owed the Saamaka People for damages ordered by the Court, the Republic of Suriname continues to drag its feet on fulfilling *any* of the Court's orders, including recognizing and titling Saamaka territory or recognizing their right to be considered a people.

The VSG has continued to fight, lodging complaints and reports with the Court, and still hopes for further concrete action from the government. But, from a Saamaka perspective, the 2007 victory increasingly looks Pyrrhic.

The Saamaka People decided, soon after the 2007 judgment, to use a small part of the money they received from the trial to finance a Saamaka-language edition of *First-Time*. Sally and I agreed to do the translation (earmarking the money from the judgment for the book's production and transport to Suriname), and it became the first book ever published in the Saamaka language.[9] The VSG bought three thousand copies to distribute in their schools. This should make clear just how much the Saamaka People care about their history—for it is Saamaka oral historians who provided the main texts in this book—and it shows how much they want this history, *their* history, to be passed on to the coming generations.

In introducing the Saamaka version, one of our most delicate tasks was to explain, to an audience that was not yet born when the original texts were recorded (and in their daily life is more concerned with their smartphones and *Fesibuku* than with *Fesiten*), the once-pervasive uses of history in everyday life, the grave spiritual dangers that surrounded the transmission of (or merely the speaking about) First-Time knowledge. In our Saamakatongo version, we reminded young readers that before the Suriname civil war,

> drinking water had to be carried in buckets from the river, it wasn't piped into the villages. You went on a special path outside the village to find a breadnut leaf to squat over to shit. There were no telephones. No electric lights or refrigerators. There were only a few outboard motors. To get to Paramaribo, you had to take a canoe (often for several days) to Afobaka before you could find a bus. Only one village, that of the gaama, had a gasoline generator that worked a couple of hours a day. Most women had been "to see the city" for a few days only once in their life. There were no tourists. Women went bare-breasted [etc., etc.]

But trying to explain to young Saamakas the meaning that First-Time knowledge once held proved much more challenging than alluding to the physical details of life in the villages. For example, the idea that many of the Saamakas we knew in the 1960s and 1970s were genuinely frightened

---

9   Richard Price, *Fesiten*, trans. and adapted by Richard Price and Sally Price (La Roque d'Anthéron: Vents d'ailleurs, 2013).

of Whitefolks or other outsiders is more or less difficult to be persuasive about, depending on the sophistication, age, and life experience of today's Saamaka reader, given that tourist lodges and gaggles of Dutch tourists are now common in Saamaka villages. Yet these realities, the idea that "those times—the days of war, the days of Whitefolks' slavery—shall come again" or the belief that "First-Time kills," forms the core of the encounters that animate *First-Time* and help give that book its dramatic edge. And they form the core of the serious epistemological problems raised by the book.[10]

Saamaka readers today, including the leaders of the VSG, tend to take *Fesiten* as a definitive history book, an account of what really happened, in an age when they see their oral history fast disappearing. The fact that *First-Time*, even in its Saamaka-language incarnation, insists that it conveys partial truths and emphasizes perspectivality and the production of history, will probably be of little interest to most Saamaka readers—although we still nurture the hope that it will encourage critical thinking among some.

Sally and I were especially pleased to have had an opportunity to give something back to Saamakas (and at their own urging).[11] We know from prior experience that Saamakas end up using our books in ways that we could never have predicted—from the use of *First-Time* as a talisman by warriors who believed it brought them invulnerability to the army's weapons during the civil war of the 1990s,[12] to the use by the grandsons of carvers represented in *Afro-American Arts* of images on which to model a new generation of tourist carvings,[13] to the use of that same book by Saamakas and outsiders in an international art forgery scheme.[14] We ex-

---

10 See for example, Michel-Rolph Trouillot, "The Caribbean Region: An Open Frontier in Anthropological Theory," *Annual Review of Anthropology* 21 (1992): 19–42, see especially pp. 24–25.

11 It may be worth noting that in Los Olivos, we were able to give nothing back (except our continuing, largely long-distance friendship with people there), while in Martinique, where we lived for decades, we frequently participated in civil society events and maintained ongoing relationships, in part through *Le bagnard et le colonel*, which was republished in 2016 by Vents d'ailleurs and which served at least as a kind of photo album of the 1960s for many of our neighbors.

12 Richard Price, "Preface to the 2nd Edition," *First-Time: The Historical Vision of an African American People* (Chicago: University of Chicago Press, 2002), xiv.

13 Sally Price and Richard Price, *Maroon Arts: Cultural Vitality in the African Diaspora* (Boston: Beacon, 1999), 168–69.

14 Price and Price, *Enigma Variations*.

pect many more surprises, and personal repercussions, over the years from the publication of the Saamaka version of *Fesiten*.

We have now spent a good deal of the past thirty years as part-time anthropological activists, giving our best on behalf of Saamakas whenever asked (and often on our own). But, in the end, our endeavors don't seem to have done much to change the course of history. Saamakas continue the bumpy process of integration into the national society, mainly at the bottom of the social heap. They remain culturally vibrant but, in terms of Maroon sovereignty and independence, increasingly indifferent.

CHAPTER EIGHTEEN

ANSE CHAUDIÈRE
(1987–2018)

How to capture, in a few pages, more than thirty years based in rural Martinique, looking out at sunsets over the Caribbean and sleeping under the moon and stars?

Our social world was decidedly eclectic, beginning with fishermen's families we'd known in the 1960s, with whom we kept up through weddings, funerals, and countless midday meals together. We were especially close with Emilien and Merlande, and eventually with Emilien's sister Liliane, who returned to Petite Anse after many decades working as a tax inspector in Paris. Emilien and Merlande introduced us to their friends Maurice Jeanne-Rose, a jack-of-all-trades at the Hotel Méridien, and his wife, Josephe, a former higgler, and they often invited us for holiday celebrations in their home in central Martinique, built by Maurice using leftover materials from building projects at the hotel. (He loved to say, "There's nothing you can tell me that I don't already know about White-folks!") Maurice also helped us sell the surplus *giraumons* (Caribbean pumpkins) from our garden to the hotel's dining services—once a whole pickup truck's worth.

Many of our friends were left-leaning independentists associated with the Cercle Frantz Fanon—its president, artist Victor Permal, and his historian wife, Marie-Christine, who lived in a beautiful creole house on the lower slopes of Mont Pelée; Gilles Alexandre, whose bookstore was a meeting ground for Martiniquan intellectuals; Gilles's wife, Frédérique (Frantz Fanon's niece, who worked in government); Alex Ferdinand, director of the independentist radio station RLDM and formerly married to Liliane Larcher; and human rights lawyer Raphaël Constant, who helped us to free Tooy from prison in Guyane. There were professors at the Université des Antilles-Guyane: Véronique and Yannick Tarrieu who taught English lit; historian Miriam Cottias, who had been my student at Nanterre; anthropologist Gerry L'Étang; and others. We spent memorable times with Édouard and Sylvie Glissant both in Paris and at their home and ours in Martinique, as well as with two close friends of Édouard—Victor Anicet, an immensely creative ceramicist, and Jean-Luc de Laguarigue, an artistically gifted photographer. Aimé Césaire, whom we visited with at least yearly, always in his office in Fort-de-France.

Presenting our book about Romare Bearden to Césaire, 2007.

Journalist Adams Kwateh, born in Senegal, who covered cultural events for the newspaper *France Antilles*. Pascal Lavenaire, director of Martinique's most listened-to radio station. Guadeloupe-born Dominique Taffin, director of the departmental archives. Anthropologist Baj Strobel, who wrote a wonderful book about St. Lucian goldminers in Guyane and translated *First-Time* and *Maroon Arts* into French. Independentist leader Alfred Marie-Jeanne, who loved to recount when he spotted us at one of his political rallies how I once told him that we had no desire to become French, but that the day Martinique became independent we would be the first in line to exchange our U.S. passports for Martiniquan ones. Our Anses d'Arlet mayors were socialists—first Olga Delbois and later Eugène Larcher; we were also friends with the socialist mayor of neighboring Diamant, Serge Larcher, whose father had been an important interlocutor about the Election Day massacre of 1925 for *The Convict and the Colonel.*

The marriages, funerals, and other affairs of the Désert family, who kept sheep and goats across the road from our house, were an important part of our daily lives, as were others who used trees from our land to make charcoal and then shared the result with us; just down the road, Marie and Julot Clémenté hosted memorable (and boisterous!) Chanténoël celebrations; and every few days, we would chat with Julien Erdual, who drove the local garbage truck and liked to discuss local politics as well as what was happening politically in the United States.

We frequently shared meals with all of these people (except Césaire, with whom we were more formal), eating Martiniquan dishes and drinking rum and wine. Our own specialties, inherited from meals in Petite Anse, included *féroce* (avocado, grilled salt-cod, manioc flour, oil, lime juice, and Scotch bonnet pepper), served with *'ti ponch* (*rhum agricole*, our own *citrons*, and stewed Caribbean plums from our trees, which we cooked with sugar and spices each June for a whole day over charcoal); giraumon soup (made from Caribbean pumpkins we grew); Bajan-style *coucou* (to which George Lamming gave his thumbs-up, even bringing Sally an authentic coucou paddle on one of his visits); Jamaican curried goat; a classic Martiniquan breadfruit concoction called *migan*, made with pigs' snouts in brine; and *ti-nen lanmori*, a stew of our homegrown small green bananas with salt cod, always served with a peppery cucumber garnish. Once in a while, Sally would make a deadly soursop-rum pie. The serving dishes included calabashes from our own trees.

Our dinner parties often included visitors from abroad, both family members and intellectual colleagues, such as Cuban poet Nancy Morejón, whom I first met when we'd both given lectures at Warwick Univer-

Dancing with Nancy in our old house, 1990s.

George with his new machine.

sity in England in 1985, who sometimes stayed with us when she was in Martinique as a judge in Glissant's Prix Carbet novel competition.

George Lamming also stayed with us several times; he was thrilled to be given the portable manual typewriter we had used in Saamaka (later converted to a doorstop in Martinique)—his own, an identical model that he used for all his writing, had recently broken down.

One evening, over a glass or two of Martiniquan *vieux*, we traded stories with George about Walter Rodney, the great historian and political activist from Guyana. I related how, at a 1970s international conference on slavery in Canada, Orlando Patterson gave a paper in which he mentioned that he and Walter had studied together at the University of the West Indies but when Walter, sporting a big Afro, followed with a fiery speech about pan-African politics, he made a point of saying: "It is true that Orlando and I were class*mates*, but we were never class *allies*!" And George told us, movingly, of the massive funeral procession in Georgetown after Walter's assassination by the Burnham regime in 1980 and the warm reaction to the funeral oration he gave there. (As the editor of the JHU Series in Atlantic History and Culture, I later published that text, lightly revised, as the foreword to Walter's posthumous *A History of the Guyanese Working People*. The typescript of that book had been smuggled out of Walter's jail cell, where he had been detained for months.)

George added that he spent that evening with poet Martin Carter, "who," he noted approvingly, "was a drinking man," wandering from one rum-shop to the next, talking about how the Working People's Alliance—the political party that Walter had founded and for which he was killed—might yet transform the ethnic-based politics of Guyana into a more egalitarian society. And he added that, right after the oration, he was invited by the new strongman of neighboring Suriname, Desi Bouterse, who had seized power in a recent coup d'état and proclaimed himself a Marxist, to come to Paramaribo to receive a state medal (was it the Order of the Toucan, or some other bird?). Lamming took us aback by adding that, in addition to the medal, Commander Bouterse had presented him with an inscribed book: *Afro-American Arts of the Surinam Rain Forest*, by Sally and me.

Maryse Condé and her husband-translator, Richard Philcox, were occasional dinner guests, first in Martinique and later in Paris. Rolph's sister and brother, Evelyne and Lyonel, both novelists, each visited with us. Sam Selvon, the Trinidadian novelist visiting from London, once shocked us when he pulled a whole handful of Scotch bonnet peppers from a plant in our yard and popped them in his mouth, saying that he hadn't had fresh ones for years—a taste that had been passed down from his ancestors in India. And various Caribbean scholars came through from time to time: historian Gert Oostindie who directed the KITLV in Leiden (and was our frequent host in the Netherlands); French anthropologist Catherine Benoît, whom we'd known since our year at Stanford; our old friend Patrick Menget, French anthropologist on his way to Brazil; Guadeloupe specialist Christiane Bougerol; Haitianist Laurent Dubois, whom we'd known since he was a student at Princeton; Randy Matory, whose work on Brazil and Nigeria we admired; historian Bernard Moitt, Antiguan-born specialist in the French Antilles; historian Robin Derby and anthropologist Andrew Apter (on their honeymoon!); Michiel van Kempen, Dutch writer and literary critic who, more than anyone else, has brought the history of Suriname literature to light; Richard Drayton, imperial historian from Guyana and Barbados; anthropologist Peter Redfield, on his way to Guyane. And countless others, from George and Jane Collier, Ken Bilby, Christine Chivallon (who had written an important book about a postslavery uprising in Martinique), to Manuela da Cunha (who had hosted us at her home in São Paulo), enjoyed meals on our veranda when they were in Martinique either for business or pleasure.

Adiante, featured in Baltimore STYLE magazine, 2008.

Using only a humble utility knife, a Suriname-born woodworker creates one-of-a-kind objects.
By Lisa Simeone

Adiante Franszoon in his Baltimore studio.

Carving a niche

PHOTOGRAPHED BY KIRSTEN BECKERMAN

124 • MAY/JUNE 2008 • STYLE

Adiante also visited several times, once with his wife, Jill. We don't know how he managed to get a stunning carved table onto the plane but it became a centerpiece of our home décor.

Students from around the world who were conducting dissertation research in Martinique often came to visit soon after they arrived on the island, seeking advice about whom they should meet and what other local resources they should tap. There were a few visiting graduate students with whom we built more long-term relationships: Lucien Taylor and Lisa Barbash (who ended up at Harvard) house-sat for us one year while we were in the United States. So, too, did Emily Vogt, now a dean at Chicago Theological Seminary. And we enjoyed many an afternoon or evening with Vanessa Agard-Jones, who was doing research for her dissertation at NYU and eventually joined the Anthropology Department at Columbia.

Jutta Hepke and Gilles Colleu, who run Éditions Vents d'ailleurs and have published many of our books in French (plus two in Saamakatongo), stayed with us at Anse Chaudière for a few days, after they had hosted us at their home/workplace near Aix-en-Provence. They had begun their publishing house in Martinique years earlier but moved to France after finding Martinique a difficult environment because of racial politics.

Every few days we would take a late-afternoon walk on the spectacular two-mile-long beach at Diamant. It was also a favorite of Glissant, who characterized it as having "a subterranean, cyclical life," shrinking during the rainy season "to a corridor of black sand" and then, in the dry season, "made evanescent by the return of white sand."[1] We often used these walks to think through current writing projects, and it was on that beach, with the sea grapes and coconut palms on one side and high waves cresting and breaking on the other, that many of our best ideas were born.

With five acres of largely wooded land, there was always much to do, from felling trees with a chainsaw and cutting high grass and weeds with a brushcutter—my mother's brother Gene had given us the first one as a housewarming present—to weeding and planting. There were also periodic forays into the woods to discover termite nests and burn them before the insects invaded the house. (Once, when kerosene was unavailable, I stupidly used gasoline instead and suffered a very serious burn, causing countless trips to the hospital and permanent scars on my leg.) When we first moved in, one of Emilien's fishermen friends from Diamant spent the day digging sweet potato plants into the earth between the house and the sea—we ate those *patates* for years. There had always been lots of sweetsop trees (*pommes de cannelle*) on the hillside—Emilien remembered stopping on the walk home from primary school to feast on them a half century before. But we also planted soursop (*corrosol*), oranges, grapefruits, mandarines, key limes, avocados, papayas, pomegranates, *prunes de cythère*, coconuts, tamarinds, Caribbean cherries, bananas, guava, *quenettes* (genips), and two kinds of mangos, as well as several magnificent breadfruit trees that contributed importantly to our diet. Sometimes we brought seeds back from our travels, including a giant variety of sour-

---

1 Édouard Glissant, *Poetics of Relation* (Ann Arbor: University of Michigan Press, 1997), 121.

sop we found in Bogotá and a cashew from Belize. Over the years Sally surrounded the house with several dozen calabash trees of three varieties, including one we brought back from Guyane. And we did a good bit of other gardening, growing okra, Caribbean cucumbers, watermelon, string beans, bok choy, corn, eggplant, *maracudja* (passionfruit), Scotch bonnet peppers, giraumon (Caribbean pumpkins), and more.

Soon after we moved in, our neighbor Julien told me I needed to buy a shotgun, since snakes (the deadly fer-de-lance, Martinique's only serpent) were common in the area. So he accompanied me to a gun store in a neighboring town, where I bought a gun and cartridges. I tried it out on a tin can—and then, over the next thirty-three years, never shot it again. However, one New Year's Day the mayor phoned, waking us at 5:00 a.m., excusing himself but saying that he'd just run over a long "something" in front of our house as he was coming home from a party and advising me to pull it over to the side of the road. And one of our neighbors shot three at once, fifty meters from our place, when he lifted a piece of galvanized roofing that had been blown onto his property after a storm. We always figured that the snakes saw us even if we never saw them. Like our neighbors, we wore boots in the garden and the forest around our house, except on the trail to the sea.

Walking down that trail through the woods was always a pleasure at the end of an afternoon. A secluded sandy beach (until a tidal wave removed the sand and left smooth rocks) at the bottom of the cliff fronting the usually calm Caribbean. Then the walk back up to the house that took ten or fifteen minutes. It was hard for us to imagine a more beautiful place to live.

We made many trips from what became the Aimé Césaire International Airport after the great man's death. From our incomplete records, I reconstruct that while based in Anse Chaudière we took off for lectures (some years earning gold or platinum cards on Air France) in San Francisco, Boston, Philadelphia, Williamstown, Charleston, Riverside, Utrecht, Leiden, Paris, Montréal, Quebec, Baltimore, Chicago, Miami, Iowa City, New Orleans, Salt Lake City, New Haven, Minneapolis, Washington, D.C., Charlottesville, Los Angeles, Long Beach, Cambridge (Massachusetts and UK), Oxford, Berlin, Bonn, Bayreuth, Halle, Erfurt, Florence, Mexico City, Oaxaca, New London, Ann Arbor, Madison, Middleton, Fairfield, Binghamton, Durham, Providence, Tallahassee, New York, Jerusalem, Bogotá, Madrid, Barcelona, San Juan, Cayenne, Santo Domingo, Santiago de Cuba, Barbados, Belém, Natal, and Rio. Each

*With Sid at an inter-
national conference in
Santiago de Cuba, 1989.*

such destination—some of which we visited several times—brings back
a flood of memories, people we met, discussions we engaged, meals we
ate, sights we saw. . . .

Once, arriving to check in for a flight to New York (for the 1992 Folklife
Festival in Washington, D.C., which began in late June), we were surprised
to see Rolph just ahead of us in line. Chiding him for not even letting
us know that he was visiting, we asked after Anne-Carine and their tod-
dler, Canel. Rolph mumbled something about being in Martinique for a
conference. A few minutes later Myriam Cottias (who had taken a course
with me at Nanterre and became a professor of history at the university in
Martinique) came running in from the parking lot, greeted us with a big
smile, and kissed Rolph goodbye. The following March, when we visited
Myriam in the maternity hospital, we gave her the Saamaka-style baby cap
that Sally had sewn in patchwork for little Alexis.[2]

Shortly after seeing the dramatic images of the Berlin Wall being pulled
apart in 1989, we were invited to that city, Sally to lecture on primitive art
at the Freie Universität (which led to the publication of her "primitive art"
book in German), I to give a more formal evening lecture at the venerable

---

2 Over the years, Alexis Trouillot and his mother often visited Rolph's family in Haiti.
He is currently completing his PhD in history of sciences at the University of Paris with
a dissertation titled "The Mathematical World in the Bilad Shinqit [Mauritania] between
1714 and 1936."

Ibero-Amerikanisches Institut. After my lecture, we were approached by a young woman who asked if I remembered her, saying that she had been a student in my 1987 Caribbean class at Saint-Denis and offering to be our guide to Berlin the next day, if we were free. Sally and I were then invited to a postlecture dinner during which our host and his white-haired guests expressed blatant anti-Semitic views. We went to bed upset, thinking black thoughts about the remnants of the Third Reich.

When we met her in the morning, Nima Forouzin told us that she had fled her home during the Iranian Revolution, spent time as a student in Michigan, lived for a time in New York, and in the mid-1980s ended up in Paris, in all places without a passport—effectively stateless. With her eight-year-old son, she was now living with a German publisher. She took us by the Reichstag and through Alexanderplatz and the rest of former East Berlin, all the time telling us how difficult it was for someone who looked like her (a beautiful, dusk-colored woman) and who spoke with a slight accent to be treated with dignity in Germany. "A day doesn't go by when several people on the street don't ask me, 'Why don't you go back to your country?'" When Nima politely asked a café waiter for directions to the nearest metro, he replied to me rather than to her. She was, as she said, invisible.

During a delicious Persian dinner, which she and her son cooked for us, she told us that she was ready to move on, intending to support herself as a translator, and asked what we thought might be a good place for them to live. What, she prompted, did we think of Nigeria? We warned her about that country's political and economic instability and suggested that she might consider Brazil instead. She remarked that the only place she had felt truly comfortable, since leaving Tehran, was New York—but that she was determined not to have her son brought up as an American.

Two years later, we received a postcard from Nima, with palm trees and the ocean, postmarked Lucea, Jamaica. She said she and her son were finally happy.

There were also two extended trips to Brazil. The first was a whole semester in 1998 teaching on Fulbright grants in Bahia. Arriving just in time for Carnival (on Niko's advice that we would never understand Brazil if we didn't "do Carnival"), historian João Reis met us at Salvador's airport with Malê carnival costumes in hand and immediately swept us into the streets of Bahia for three days and nights. João also found us an apartment near the sea. He was a great host, shepherding us through the police bureaucracy, helping to get our papers in order. Walks on the beach. Exploring Salvador. Visits with João to various Candomblé *terreiros*, which allowed us to compare spirit possession in Brazil to that in Saamaka. A long weekend with a rented car to drive around the Recôncavo. Eating *moquecas*. Becoming friends with Luiz Mott, an anthropologist and gay rights activist (and gifted cook) whose life was being threatened because he insisted that Brazil's Black Rights icon, seventeenth-century Zumbi dos Palmares, had been gay. Our classes (three hours long, in Portuguese) were fun, though students couldn't read anything in English and they seemed to wander in and out of the classroom somewhat at random. I was working on a project that João had given me for the semester: to read a stack of books he'd provided about *quilombos* (communities where the descendants of maroons still live) and to write my frank opinion of the situation in Brazil, since the promulgation of the new, 1986, constitution, which granted these communities new rights.[3] Meanwhile, Sally arranged a Portuguese translation of *Primitive Art in Civilized Places* with the university press in Rio. Leah and Niko both visited, he with his Mexican *novia*, Ruth Hernández Camacho, getting ready to marry later that year. We gave lectures in various Brazilian cities and universities: Natal, Brasilia, Campinas, São Paulo, Rio, Florianopolis, and Porto Alegre (where we became friends with anthropologist Ruben Oliven, whose flair for Jewish humor always reminded us of Sid). We also spent a good deal of time with a graduate student from Michigan, John Collins, who sat in on our classes and was finishing the fieldwork that eventually led to his groundbreaking book, *Revolt of the Saints*. We had a series of discussions that resulted, over time, in a great deal of mutual learning, and we have remained fast friends. It was in part these conversations that got me interested in the increasingly active Movimento Negro. While in Brazil that semester, the news I got from Suriname made me truly worried about the invasion of Chinese loggers, with the acquiescence of the Suriname government, that was going on in Saamaka territory.

In 2003 we made another several-month trip to Brazil, again courtesy of the Fulbright Foundation, but this time in Rio, as guests of anthropologist Olívia Gomes da Cunha and her historian brother Flávio Gomes. Both extraordinary scholars, and among the first Black faculty at the Federal University, they were in the midst of a nationwide debate about whether affirmative action should be instituted in Brazilian uni-

---

3   See Richard Price, "Scrapping Maroon History: Brazil's Promise, Suriname's Shame," *New West Indian Guide* 72 (1998): 233–55; and "Reinventando a história dos quilombos: Rasuras e confabulações," *Afro-Ásia* 23 (2000): 241–65.

versities or whether such policies ended up creating racial categories that too-closely mirrored those in the United States. Among the anthropologists we came to know—Marco Antonio Gonçalves and Els Larou (who hosted us in their elegant home for our first week[4]), Peter Fry (with whom I had private contests about who could wear the loudest Hawaiian shirt), Yvonne Maggi (who directed the university press), and others—the affirmative action battles were fierce and former friends were often no longer on speaking terms. Olívia and Flávio, both specialists in all things Afro, opened many doors for us in Rio and made our stay, when we lived in Santa Teresa, high above the city, a real joy. During that visit, we also gave lectures in a number of other Brazilian cities, I on human rights, Sally on art and museums: Porto Alegre (where we were hosted by Ruben Oliven), São Luis (where Sérgio Ferretti and his wife, Mundicarmo, took us to Casa das Minas ceremonies every night, as well as to Mamuna, a quilombo under threat from the nearby Brazilian space center[5]), the planned city of Maringá, and Belém (where historian Rosa Acevedo took us up the Amazon to visit a quilombo).

Six years later, while at a symposium at the Museu Nacional in Rio de Janeiro, one of John Collins's doctoral students, Alessandro Angelini, kindly served as cicerone to his remarkable field site, the miniaturized (but extensive) city of Morrinho, built a decade earlier by teenagers in an empty lot within the *favela* of Cariocas and constructed from Lego bricks and diverse detritus. With its tiny police cars, bars, hospitals, prostitutes, armed guards, and rows upon rows of brightly colored houses, it had already captured the imagination of filmmakers and was making waves at the Venice Biennale and the MOMA. Several teenagers, friends of Alessandro, were carrying on the tradition, building further out into the hillside overlooking the city, a favela within a favela.

In 2002, and again in 2003, we traveled for six weeks to Paris, where we each gave a series of lectures at the École Pratique de Hautes Études, in-

---

4   Els later wrote a foreword to the Brazilian edition of Sally's "primitive art" book.

5   Mamuna and several neighboring quilombos in Alcântara were already under serious threat from a proposed expansion of the launch center, and we were taken to meet with protesters from the village. After President Trump signed an agreement in 2019 that permitted American rockets to launch from the center, President Bolsonaro, a firm opponent of quilombos, ordered the destruction of multiple such communities in the region. I hope that the publication of *First-Time* in Brazil, scheduled for 2022 (*Os Primeiros Tempos*, São Paulo, EdUSP) may serve as an inspiration to quilombolas, and to anthropologists, historians, and others in Brazil who struggle on their behalf.

vited by our old friend Brazilianist Patrick Menget whom we knew from Harvard graduate-student days and his wife, Latin Americanist Anne Marie Losonczy.

A 2014 trip to Cuba turned into something much more than the presentation of lectures. Pedro Ureña Rib, a master chef who had often hosted us in Guyane when he was a professor of intercultural studies there, was now serving as a diplomat for his native Dominican Republic, and he took us to some of his favorite Havana haunts. Then, after each of us had given a lecture at the Casa de las Américas, Nancy Morejón drove us in her rattle-trap Soviet-era Lada to the venerable El Vedado headquarters of the National Union of Writers and Artists of Cuba (UNEAC), founded by Nicolás Guillén, where writer Miguel Barnet presented me with the Premio Internacional Fernando Ortiz, "the highest recognition

Granma.

After the prize, with Henrietta Pryce (left) and Nancy.

awarded for the work of a lifetime"—Cuba's most important award in Caribbean studies. I was moved by the ceremony, which was featured the next day by an article in Fidel's official newspaper, *Granma*.

Our children never lived in Anse Chaudière, though of course they visited periodically—and we visited them as well, whether in England, Brazil, Mexico, Cambridge (Mass.), or wherever their lives took them. Niko's career with the Associated Press led him from Carson City, to Los Angeles, to New York, to reporting from across Latin America, and then in Iraq, Afghanistan, and other war zones, then to becoming Latin America editor based in Mexico City (where he married and started a family), then Europe editor based in London, and finally to a position as executive editor for Global Video, still based in London, and now a grandfather three times over.

Leah came through often, especially before settling in to two decades teaching at Harvard, where she was Francis Lee Higginson Professor of English; in 2019, she and her husband, Nir Eyal, took positions at Rutgers (she as Henry Rutgers Distinguished Professor of English, he as Henry Rutgers Professor of Bioethics) and are raising their son in their home in Princeton. Covid has now ended visits back and forth with our children, grandchildren, and great-grandchildren, though Facetime is serving as a very imperfect substitute.

Other family members also visited us in Anse Chaudière—my father, whom we otherwise saw once a year at his home in Chapel Hill; my mother, with whom we remained very close, spending a couple of weeks a year with her in New York; and my mother's younger brother Bobby and his wife, Mickey, whom we also saw regularly in New York.

Not long after we set up our home in Martinique, I began wondering about teaching at the local university. In spring 1989, I filled out the application for an open professorship in history and dropped off a heavy carton of my books and articles at the university for the appropriate committee to consider. In my interview, I stressed the need for the department to broaden its purview, to become more fully Caribbean, in short, less French. In the end, my application was rejected. I was told by a member of the committee that they had found my response to their inquiries about whether I could teach about Louis XIV unsatisfactory and arrogant. (It

Niko with my eighty-five-year-old mother, Zihuatenejo, ca. 2000.

On our verandah with Leah, 1990s.

was only several years later that the university began to adopt programs more in keeping with the fact that it was located in the Caribbean.)[6]

Around the same time, we met Dave and Jeannie England, a British couple our age who were living just over the mountain by the sea in the town of Diamant. They told us that when in their early twenties, they had gone out from England (she, a potter, had grown up in Wales, he in Northern Ireland) to St. Lucia, where they had established a business working with local craftsmen (woodcarvers, potters, basketmakers) to sell their wares. They also dabbled in leftist politics and befriended George Odlum, who ran the main opposition newspaper. Though they looked rather like hippies and defied the role that respectable White people were supposed to play in that neocolonial society, they managed to put their two daughters, Suzy and Jessie, through the best local schools and, eventually, the University of the West Indies in Jamaica, where one got an MPhil in political science and the other, continuing at Cambridge, a PhD in archaeology. In 1983, with political tensions running high in the eastern Caribbean (and the U.S. invasion of Grenada only weeks away), the Englands were suddenly accused of terrorism on the vaguest of charges connecting them to Cuba and Libya, and in a single night, they were hustled off the island. Until their deaths from lung cancer in 2006 and 2014 (they were both inveterate smokers), they remained our close friends, as do their daughters, who live in Martinique, to this day.

Each year, during the Christmas holidays, when a maximum cohort of children and grandchildren were back on the island, we held calabash bowling parties with the England clan. After a well-lubricated dinner on our verandah and after the younger generation, armed with flashlights, had climbed trees and gathered dozens of calabashes of different sizes and shapes, we would descend to the terrace closest to the sea for a raucous session of the *boule*-like game invented by Sally, which would last well into the night.

Jeannie was the one who gave our house a name. She made a pottery sign with the words Manicou Crique, and a cute picture of a Martiniquan

---

6   When teaching a course on the Caribbean at the University of Paris (St. Denis) in 1987, I had asked my undergraduate students, who were mostly second-generation Antilleans, to write down what proportion of the Caribbean they thought was French. The average answer was 55 percent. The true answer was 2 percent.

opossum (*manicou*), recognition of the many such animals who raided our fruit trees at night. If you can catch them, they're delicious, so we concocted a trap—two plastic soft-drink crates (borrowed from Emilien's café) surrounded by chicken wire, with a funnel-shaped entrance topped by an old kitchen pot and a couple of aluminum spoons. A long string ran from the pot handle, through a plum tree, and then to our bedroom window. Overripe bananas served as bait. The very first night, around midnight, the sound of clattering spoons woke us, so I jumped up, pulled the string, and ran outside, stark naked, to secure the pot with a piece of wire. The next day we put the contraption and its inmate in the back of our pickup and brought it to Emilien, who said he would feed bread to the critter for a few days to clean him out and fatten him up.

But when we arrived for the much-anticipated midday meal, Emilien told us that the possum had chewed his way out of the cage during the night and disappeared, so we had to settle for fish. During the meal, I looked up and saw the possum sitting peacefully on a beam above the table, watching us eat. Emilien quietly asked me if I liked to kill things, to which I said no, and he said he felt the same way but that he knew someone who did. Soon, a local fisherman named Arounard showed up, grinning broadly at the task he'd been assigned. He grabbed the possum by the tail, spun it around several times to dizzy it, and took it outside to butcher. It was the first possum we'd eaten since our original visit to Petite Anse in the 1960s. We caught (and ate) several others over the years.

In 1993, we took a brief but memorable trip to St. Lucia, across the channel from our home in Anse Chaudière, to celebrate the revocation of the special law that had been hastily passed in 1983 to banish Dave and Jeannie (and their daughters) from the island. After a change of government, Odlum had told them they could return without fear of arrest, and he organized a party in their honor, to which we and a number of their St. Lucian friends were invited. We, the Englands, and a few other friends from Martinique crossed the channel, a string band from Anse La Raye played through the night, and it was a very West Indian celebration. The next day Odlum took Sally and me down to his brother's place in the south of the island and, after a few Piton beers looking out at the sea together, persuaded us to write a long piece for his newspaper about Toni Morrison, who'd just won the Nobel in literature. "St. Lucians," he said, "don't know her work. Introduce her books to them!" (St. Lucians had a

A meal chez nous, with Nancy Morejón, George Lamming, Dave England, 1990s.

special interest in the prize, not only because Derek Walcott had won it the previous year but also because Sir Arthur Lewis had won the Nobel in Economics in 1979—making the island the only one in the Caribbean with two Nobel winners.) Back home, we raced through our library of Morrison books and faxed him the article just before his deadline, a few days later.[7]

That year, we also traveled to the Netherlands and then to Germany. The Dutch visit brought together several of Harry Hoetink's old friends to celebrate his retirement and resulted in a book dedicated to him. I remember one morning sitting with Sid, having coffee and chatting, and thinking to myself, with amazement, that if a stranger walked by, they would have no idea there was any "history" between us.

The Germany visit also had a history. Shortly before her death in 1972, Frances Herskovits, Melville's widow, had told me (at the annual meeting of the American Society for Ethnohistory in Athens, Georgia) how they had made a large collection of Saamaka objects for the Hamburgisches

---

7   Richard Price and Sally Price, "Toni Morrison Wins 1993 Nobel Prize for Literature," *Crusader* (St. Lucia), Saturday, October 23, 1993, 11.

Museum für Völkerkunde in 1929. She explained that in the late 1940s they had received a letter from a curator reporting that a good half of the collection had been burned in a wartime fire caused by an Allied bombing raid. They hadn't ever managed to get back there to see what was left, and she urged me to visit. Five years later, when Sally and I finally traveled to examine the collection, we found that eighty-six pieces had survived (of the 193 originally in the collection). In 1991, the museum's curator wrote to ask us to contribute a chapter about the collection to a catalog, to be printed in connection with a 1992 quincentenary exhibition, "the only one in Germany," she said, "to be devoted to the people no one loves, that is the Blacks."[8]

So, we traveled from Harry's get-together in Holland to Hamburg to view the exhibit. What I found most revealing was a monumental "welcoming" photomural that covered the museum's wall just outside the exhibition rooms. It was intended to show the most famous Blacks in the Americas and included Michael Jackson, Sammy Davis Jr., Mohammed Ali, Whoopi Goldberg, Arthur Ashe, Pelé, Martin Luther King, Charlie Parker, Louis Armstrong, and Sidney Poitier. Taking it all in, I asked myself who was missing. Knowing that museums almost always opt for images that are happy rather than disturbing, I was nonetheless astounded. Neither of the two most famous Black Americans in Germany was among the thirty-two figures depicted in the mural.

The first omission was the star of the 1936 Berlin Olympics, Hitler's showcase for the superiority of the Aryan race. Despite (as Hitler said of him) "having antecedents who came from the jungle,"[9] Jesse Owens won four gold medals, before a crowd of 110,000 screaming people. Who was the second omission? The Black Bomber himself. The 1938 heavyweight championship rematch between Joe Louis and Max Schmeling was arguably the most famous boxing match of all time. It had the largest audience in history for a radio broadcast. Following his defeat of Louis in their 1936 bout, Schmeling had become a national hero, with the Nazis touting his victory as proof of Aryan superiority. Just before the rematch,

---

8   See Richard and Sally Price, "Widerstand, Rebellion und Freiheit: Maroon Societies in Amerika und ihre Kunst," in *Afrika in Amerika*, ed. Corinna Raddatz (Hamburg: Hamburgisches Museum für Völkerkunde, 1992), 157–73.

9   Albert Speer, *Inside the Third Reich: Memoirs* (New York: Simon and Schuster, 1997 [German orig., 1969]), 73.

Louis visited the White House, where President Franklin D. Roosevelt told him, "Joe, we need muscles like yours to beat Germany." Louis later admitted: "I knew I had to get Schmeling good. I had my own personal reasons and the whole damned country was depending on me." When Schmeling arrived in New York for the rematch, he was accompanied by Nazi Party officials who issued statements that a Black man could not defeat Schmeling and that, when Schmeling won, his prize money would be used to build tanks in Germany. (The Anschluss had already taken place; Austria had already been overrun.)

The rematch was held in Yankee Stadium before a crowd of more than seventy thousand. It lasted two minutes and four seconds. Louis battered Schmeling with a series of swift attacks, forcing him against the ropes where he gave him a paralyzing body blow. Schmeling was knocked down three times and only managed to throw two punches in the entire bout. On the third knockdown, Schmeling's trainer threw in the towel and the referee stopped the fight. Poet Langston Hughes wrote that when Louis won, "thousands of colored Americans thronged out into the streets all across the land to march and cheer and yell and cry. . . . No one else in the United States has ever had such an effect on Negro emotions—or on mine. I marched and cheered and yelled and cried, too."[10]

So Germany chose not to show either Jesse Owens, four-time Berlin Olympic Champion, or Joe Louis, who had been heavyweight champion of the world for eleven years, in their photomural of famous Black Americans. I was reminded of the title of an essay by Jim Boon: "Why Museums Make Me Sad."[11]

One day in 1995, walking the beach at Diamant, we got the idea for an article about the efforts of some of Martinique's leading intellectuals to rewrite the history of the island. Several nights before, we had driven to the city to see Patrick Chamoiseau's film *L'Exile de Béhanzin* and in the

---

10 Langston Hughes, *I Wonder as I Wander: An Autobiographical Journey*, 1956, in *The Collected Works of Langston Hughes*, vol. 14 (Columbia: University of Missouri Press, 2003), 307.

11 James A. Boon, "Why Museums Make Me Sad," in *Exhibiting Cultures: The Poetics and Politics of Museum Display*, ed. Ivan Karp and Steven D. Lavine (Washington, D.C.: Smithsonian Institution Press, 1991), 255–77.

wake of that read Raphaël Confiant's book on Césaire, Maryse Condé's *Traversée de la Mangrove*, and Confiant and Chamoiseau's *Lettres Créoles*. We decided to write a critique, eventually calling it "Shadowboxing in the Mangrove."[12] Meanwhile, I was working with increasing intensity on my Médard project, interviewing participants in the 1925 Election Day massacre, seeking out surviving artworks made by this mysterious man.

The next year, Anil Ramdas, a hip cultural studies journalist for the leading newspaper in the Netherlands, traveled to Martinique to interview us, staying for three days. He had somehow formed the bizarre idea that my/our books, laid end to end, could be used as a metonym for the trajectory of the social sciences during the past thirty years. And he didn't find it a pretty sight. I had started, he said, as a social scientist incarnate, publishing in classic anthropological monograph form. (And indeed, my published dissertation did fit this bill.) He claimed that I next moved through textual experimentations with page layout and typefaces, in an attempt to disperse my ethnographic authority and share it with the voices of the previously underrepresented. (Again, I pled guilty—*First-Time* was very much concerned with representing "partial truths," presenting alternative narratives and multiple historical voices that, in Natalie Davis's words, "allow one to imagine new possibilities for both history and memory."[13]) And *Alabi's World*, though more linear in form than the previous work, used four different typefaces to emphasize the inevitable perspectivality of my various historical sources. Ramdas then took note of how the coauthored books that Sally and I next began writing took on a fragmentary form, mixing diary, memoir, and line drawings. *Two Evenings in Saramaka*, for example, was written in the form of a screenplay, with designated voice and stage directions, and *Equatoria* was in the form of a diary set off against excerpts and fragments from other people's writings, combined

---

12 First published as Richard Price and Sally Price, "Shadowboxing in the Mangrove," *Cultural Anthropology* 12 (1997): 3–36, and later anthologized, this paper led to much controversy and we revisited it several times, most recently in Richard Price, "*Créolisation*, Creolization, and *Créolité*," *Small Axe* 52 (2017): 211–19; and Sally Price, "Beyond Francophonie: Contextualizing *Éloge de la Créolité*," *Small Axe* 52 (2017): 200–211. We had shared a prepublication draft of the paper with Glissant, and after a dinner at his Riverside Drive apartment in New York, he told us he didn't disagree with any of our criticisms of his buddy Chamoiseau. "But did you need to be so *dur* [hard or tough]?"

13 Natalie Zemon Davis, "Who Owns History?" *Studia Historica* (Helsinki) 61 (1999): 19–34, quote on p. 26.

with Sally's pen-and-ink sketches, the whole taking on the form of a collage or montage. And finally, Ramdas noted, we had cast our ethnographic research in the form of a novel—*Enigma Variations*—in which characters named Rich and Sally were the antiheroes and where the authors shamelessly played with fiction and reality and with notions of verisimilitude and authenticity and in which they even staged a seminar in the Princeton Art History Department where professors and students debated Carlo Ginzburg's analysis of Freud's discussion of Morelli and Sherlock Holmes and prehistoric hunters—the whole nine yards—all in connection with that famous (fictional) severed ear that was mailed to a demure maiden lady in a cardboard box. For this Dutch journalist, the Prices' lifework represented a cautionary tale of gradual but inevitable decline, from modernist scientific certainties to postmodernist confusion and disillusionment. As we watched the sunset over the Caribbean on our last evening together, Ramdas decided to call his piece "De avondrood van antropologie" (The twilight of anthropology).[14]

That year we also traveled to the annual meetings of the American Anthropological Association in San Francisco. I had sent my Médard manuscript to Deb Chasman, editor at Beacon Press who had published my 1992 book with Sid, and she was enthusiastic about the new work. At the meetings, she offered me an advance that seemed enormous: $16,000. I had also sent the manuscript to David Brent at Chicago, who had published Sally's very successful *Primitive Art in Civilized Places* as well as our considerably less successful (in terms of sales) *Two Evenings in Saramaka*. We were at a small table in the hotel bar, when a (possibly inebriated) David actually got on his knees (as if proposing marriage in an old film) and loudly implored me to give the book to Chicago rather than Beacon, though he said he could not possibly match their advance. In the end, I signed with Beacon. That evening, Sid came over to us and tried to give Sally a peck on the cheek, but she pulled away. After shaking hands with me, he invited the two of us to meet him for coffee the next morning at 9 a.m. Sally declined, but I said OK. A few minutes later, we were chatting with Nancy Choderow, a friend of Sally's from Radcliffe who'd become a feminist psychoanalyst and well-known author. Nancy knew all about our break with Hopkins, so I told her about Sid's invita-

---

14 The editors in the Netherlands later changed his title to the more lurid "Verraad in de jungle" (Treason in the jungle). Anil Ramdas, "Verraad in de jungle," in the *Zaterdags bijvoegsel* of the *NRC-Handelsblad* (Rotterdam), May 25, 1996, 1–2.

tion. She explained that the reason Sally and I had responded differently was simple: "You have a Jewish mother, Sally does not." When I met Sid the next morning, he simply plied me with jokes: There was this circle of nuns walking around clockwise and this circle of prostitutes walking counterclockwise . . . (I don't remember the punchline). I felt then, as I felt during all my subsequent interactions with him, that I wanted to act cordial but in no way grant him what he so clearly desired: my forgiveness and a rollback to the way we had once been with one another, as if nothing had happened between us.

Not too long after, Rolph, who had periodically phoned me in Martinique over the years to get advice about his career (in particular his salary), called, distraught, to discuss whether he should leave his position at Johns Hopkins (as Krieger/Eisenhower Distinguished Professor of Anthropology and director of the Institute for Global Studies in Culture, Power and History) to take up the offer of a professorship at Chicago. He complained, with bitterness, that "Sid is doing the same thing to me that he did to you." I told him gently that I didn't think it was quite the same, in that a professorship at Chicago was waiting for him, but I supported what I took to be his desire to move on.

⬅

So who was this "Médard," whom I have mentioned as a "folk artist," and why did he obsess me for so many years?

In 1978, on our way home from Suriname fieldwork, we had stopped off for a few days, as usual, in Martinique, to visit Emilien and Merlande, who were running their café/general store next to the sea. We quickly noticed—among the rum bottles, high up above the narrow counter that served as a bar—a painted wooden statue we'd never seen. Emilien said it was "a general" and that they'd inherited it from Merlande's godfather, who had died that year. The statue had been made, Emilien told us, by a certain Médard Aribot.

I began to ask around about this Médard, and one thing kind of led to another. Indeed, it took some twenty years of on-and-off fieldwork before I published the results.[15]

---

15 R. Price, *Convict and the Colonel*. The book was "blurbed" by George Lamming, Roger Abrahams, Rolph Trouillot, Lucy Lippard, Maryse Condé, and others. For reviews, see Richard Price and Sally Price, Books, http://www.richandsally.net/the_convict_and _the_colonel_8370.htm.

With Médard's colonel.

As I talked to people about Médard, who it turned out had died only in 1973, I learned that this taciturn, unschooled man had lived in a cave by the sea near the town of Diamant, just over the mountain from Petite Anse, . . . that he was a kind of Robin Hood (stealing from the French National shipping company, from the gendarmerie, and even from the attorney general [a pair of pants drying on his clothesline]), . . . and that he redistributed this booty to his poor neighbors. He was also a self-taught artist who sculpted marvelous steamships, pianos, kings, and military figures from scraps of wood and other detritus, displaying them at the annual fêtes of neighboring towns and sometimes peddling them in the island's capital. He was called by many of our fishermen acquaintances a "genius" and remembered with fondness for his eccentric way of life. But the main thing he was remembered for was having sculpted the "general" displayed in Emilien's bar, which older men told me was in fact the image of a certain Colonel de Coppens, the *béké* (planter-descended) one-time proprietor of Diamant's rum distillery and the rightist mayoral candidate in the 1925 municipal elections. As Emilien's older brother Ernest told me in 1983, "Colonel Coppens—he's the one who sent Méda' to forced labor. It was because of that *'photo'* [sculpture]. . . . Hard labor, for life! For a man who had no education . . . a complete innocent. A man like that, to send him to the penal colony. . . . He hadn't hurt a soul—all he'd done was make that *'photo.'*"

From speaking with many people, some of whom had been present during the elections of 1925, I slowly pieced together a version of what local fishermen call "The War of Diamant" and learned that the crowd of voters—several hundred socialists blocked from the voting booth by barbed wire, a machine gunner, and other forces of the French State that wished to ensure the victory of Coppens over a local Black socialist—had marched around the building brandishing Médard's statue of Coppens and that Coppens had then given the order for the troops to fire, killing ten men and wounding eleven who were simply trying to exercise their right to vote. And I was told repeatedly, it was for having sculpted this bust that Médard was condemned in perpetuity to the dreaded *bagne* (penal colony) of Guyane.

As I investigated further, finding no traces of this incident in local schoolbooks or history books, I turned to the Departmental Archives, where I indeed found newspaper reports of the 1925 killings. (It was the largest single massacre of citizens by the State in all of Martinique's troubled twentieth-century history.) But when I tried to find information about Médard, I came up completely dry.[16] And two "authoritative" sources—the island's only newspaper, *France-Antilles*, and its major official scholarly journal, *Cahiers du Patrimoine*—each published articles concluding that the story (based on oral history) of Médard having sculpted a bust of the colonel that had been used in the 1925 election protests and of his having been sent to the bagne—which I had published in an article in 1985[17]—were in fact nothing more than "popular legends, backed up by no archival facts."[18]

In 1985, when we were on leave from Hopkins in Paris, I asked historian Bob Forster, who was also on leave from Hopkins, for advice about working in the Archives d'Outre-Mer, then located in the capital, and he kindly introduced me to the director of the archives—a sixty-four-year-old woman who, when I addressed her as "Madame" corrected me: "Jusqu'ici, c'est Mademoiselle." She proved to be a savior, not only finding for me the large cardboard carton overflowing with photos, police reports, cablegrams, and other direct evidence relating to what the archives labeled "the affair of Diamant" but eventually giving me access

---

16 The director of the Departmental Archives also had her staff search all relevant sources—*The Official Journal of Martinique*, which provides records of all those appearing before criminal courts, all newspapers, and so forth, never finding a single mention of the man.

17 Richard Price, "An Absence of Ruins? Seeking Caribbean Historical Consciousness," *Caribbean Review* 14, no. 3 (1985): 24–29, 45.

18 "Médard Aribot, Artist or Convict? His Life Seems Closest to a Marvelous Folktale, However Sad. Was He a Convict? There's Nothing That Proves It . . ." (Dominique Rabussier, "Médard Aribot, artiste ou bagnard?" *France-Antilles Magazine*, August 14–20, 1993, 48–49, and August 21–27, 1993, 48–49; "La rédaction" [two historians], "P.S.," *Cahiers du Patrimoine* nos. 7–8 [1990]: 113.)

(quite illegally, since the requisite number of years had not passed for me to peer into it) to the notebook written by the prison wardens detailing Médard's highly rebellious years in the bagne of Guyane.

The 1925 report written by the chief of the police brigade in Diamant that fateful Election Day confirmed that the crowd had brandished Médard's statue of the colonel. And a decade later, I was able to present two contrastive versions of history (in two vertical columns, running over many pages, labeled "The Left" and "The Right") in *The Convict and the Colonel*. Combining fishermen's oral history, newspaper accounts, and the rich materials from the Paris archives eventually permitted a rather full view of "The War of Diamant" and Médard's role in it.

The book begins with the "War of Diamant," then moves on to the search for Médard's remaining artworks (important *lieux de mémoire* for the fishermen and peasants who kept them in their homes) and concludes with a lengthy consideration of the changes taking place in Martinique regarding historical consciousness, the ongoing process of *francisation* in this postcolonial space, and the role of literature and the imaginaire in history. One of the foci of the third section is the singular house that Médard built when he returned from Guyane in the early 1950s, after the closure of the bagne—a miniature, colorful, gingerbread structure by the sea in Diamant that became a favored tourist destination and was featured on the cover of the *Guide Gallimard de la Martinique*. Now classed as a *Monument historique de la France*, the house serves as the main public reminder of Médard and the massacre of 1925. (It was badly vandalized in 2014 and was very poorly reconstructed since.) In the book, I trace the changing meaning of the house to local people, to the Martiniquan public, and to French tourists, describing these shifts as part of the more general process that I call "the postcarding of the past."[19]

Sally and I were eager to make the book available to our Martiniquan neighbors, its central protagonists, so Sally volunteered to translate it into French.[20] And soon after the arrival of *Le bagnard et le colonel* in Martinique, the book was launched amid considerable media hoopla at

---

19 For the very latest twist in the story of the house, see Richard Price, "Médard Meets Mighty Mouse," *New West Indian Guide* 91 (2017): 261–64.

20 *Le bagnard et le colonel* (Paris: Presses Universitaires de France, 2000; 2nd ed., La Roque d'Anthéron: Vents d'ailleurs, 2016).

a beachside hotel in Diamant, in an ambience that veered between the moving and the carnivalesque. For the first time in the history of Martinique, the "War of Diamant" became a topic that could be discussed in public. Improbably, some five hundred people from all over the island showed up, spilling out of the packed dining hall. Fishermen and their families from Petite Anse rubbed shoulders with professors from the university and politicians of various persuasions. Around 8:00 p.m., the mayor of Diamant opened the proceedings by speaking solemnly of "*le devoir de mémoire*" (the duty/obligation to remember), a buzz-phrase in recent French commemorations. Several academic panelists spoke to the book's contents, Sally and I made a few remarks, and the debate was thrown open to the floor.

It wasn't until shortly before midnight that a woman rose to give the final testimony of the evening. Voice shaking with emotion, she introduced herself as Yvette Galot, a member of the town council. Stopping several times to wipe away tears, she described how her grandfather had been shot dead on the street that bloody day in 1925. When she was a schoolgirl, she continued, children teased her about being the granddaughter of a traitor and a troublemaker. But her father had told her never, never to be ashamed of what her grandfather had done, that he was a patriot. This book, she said, bore out her father's words, putting meat on the bare bones he had been able to give her, and for that she was eternally grateful.

Preceding this *témoignage* from a person whose life had been touched by the events of May 1925 were several hours of miscellaneous commentary, debate, and raucous argument, including contradictory testimony about Médard: "Why did you choose to celebrate the life of a criminal?" "No! Médard was a saint and a Robin Hood." "Médard never uttered a word in his life, I can assure you." "Ridiculous! I spoke with Médard many times." "Médard was a short, little fellow." "No, Médard was tall and strong." A junior high school teacher from Diamant described how, when she wrote the Diamant chapter of the recently published *Histoire des Communes*, the publisher in Paris, who had once visited Martinique, insisted that she change what she'd written about "la maison du bagnard" (the house of the convict) to be about "le temple chinois" (the Chinese temple)—which gave me a chance to report that a few days earlier when I was in front of the house with a television crew preparing a report for the book launch, a tourist got out and eagerly explained to me that the house was in fact "a Hindu temple where they practice 'coolie voodoo,' with animal sacrifice and blood all over the place." There was heated discussion about whether Médard's statue of the colonel, which I held in my arms throughout the event, contained magical powers designed to swing the elections, with one man saying that he certainly wouldn't touch it without first turning his shirt inside out. In fact, a number of descendants of the victims of the massacre were present and testified. Each, in his or her way, said that the book had allowed a part of their history that had long been suppressed to become their own once more. It gave them authority for the first time to speak and to be believed.

So, in this case, an anthropologist's insistence on history—despite the State's denials—had practical, salutary effects, freeing previously suppressed discourse to be voiced with pride. The town hall of Diamant now has a wall on which the names of the dead and wounded in the 1925 Election Day massacre, taken from my book, are inscribed. And the town now solemnly commemorates the event annually.

By the late 1990s, the little house we were living in, built artisanally by the original owner, was showing signs of wear—termites in the roof, inadequate space for our several thousand books, and general dilapidation. It seemed poised to be blown away by a hurricane, in which case we would have had insurance money for a replacement, but since that storm never materialized, we decided to rebuild anyway. At a party at the Englands, we met Mike Parker, a British architect who'd settled in the island, who agreed to help us realize a plan that Sally had been playing with over the years. And by 2000, we moved into the new two-story structure, this one with hot running water.

That millennial year proved eventful in other ways as well. In the spring, we spent a week at a conference at the University of Puerto Rico (where Toño arranged our first meeting with artist Antonio Martorell) and participated in a week-long seminar on Afro-American Studies, organized by Kevin Yelvington, in Santa Fe.[21] Sally was elected a member of the Royal Netherlands Academy of Arts and Sciences, one of only three foreign anthropologists (including Claude Lévi-Strauss). Rolph Trouillot invited me to speak at the University of Chicago, and we had a heartfelt conversation afterward, accompanied by caviar and champagne, going

---

21 See Yelvington, *Afro-Atlantic Dialogues.*

Looking up from the sea.

over our respective trajectories, in his glass-paneled, high-rise apartment on Lake Shore Drive. It was the last time I saw him before he suffered a devastating aneurism in 2002. Ten years later, Brackette and I organized a memorial session for Rolph at the annual meetings of the American Anthropological Association—hundreds of his friends and students attended and a number of his Hopkins classmates spoke movingly about his legacy.[22]

That same year, back in Martinique, Merlande succumbed to a multi-year battle against cancer, remaining in good spirits till the end. Our long-term relationship with Emilien shifted more to our house, where he often came for a meal, but I went over to his place in Petite Anse as well—to watch Real Madrid on his large-screen TV. We also watched many World Cup games together, rooting for Brazil. (The backstory is that my Mar-

22 My obituary of Rolph was published in *American Anthropologist* 115 (2013): 717–20.

tiniquan agemates tend to be fans of Brazil, rather than France—though younger local fans are enthusiastically *bleu-blanc-rouge*. This is because when TV started in Martinique, Brazil was both the best in the world and the best team with players who looked like them. So the switch, on the club side, to Real Madrid came naturally, with Roberto Carlos, Ronaldo [*O Fenômeno*], and others leading the way.) Just after 9/11, we took Emilien on a visit to New York, staying in midtown Manhattan at my mother's apartment—we'd done the same with Merlande years earlier.

In retrospect, that year—which saw the publication of my Martinique book in French and our building a new house—began a gradual but sustained retreat from the frequent interaction with our neighbors that we had long maintained, and it marked a certain inward-turning in our life. Sally and I found we were spending less time in Petite Anse and more on our writing and our fieldwork in Guyane and Paris. (One tradition we maintained though: attending wakes in Petite Anse, as well as the *bourg*. Since the 1960s, when we often attended all-night wakes lit by kerosene lanterns that included magnificent call-and-response *contes* told by aging raconteurs, they had become large communal gatherings, with local politicians as well as far-flung relatives in attendance, sharing greetings and food and drink—an important moment for us to keep up at least a semblance of long-standing relationships.)

We'd also launched a new project we'd been thinking about for a couple of years—tracking down and writing about Romare Bearden's little-known Caribbean paintings. It had a serendipitous origin. When we were trying to find a cover image for *The Convict and the Colonel*, Sally had looked through the catalog of a Baltimore Museum of Art exhibition that we'd attended in 1980, *Romare Bearden: 1970–1980*.[23] In the "Listing of Works" at the back of the book, she was surprised to see how many of his watercolors depicted the Caribbean, and we realized that he'd actually had a home in St. Martin. This was not part of the general knowledge about Bearden, and we decided to pursue it as a new project, beginning by an attempt to locate as many of his Caribbean paintings—some of which dated from his brief trips to Martinique—as possible, and to speak with as many of his friends as we could about the meaning of the Caribbean in his life and work. Our compass was set. Over the next few

---

23 Jerald L. Melberg and Milton J. Bloch, eds., *Romare Bearden: 1970–1980* (Charlotte, N.C.: Mint Museum, 1980).

Looking down from the house.

years, we visited St. Martin, crossed the channel to St. Lucia to spend time with Derek Walcott (who had been Bearden's friend), and spoke with Bearden's friends and associates in New York, the Caribbean, and France.[24]

The following years in Anse Chaudière were rich with new research and writing projects: a book about the Herskovitses' 1920s Suriname diaries (which our friend Kevin Yelvington had alerted us to and photocopied for us at the Schomburg Center in New York); our French-

---

24 Our book, lavishly illustrated in color, was published in both French and English editions in 2006: *Romare Bearden: The Caribbean Dimension* (Philadelphia: University of Pennsylvania Press) and *Romare Bearden: Une dimension caribéenne* (La Roque d'Anthéron: Vents d'Ailleurs). The list of Bearden's friends who kindly shared their reminiscences with us—from his main man in Harlem, writer Al Murray, to his poet admirer in St. Martin, Lasana Sekou—can be found in the book's acknowledgments.

language book about Maroons in Guyane; my intensive work with Tooy; my ongoing human rights efforts on behalf of Saamakas; and a book, written with Sally, about our 1960s fieldwork in Saamaka.

We experienced 9/11 in Martinique. Our closest neighbor, Marie, phoned and simply said, "Turn on your TV!" As we watched in horror, I kept thinking how fantastically clever whoever had planned the hijackings had been. That evening, Radio Caraïbe International (the most listened to station in Martinique) called and begged me for an interview. "There are only six Americans who live in Martinique. You're the most famous one. Please tell us how the news made you feel." I wasn't about to cry for them. . . . A decade later, RFO (the main TV station on the island) sent a crew of three to our home to film us watching the 2012 election results and talk to us about Obama's victory over Romney. Unlike 9/11, that was one event we were pleased to celebrate with the island media. (In 2008, we had done several TV interviews to explain to Martiniquans the significance of Obama's candidacy, about which the whole island was enthusiastic.)

In 2005, we had a memorable visit to Puerto Rico, where I launched the Spanish-language version of *The Convict and the Colonel*, for which Toño Díaz-Royo had written an introduction, adding personal experience from his clinical practice about madness and colonialism.[25] When we arrived, we saw that the walls near the university were festooned with slogans honoring Filiberto (Ojeda Ríos), whose funeral—the day before our arrival—was the largest in Puerto Rican history. Filiberto had been commander-in-chief of the Boricua Popular Army (a.k.a., *Los Macheteros*) and the FBI's most wanted criminal because of the 1983 Wells Fargo depot robbery in West Hartford, Connecticut, when he and his companions stole $7.2 million, the largest cash heist in U.S. history, for the cause of Puerto Rican independence. While awaiting trial, he had escaped, had gone into hiding, was sentenced in absentia to fifty-five years in federal prison, and had just been located by the FBI at a remote farmhouse in Puerto Rico. His barbaric and cowardly murder by the federal agents instantly made him a martyr and Puerto Ricans from all parties—left and

---

25 Richard Price, *El presidiario y el coronel* (San Juan: Ediciones Callejón, 2005). Driving us to the post office near his home in Trujillo Alto so we could mail a letter, Toño—a committed independentist—remarked that he always hated having to go into a U.S. post office since the employees were all pro-statehood.

right, statehood as well as independence—marched at his funeral. The newspaper interviews in San Juan about my book inevitably compared Médard's rebellious acts to Filiberto's.

During our stay, Toño took Sally and me to the Cayey studio of his friend Martorell, where we had the opportunity to see the artist's work in progress and the scores of file drawers about Martorell's art and writings that Toño was organizing as part of his massive biographical project on the maestro.[26] He also introduced us as "professors" to an extremely shy woman who prepared coffee for us. She told us she'd never before met a professor. When we left, we asked Toño who she was, why she seemed so socially awkward. He told us that, as a late teenager, she'd been one of the original Machetero crew who'd pulled off the 1983 robbery and had only a few months before been released from prison on the mainland, where she'd been for all her adult life. Martorell, as a humane and political act, was taking responsibility for her readjustment to society.

By the second decade of the new millennium, deaths of close friends and relatives were becoming common. Emilien, who had been having troubles with balance, died from a fall in his home. Soon after, his sister Liliane, suffering from depression, hanged herself from a mango tree in Petite Anse—we were devastated. Édouard Glissant and Derek Walcott both passed. My father was in the care of my sister in western Massachusetts when he died at age ninety-six, but we were visiting with my mother (as fate would have it, in Valhalla [New York]) when her heart gave out and she died in our arms at the age of ninety-seven. In 2015, we got news of Sid's death.[27] My feelings were mixed—on the one hand, relief that he would no longer be giving interviews in which he erased my role at Hopkins and in Caribbean studies,[28] on the other, feelings of loss of a mentor and one-time friend. Sally's feelings were less mixed.

The next year, the University of Puerto Rico held a two-day event com-

---

26 See Antonio Díaz-Royo, *Martorell: La aventura de la creación* (San Juan: Editorial Universidad de Puerto Rico, 2007).

27 When Sid died, from a fall down the stairs, he was working on a review I had asked him to do of a seven-hundred-page book about slavery in German, for *New West Indian Guide*. He had told me he would read one page every day—he must have been around page four hundred.

28 One reader of this manuscript, who knew Sid well, wrote me that what he had attempted was nothing less than a (failed) "*dammatio memoriae* [designed] to erase all traces of your work from the discipline."

With Antonio Martorell in his studio (Ponce, Puerto Rico, 2016).

memorating the donation of books from the collections of Sid Mintz and Gordon Lewis to its library. I presented the Third Annual Gordon K. and Sybil Farrell Lewis Memorial Lecture, and Sally gave the Sidney W. Mintz Memorial Lecture, in which she reminisced warmly about our friendship during 1964–84 but pointedly ended her narrative in 1985.[29] Jackie, as well as Sid's children, flew down for the ceremony. Toño took us for a memorable visit to Martorell's studio in Ponce, where the maestro took a couple of hours to lead us through some of the wonders that had sprung from his fertile imagination.

My long-time colleague in Maroon studies, Dutch anthropologist Bonno Thoden van Velzen, suffering from terminal bone cancer, expressed the hope that I would be willing to provide a foreword to his final book, to be called *Prophets of Doom*. Bonno and his wife, Ineke, who had died in 2011, were the senior anthropologists of the Okanisi (Ndyuka) people, much as we were with the neighboring Saamakas.

I struggled with that foreword, grappling with a question that had long puzzled me: Why does the view that Sally and I have of Saamaka soci-

---

29 Sally's lecture is available on the left column of our website, www.richandsally.net. We had been friends with Gordon and Sybil for decades, often visiting them when we were in Puerto Rico.

ety and the view that Bonno and Ineke have of Okanisi society differ so much, ours being (I think) more oriented toward the normal if sometimes heroic, theirs more toward the darker side of humanity . . . ours depicting mostly well-adjusted, relatively content and egalitarian people, theirs more often manipulative, jealous, violent, and fearful ones. I thought back to the suggestion of my first mentor in anthropology, Clyde Kluckhohn, who had argued that every anthropological monograph should be preceded by a summary analysis, written by the author's psychoanalyst. But I also considered the possibility that the answer might be found, not in the investigators' personalities or theoretical approaches but rather in the societies themselves—differences in what used to be glossed as "national character." I believed that it was well established that Okanisis had, for at least a century and half, had more social inequality (and greater cosmological hierarchy) and more frequent witchcraft accusations (and convictions) than Saamakas; that their prophetic cults had been more frequent; and that the often violent demonic outbreaks, including those that continue to plague Okanisi schoolgirls into the present, were far less present in Saamaka. So some combination of anthropologists' personalities and facts on the ground (but in what sort of mix?) must, I thought, come into play in explaining the difference.

At the same time, I knew that fieldwork by the Thodens and Prices was, from the first, quite different. Sally and I immersed ourselves in the daily lives of our neighbors, dressing, cooking, and gardening like them, learning skills involved in hunting, fishing, calabash carving, sewing, and so forth. Bonno and Ineke made a much clearer distinction between their lifestyle as researchers and that of their Okanisi hosts. During a 2015 interview with Brazilian anthropologist Olívia da Cunha, Bonno mentioned—and firmly denied—a rumor that spread among his anthropological colleagues and made him, he said, "unhappy" (he seemed to consider it scandalous): "That Ineke was walking bare-breasted through the village."[30] Even back at home, Bonno and Ineke led a rather formal European-style life, with portraits of distinguished ancestors on the walls of their stately home in Bosch en Duin and then in their postre-

---

30 Olívia Maria Gomes da Cunha and H. U. E. Thoden van Velzen, "Through Maroon Worlds: A Conversation with Bonno Thoden van Velzen," *Canadian Journal of Latin American and Caribbean Studies* 41, no. 2 (2016), 254–78, quote on p. 262.

tirement house in Huijbergen,[31] while our lifestyle was that of more re-laxed 1960s-influenced Americans. After conducting her interview with Bonno, Olívia made an interesting reflection: "Just as we learn that in Ndyuka [Okanisi] cosmology the omnipresence of death and the dead is always signaled by the singular combination of forms of memory and forewarnings of danger, so the recollection of field experience is not just a trajectory; it is also a tragedy."[32] I believe that this sense of foreboding and tragedy, which seems related to Bonno's continued preoccupation with doom in Okanisi history, pervades his work.

To what extent is the sunnier picture of Saamaka life and culture that Sally and I maintain, as seen for example in *Saamaka Dreaming*, a corol-lary of our own personalities or the reflection of realities on the ground? As with the related questions posed in our 1960s Andalusian fieldwork, the art of ethnography continues to hold many mysteries.[33]

---

31 On our last visit to Bonno, in 2018, he drove us a couple of kilometers from his house to see the famous Wall of Brabant which, unsurprisingly, made me think of the setting of *Lohengrin*.

32 Gomes da Cunha and Thoden van Velzen, "Through Maroon Worlds," 272.

33 The closest look into our own ways of conducting the delicate act of ethnography can probably be found in *The Convict and the Colonel, Travels with Tooy*, and *Saamaka Dreaming*. It is in those books, rather than this memoir, that the density of days in the field, what a committed anthropologist does with their time, is most easily seen—at least our version of it.

CHAPTER NINETEEN

RUE VOLTA

(2008–2019)

We spent many months during the first decade of the new millennium in Paris, as Sally worked with art historians, museum curators, anthropologists, and others who were involved in planning (or opposing) Jacques Chirac's dream of a major museum of non-Western art. Sometimes we crashed in friends' apartments, sometimes we took short-term rentals. By the time her book was published in English and she began thinking about a French edition, other books of ours were also coming out in French, so we decided to find a place of our own in a city that had always been special for us, beginning with the first year of our marriage.

Our apartment on the rue Volta, in the gentrifying Haut Marais, was loft-style, bathed in light, and perfect for our needs.[1] It quickly became a place to entertain friends, as we got acquainted with the offerings, from artichokes and eels to ducks and whelks (without even mentioning the fantastic cheeses and charcuterie), in the wonderful outdoor markets just a short walk away. People we knew from Martinique came through often—Maryse Condé, Sylvie Glissant, Mathieu and Camille Glissant, Catherine Benoît, Dominique Taffin, and many others—and we revived friendships from earlier times in Paris (sociologist Kristin Couper, mathematician Marie-France Vigneras, historian Myriam Cottias . . .). There were many new friends as well: Africanist art historian Étienne Féau, artist William Adjété Wilson, anthropologist/psychologist Lorenzo Brutti, historian Nelcya Delanoë, and Haitianist anthropologist Natacha Giafferi, as well as Guadeloupean activist and physician Serge Romana (who got us involved in the activities of Antillean associations in the Paris area), and Saamaka linguist Vinije Haabo (who visited from his home in the Netherlands).

The social event that should have been "the cherry on the cake" (as the French would put it) in our apartment never actually materialized. In 2014, we had, quite unexpectedly, received notice that we were each being awarded the title of Chevalier de l'Ordre des Arts et des Lettres by

---

1 Our street was named after Alessandro Volta, Italian inventor of the electric battery in 1800—the volt is named for him. The following year, he demonstated his device before Napoleon, who gave him a medal and made him a count.

42, rue Volta.

France's minister of culture. The induction ceremony could, according to the instructions, be held at home, if a higher-ranking member of the Ordre was present to pronounce certain specified words and pin on the beribboned medals to make us knights. After Maryse Condé agreed to do the honors, we bought a case of champagne and extra champagne glasses, prepared hors d'oeuvres, and invited friends and colleagues. Without taking any of this very seriously, we realized it would be a good excuse for a party. However, the day before the event, the cranky little elevator in our building got stuck and refused to budge, and there was no way we could get Maryse, who was already having serious difficulty walking, up the four flights of stairs. (When Maryse and Richard had come over for dinner a few weeks earlier, she joked that she needed to hold on to two Richards, one on each side, to navigate the five blocks between our apartments.) We canceled the event and never rescheduled.

Once we felt settled into the rue Volta, we kept a fairly regular rhythm of spending April–June and September there, and we tried to group our European lecture trips into those months. My partial records show that we flew (or took the train) for lectures in Rome, Geneva, Neuchatel, Vienna, Prague, Zurich, Madrid, Barcelona, Bayreuth, Berlin, Copenhagen, Lund, London, Essex, Rotterdam, Utrecht, and Leiden—with several trips to many of these places. (In fact, since it was cheaper to fly to Brazil via Paris than from Martinique, we flew there from rue Volta several times, including a trip to Natal to jointly present, in Portuguese, the opening plenary lecture for the 2014 Association of Brazilian Anthropologists.) And each time we published a book in French we would give presentations—at universities, bookstores, human rights associations, museums, the Ministry of Outre-Mer, the Maison de l'Amérique Latine, and so forth in Paris. (In 2016, I spoke to an audience of several hundred Antilleans—half Martiniquan, half Guadeloupean—in the Hôtel de Ville of Paris, presenting the new edition of *Le bagnard et le colonel*.) Our lectures elsewhere in France included trips to La Rochelle, Avranches, Nantes, Bordeaux, Dijon, Marseilles, Toulouse, and Rouen.

Our neighborhood, triangulated between métro stops Arts et Métiers, Temple, and République, was rich with history and excitement. Two blocks from our apartment was the oldest Chinese settlement in Paris, filled with grocery stores and inexpensive (Wenzhou-style) restaurants. Around the corner was L'Ami Louis, the super high-end bistro favored by Bill Clinton and Jacques Chirac (we never tried it). A half-timbered house on our street, once believed to be the oldest extant home in Paris, dating from the fourteenth century (but which researchers in the 1970s determined was actually a medieval replica from the seventeenth century), had the best Pho restaurant in the city, a veritable hole in the wall for which there was always a long line of people waiting to get in. The corner boulangerie was run by a friendly Camerounais, who had won a prize for the best croissants in Paris. The grassy Square du Temple park a couple of blocks from our apartment, site of the twelfth-century Knights Templar European headquarters, always reminded me of Parsifal and the Holy Grail, as well as their bloody Crusades. The upscale rue de Bretagne, with its tony shops and outdoor cafes and the Marché des Enfants Rouges, was just a few steps away. And the Place de la République, a five-minute walk and the preferred starting place for most Parisian political demonstrations and marches, always had something going on.

A few days after we moved in, we were buying artichokes in the nearby Marché des Enfants Rouges, said to be the oldest market in Paris, when the bearded vendor saw Sally's Obama button and made a comment. As we began to chat, he told us he'd left his native Egypt when he was nineteen, that his sister, who had a doctorate in pharmacy from Egypt and another earned in the USA, had been in Kansas City for forty-five years, and ran the pharmacy department of the city's largest hospital. His story reminded me of an article I'd read that morning in *Le Monde*: Lilian Thuram, the great, recently retired Guadeloupe-born footballer, was quoted about what it meant to be French and Black. He described meeting a five-year-old boy, born in France, who told him he was *ivoirien* (from Ivory Coast) and asked Thuram his nationality. "I said that I was French and he shot back, '*Mais non*, you're Black!'" "How many French people," Thuram wondered, "would spontaneously assume that someone named Karim or Zinédane [or, he implied without having to say it, who was Black] was French—if he wasn't a star on the French football team?"[2]

Each May 23, we would attend Serge Romana's CM98 association's giant fête in the Place de la République celebrating the memory of the victims of colonial slavery, where as VIPs (since we gave annual lectures to the association) we could go backstage and meet the members of Kassav', Tabou Combo, or whatever other famous band he had persuaded to give a massive free concert—we would mingle with other supporters, such as Christiane Taubira, the dynamic minister of justice from Guyane. Always lively![3]

The rest of Paris beckoned as well—from museums and cinemas to our more favored activity of walking the streets. There are certain places we returned to again and again—a particular Chinese restaurant in the 13th arrondissement; our favorite bistro in the 20th; a Spanish place in the 10th, where we watched many a Real Madrid match and ate tapas; the

---

2   Mustapha Kessous and Stéphane Mandard, "Lilian Thuram, 'Combien pensent qu'un Karim est d'ici ?'" *Le Monde*, October 18, 2008. At the time, Karim Benzema was a promising young striker on the French national team and Zinédine Zidane the star of their World Cup triumph in 1998 who captained their team to the 2006 final.

3   CM98's ambitious plan, approved by President Hollande, for a memorial in the Tuileries Garden with the names and communes of all the enslaved who were freed in 1848 (some two hundred thousand people), seems, under President Macron in spring 2022 (as this memoir goes to press), finally ready for realization.

Canal Saint-Martin; Belleville; the Place des Voges; the rue Mouffetard; the Place des Abbesses, where we began our married life. . . .

But often enough when we were in Paris, the weather would turn cool and grey. And we would think about taking four or five days in our other favorite European place, Spain. So, we would book a cheap flight to Madrid or Sevilla, rent a car, and visit friends in Los Olivos or tour areas of Spain we hadn't known. (Our 1960s friends from Los Olivos, after their economically driven migration to Barcelona, had—by the time we lived on rue Volta—retired back to the pueblo, where they modernized their family homes and settled back in.)

Obtaining and maintaining residence papers (*cartes de séjour*) was, to put it politely, a constant struggle over the years. (Martinique, though part of France, is not party to the Schengen Convention, so a carte de séjour from there doesn't work in continental Europe.) After the initial acquisition of a visa at the French embassy in Washington (a bureaucratic adventure in itself) and arrival in France, the fun would begin: chest X-rays, interviews, complex proof of financial health and housing, medical insurance, and more (all translated into French by costly government-designated translators), followed by interviews (scheduled months in advance) at the central police station. In the 1960s, the procedures, as we remember them, were relatively casual, but by the 1980s, they had become truly draconian; as a lycée student, Leah narrowly missed being deported for technicalities that we have mercifully wiped from our memories (or perhaps never fully understood).

But there were also lighter moments in our dealings with French bureaucracy, including in Martinique. In 2008, visiting the outpatient wing of the public hospital for treatment of a wrist she had broken while harvesting grapefruits, Sally always wore a campaign pin for Obama, who was immensely popular in Martinique, because the people working at the bill-paying windows would see the pin, call her to the front of the very long line, ask her to get them an Obama bumper sticker, and allow her to pay without waiting.

There was also a serendipitous encounter in Martinique with a dentist who, it turned out, was a frustrated political activist. After engaging Sally in a lengthy discussion of the war in Iraq as he worked on her teeth, often pausing for pure conversation, he asked if she might be willing to pay him, not with euros, but rather with the (worthless) 250-dinar note sporting Saddam's picture that she'd shown him, a present from Niko,

Niko in Baghdad, 2003.

who'd brought it back from Iraq, soon after he was embedded with troops in the wake of Shock and Awe.

Or again, after we'd reapplied the required number of times for one-year residence cards in Paris, we were authorized to request (with substantially more documentation) ten-year cards. Managing to get appointments at the police station together on the same day, we sat in the waiting area all morning and were both finally called to be interviewed, at separate, glassed-in counters. But there we were told that the legislation had changed and we wouldn't be eligible for ten-year cards for another three years. As the women handling our cases made multiple back and forths to consult with an official we couldn't see in a back office, we got ready to leave, resigned to return home without the ten-year cards, and Sally put on her jacket. She'd bought it in a pop-up store in the Marais from a strange little man whose day job was designing tutus for the Paris ballet but who'd created this one-of-a-kind garment—an innovative patchwork of vintage mail sacks that had been discarded by the post office. The two women eyed it with fascination and asked her to come back to the counter so they could see it more closely. "*Fantastique!* It's a true *pièce de collection!*" they exclaimed, "something you'd only see in a top fashion magazine." We'll never know whether

Sally's jacket.

it was the jacket that, in the end, made them change their minds and
OK our requests for ten-year cards. But we don't see what else could
explain their about-face.[4]

Once we had the treasured ten-year residence cards, we became eligible to participate in the French health service, operated through *cartes
vitales*, credit-card-style cards used to get free care from doctors and
pharmacies through the state-run program. My own request was made
using the social security number that I'd gained from my employment in
French universities in the 1980s, but Sally's was denied. Multiple written
letters and subsequent visits to health-service offices produced various
reasons (they'd never received her application, she'd filled it in incorrectly,
it was missing a particular item, etc.). Finally, she was informed that there
was an "anomaly" between her ten-year residence card, which said, "Sally
Hamlin, épouse Price" and her U.S. passport, which said, "Sally H. Price."
She would have to go back to square one and apply for a new ten-year

---

4 These two women were not alone in their excitement about the jacket. Sally never
wore it without someone approaching her (in the street, in the metro, in the market) to
express their fascination with it. Nostalgia for the earlier postal sacks? We don't pretend
to fully understand the French mindset.

residence card under a name that matched her passport. She did her best to explain that privileging her birth name was the decision of the French and that "Hamlin" was abbreviated to H. upon her marriage, but she continued to receive rejections. That's when she decided to go to work as an anthropologist and give the French a lesson about cultural approaches to naming. Her letter, addressed to the woman whose name was on her last rejection, began by explaining that officials in the *préfecture* refused to change the way her name appeared on the residence card. It went on (in French):

> While in France a person's birth name is given first, the United States follows a different practice. Thus my U.S. passport lists me under my married name (Price), reducing my birth name to a middle initial. Consider the following: My birth certificate (see attached) listed me as Sally Randolph Hamlin, but upon my marriage I took my husband's last name (Price) and dropped my earlier middle name (Randolph). My passport then abbreviates "Hamlin" to "H."
>
> In order to understand the system, consider the history of the person whom I expect to be the next president of the United States. She was born "Hillary Diane Rodham." Upon marriage to Bill Clinton, she became "Hillary Rodham Clinton" or "Hillary R. Clinton" or "Hillary Clinton."
>
> Or again, note the history of my mother's names. She was born "Pauline Louise Randolph," normally shortened to "Pauline L. Randolph" (see my birth certificate, attached here). Following her marriage to my father, Arthur T. Hamlin, she became "Pauline R. Hamlin" (see her signature on my marriage certificate). . . . The equivalent of "Sally H. Price."
>
> I will appreciate your taking these facts under consideration; I would hate to think that France would deny a *carte vitale* simply because naming conventions in the United States do not match those in France. (Note that the form of my name did not prevent Aurélie Filipetti, France's minister of culture, from awarding me a medal as "*Chevalier de l'ordre des arts et des lettres*" for my contribution to French culture; would you like me to ask the minister for authentication of my identity?)
>
> With thanks for any attention you can give to this matter. . . .

There was no answer to this email, but the carte vitale soon arrived in our mailbox.

Among our encounters with the French State during our time living in Paris, the most tumultuous concerned the French edition of Sally's book on Jacques Chirac's museum of non-Western art.

During the several years leading up to the 2006 opening of the Musée du Quai Branly, the staff generously welcomed Sally's many visits, granted her every interview she requested, and facilitated her research with supporting material. And she was invited to speak at the large symposium in the Lévi-Strauss auditorium that marked the museum's first anniversary, an occasion at which Stéphane Martin (president of the institution) greeted her with a smile and a kiss on each cheek: "The problem, Sally, is that you've written your book too soon. The museum isn't finished yet."[5]

The wrap-up speaker at that symposium, at the end of a very long day, was Édouard Glissant who, afterward, invited Sally and me to join him and Sylvie at the venerable Café de Flore in Saint-Germain-des-Prés. We taxied over, ordered coffee, and began chatting, but Édouard, who was diabetic, kept ogling the pastries in the vitrine behind us, pleading with Sylvie, "Just a little piece, please!" But she was strict and Édouard had no cake. Sally mentioned that her book about the museum was about to appear in English, and she was hoping to get it published in French, at which Édouard picked up his phone and, of course without ever having seen the book, speed-dialed his editor at Seuil: "Laure, there's a terrific book by Sally Price about the Quai Branly that you just must publish . . ." Unfortunately, Laure Adler left Seuil a few days later, and Édouard moved on to Gallimard.

The American version had been well received.[6] But it soon became clear that because all the major publishers in France produce catalogs

---

5   He of course hadn't seen the book, which wasn't published until three months later.
6   Sally Price, *Paris Primitive: Jacques Chirac's Museum on the Quai Branly* (Chicago: University of Chicago Press, 2007). See, for example, the reviews by Kate Duncan, *Journal of Surrealism and the Americas* 2 (2008): 268–72; Fabrice Grognet, *L'Homme* 189 (2009): 280–82; Elizabeth Harney, *African Arts* 42, no. 3 (2009): 89–90; Sidney Kasfir, *American Ethnologist* 36 (2009): 181–83; Ronald C. Rosbottom, *French Review* 82 (2008): 414–15; Lawrence Straus, *Journal of Anthropological Research* 64, no. 4 (2008): 597–99; and James Volkert, *Museum*, July–August 2008, 23–24, 82.

and other publications for the MQB, the idea of taking on a book that contained criticism of the museum was simply not possible for them.[7] Nonetheless, in June 2009, thanks to skillful negotiations by the University of Chicago Press, and a somewhat maverick editor at Éditions Denoël (part of the Gallimard family of publishers), a contract for a French edition was offered. That's when the real fun began.

The first sign of trouble had come even before the book was published in English when a distinguished colleague who had offered to write a blurb for the Chicago edition suddenly changed her mind. The MQB's director of research warned her, she explained, that praise for the book could jeopardize the project she had underway at the museum.

Once the book appeared in English, the editor of the MQB-run journal *Gradhiva* solicited a review, but by the time the review was submitted the person who had voiced a warning about the negative consequences of a supportive blurb had become its new editor, and the review was held for three years without being accepted or rejected.[8] Indeed, the book was never mentioned at all in *Gradhiva* and (when we last checked) is not available in the reading room of the museum.

January 2010, with the translation partially completed, Denoël suddenly cancels the publication, pleading financial straits brought on by the global economic crisis. The editor who had accepted the book is let go on the same excuse. But thanks to the University of Chicago Press, which agrees to forego the first advance on royalties, and the translator (Nelcya Delanoë, a historian of the United States and North American Indian cultures), who generously accepts a reduced fee, it is reinstated within weeks.

July 2011, the book has been translated, the cover has been designed, the back-cover text has been finalized, meetings have been scheduled with three public relations people to plan promotional activities, interviews have been set up on French radio stations, Denoël has sent Sally a ticket on Air France for her promotional trip back from Martinique in

---

7   For example, the foreign rights agent at University of Chicago Press, who was tasked with selling the book to a French publisher, wrote Sally that "*Actes Sud* replied that they could not publish a French edition of *PARIS PRIMITIVE* as they work very closely with the Musée du Quai Branly" (email of June 11, 2009).

8   Four years later, it was published in the United States: Geoffrey White, "Civilizations on the Seine: Sally Price's *Paris Primitive*," *Museum Anthropology Review* 6 (2012): 38–62.

September, and bound proofs have been sent out to journalists (as well as, apparently, to the MQB).

July 13, 2011, Sally receives an email from the book's editor: "A big problem has just arisen about your book." "What sort of problem?" "The book has been postponed [*reporté*]." "Postponed till when?" "*Reporté à jamais* [Forever!]" Gallimard, he says, has decided it's not financially viable. Sally says the whole story sounds fishy . . . she wants to speak to him in person. "No, I wouldn't want to spoil your July 14th holiday," he says, "but I could meet you on the 15th." Sally underscores her lack of interest in celebrating Bastille Day and insists he come to the rue Volta the next morning so that I can participate in the discussion.

July 14, 2011, we're told that the decision to scrap the publication was based in part on the refusal of the Réunion des Musées Nationaux (the government office that controls museum shops in France, a major outlet for books on French museums) to purchase a single copy—they normally would have made a bulk purchase of one thousand (or was it fifteen hundred?). That night, we're invited for a Bastille Day dinner at the home of a colleague who'd spent several years as a senior participant in the planning stages of the MQB. Also present: a former curator at the museum of African and Oceanic art who had been helpful to Sally in making sense of the structure of the French museum world. When we recount the events of the day, both of them are simultaneously unsurprised and scandalized.

Friday, July 15, 2011, Sally contacts David Brent, who had originally accepted the book for the University of Chicago Press, and Ines ter Horst in the Foreign Rights Department, who had engineered the contract with Denoël. David says that he'll phone Pierre Nora at Gallimard. "I think we can win this. Gallimard owes Chicago big!" he says, an allusion to the fact that he often serves as the publisher for Gallimard's social science titles in English.

Monday, July 18, 2011, David emails to say that the book has been saved. And so, after a roller-coaster weekend, the French edition of the book is resuscitated for the second time and we return to Martinique.

In September, we fly to Paris, where the French edition has hit bookstores and journalists have made appointments for interviews.[9] A very

---

9 Sally Price, *Au musée des illusions: Le rendez-vous manqué du quai Branly* (Paris: Denoël, 2011).

brief review in *Le Figaro* states that the book has "come too late" and that it "borders on dishonesty" since, as the translation of a 2007 book, it is "masquerading" as an evaluation of the present state of the museum. The review then goes on to heap praise on the museum and its president, Stéphane Martin ("the author of a fascinating and impartial book on the museum," who has been able to build the MQB "around listening and respect"), and it asserts that people from the cultures represented are "unanimous" that the museum, "far from acting as a site for rare, precious, or exotic plunder, is a place of dialogue between equals." Sally, it concludes, is a "slightly paranoid *altermondialiste*, [who] prefers to see in the museum's success the result of our [French] alleged superiority complex."[10] An equally short paragraph in *Le Monde des livres* faults her book for—again—"coming too late [since] the situation has evolved."[11] The twenty-four-page afterword she wrote for the French edition, which updates activities at the museum, appears not to have impressed either reviewer.[12]

Tuesday, September 13, 2011, Sally is a guest on *Tout un Monde*, an important hour-long program on France Culture Radio, whose host, Marie-Hélène Fraïssé, has invited both Sally and Yves Le Fur, the museum's director of permanent collections. After Sally gives her opening remarks, Le Fur launches his attack, his voice sputtering with contempt. He first accuses her of "demonizing" art dealer Jacques Kerchache (a close friend of Chirac's, notorious for his unethical collecting practices) and then homes in on her treatment of the Parisian art dealer, Hélène Leloup, who sold the museum (for 4 million euros) its most prized object, the statue from Mali that greets visitors at the entrance to the permanent collections. Sally had cited a 2006 article in *Technè*, the distinguished journal published by France's center for museological research and restoration, which recounted how Leloup had bought the statue in Paris in 1969 from a Malian dealer. And she had contrasted that account

---

10 Eric Biétry-Rivierre, "[review of] *Au musée des illusions: Le rendez-vous manqué du quai Branly*," *Le Figaro*, September 7, 2011.

11 Philippe Dagen, "Haro sur le Quai Branly," *Le Monde des Livres*, September 9, 2011.

12 The only Francophone review that praised (or, in fact, even mentioned) the new afterword was from outside France, in Canada, calling it "rich in information about events since the American edition was published, allowing Sally Price to take her critique further and deeper" (Laurent Jérôme and Laurence Desmarais, *Recherches amérindiennes au Québec* 42 [2012]: 155–59).

to the story told by Leloup (on a CD made for the museum and on sale in the museum bookstore[13]) that she had discovered the statue by herself in a remote cave in Mali, "entering on hands and knees, being careful to avoid the killer bees that guarded the entrance."[14] Le Fur, red-faced and sweating, is on a roll and continues insisting that Sally's story was a brazen fabrication. Sally feels like she'd been punched in the gut, and Fraïssé has trouble restoring calm.

Sally also gave quite a few interviews for the press. A journalist for the newspaper *Le Parisien*, for example, met with her for a full hour and said the results would appear within a week or two. A journalist for the magazine *Jeune Afrique* asked questions with his readership in francophone African countries in mind. A woman who wrote for the widely circulated magazine *Télérama* talked with Sally for an hour and a half and told her the discussion would be part of an upcoming article on the museum's first five years. A journalist from France's most important regional newspaper, *Ouest-France*, came to our apartment for a fascinating several-hour discussion of French cultural politics, based on arguments in the book.

But only one of the many interviews she gave was ever published—the one in *Jeune Afrique*. And when Sally, frustrated, inquired of the journalists who had interviewed her, the reply was that their editorial director told them that criticism of the museum was not in the publication's interest.[15]

As for television, a journalist for RFO (a state-sponsored network) who had, a year earlier, put together an interesting program on *Voyages avec Tooy* emailed Sally several times to say how much he was looking forward to reading her book. But once the review in *Le Figaro* was published, he stopped communicating and her emails were greeted with silence.

Many French friends and colleagues in France (as well as others in francophone Africa, whence many of the MQB's objects had been looted)

---

13 Sally Price, *Au musée des illusions*, 228–30, 294–96.

14 See Augustin Viatte, 2006, *L'autre musée: Quai Branly*, CD (and paperback) available from amazon.fr.

15 The rare reviews in French scholarly journals were more matter-of-fact, often along the lines of "although announced as 'a friendly critique by the most French of American anthropologists,' Sally Price doesn't mince words" (Carole Boulbès, "Sally Price. *Au Musée des illusions: Le rendez-vous manqué du quai Branly*," *Critique d'art* 39 [2012], https://doi.org/10.4000/critiquedart.2613.

have thanked Sally for her willingness to criticize the museum, asserting that although her views are shared by countless observers (including many participants in the museum's development), no one in France would take the risk of publishing them.[16]

From the first, President Chirac repeatedly billed the MQB undertaking as a way to realize a "dialogue of cultures and civilizations." Of course, any dialogue is based on specific ideas about who speaks and who doesn't. The virtual censorship of ideas that, in contrast, were found interesting by reviewers of Sally's book outside of France—and by countless individuals in France who spoke to us privately—makes clear that public participation in this particular dialogue requires acceptance of the museum's view that everything it does is, as Stéphane Martin frequently says, *"Formidable*!!" The triumph of the State.

---

16 For more on the politics of publishing in France, see Norimitsu Onishi and Constant Méheut, "Pedophile Scandal Can't Crack the Closed Circles of Literary France," *New York Times*, November 28, 2020.

COMING HOME?

CHAPTER TWENTY

By the 1990s, based in Martinique, I was already concerned about the ways that former lifeways were rapidly becoming postcarded, the extent to which modernization—the construction of French *grand-surface* supermarkets, chain stores, car dealerships, restaurants, and hotels—was sweeping through the island and the extent to which Aimé Césaire's fear of a "genocide by replacement" (French immigrants—young people as well as retirees) was already being realized.

In fact, as early as the 1950s, Lévi-Strauss had foreseen the warning signs by contrasting old-time Martinique with modernizing Puerto Rico.

> In Martinique, I visited some rustic and run-down rum distilleries in which the equipment and techniques had stayed unchanged since the eighteenth century. In contrast, in Puerto Rico, the factories of the company that has a virtual monopoly on sugar cane were agleam with white enamel tanks and chrome-plated faucets. And yet the rums of Martinique, taking on flavors from the bottoms of old wooden barrels loaded with sediment, are suave and fragrant, while those of Puerto Rico are crude and brutal. Might not the finesse of the Martiniquan rums be the result of the impurities that the archaic methods have left in place? In my view, this contrast illustrates the paradox of a civilization [our own], whose charms come essentially from the residues that it carries in its wake, without our being able to stop ourselves from trying to clean them up.

And he wondered whether our capitalist way of life "isn't constituted to destroy that which gives it its charm."[1]

I ended my 1998 book about Martinique with similar thoughts about nostalgia, quoting Walcott questioning his own motives:

> . . . that other life going in its "change for the best,"
> its peace paralyzed on a postcard, a concrete
> future ahead of it all, in the cinder-blocks
> of hotel development. . . . .
> I watched the afternoon sea. Didn't I want the poor

---

1 Lévi-Strauss, *Tristes tropiques*, 459–60.

to stay in the same light so that I could transfix
them in amber, the afterglow of an empire,
preferring a shed of palm-thatch with tilted sticks
to that blue bus-stop? . . . .
Art is History's nostalgia, it prefers a thatched
roof to a concrete factory. . . .
Hadn't I made their poverty my paradise?[2]

The honest anthropologist, I wrote, must question his motives as well. And I noted that Clifford Geertz, writing—somewhere between exhaustion and ennui—of being an anthropologist at the end of the twentieth century, had argued that "to convey this, what it is to be an anthropologist not off somewhere beyond the reach of headlines but on some sort of fault line between the large and the little . . . what is needed, or anyway must serve, is tableaus, anecdotes, parables, tales: mini-narratives with the narrator in them."[3] But I also asked whether we didn't need more, whether along with Glissant we didn't also want to accept the challenge "to struggle against a single History and for an interactivity of histories, to rediscover at once one's true time and identity, and to question in completely unexpected ways the nature of power."[4] Noble thoughts!

As we continued with our lives in Anse Chaudière, watching the process of ever-increasing modernization and the slow disappearance of the Martinique we had once loved (as people and institutions became increasingly French and decreasingly—in our eyes—Caribbean) and experiencing the loss of many of our closest friends, there was less and less to bind us to the place. Not only were Césaire, Walcott, and Glissant gone but so were Emilien and Merlande, Maurice and Josephe, Dave and Jeannie, Liliane, and so many more. We'd been keeping up with many of our friends—Gilles Alexandre (who in 2018 was forced to close the only real bookstore in Fort-de-France, which had functioned since 1910); Jean-Luc de Laguarigue; Madeleine and Renaud de Grandmaison; Adams Kwateh; Alex Ferdinand; Raphaël Constant; Victor and Marie-Christine Permal; Dominique Taffin (who left for Paris in 2019); Dave and Jeannie's daughters, Suzy (who had married Mike Parker, architect of our house)

2 Derek Walcott, *Omeros* (New York: Farrar Straus & Giroux, 1990), 227–28.

3 Clifford Geertz, *After the Fact: Two Countries, Four Decades, One Anthropologist* (Cambridge, Mass.: Harvard University Press, 1995), 65.

4 Édouard Glissant, *Le discours antillais* (Paris: Seuil, 1981), 159.

and Jessie (and her husband Thierry); Julien Erdual and our several other neighbors, with whom we'd shared so many events—weddings, funerals, Christmas parties, Carnival, Easter crabfeasts . . .

But with age, we were finding that our chainsaw, brushcutter, and other tools were becoming increasingly burdensome to handle in the never-ending effort to keep our property free from the invading scrub forest. And the feral goats that had started four or five years earlier to descend from the mountains and eat everything we planted were becoming a genuine nuisance.

In any case, as we approached the edge of octogenarianism, we decided that it was time to number our days in both Paris and Martinique. In fall 2018, we visited Florida, found an attractive home on Tampa Bay, and settled ourselves on Coquina Key, where we could watch dolphins and manatees, egrets, herons, ospreys (often carrying a fish in their claws), and diving pelicans; kayak around the island; do occasional fishing off our dock; and enjoy the orange-red sunrise over the water.[5]

It's a place where we feel closer to the Caribbean than we would have elsewhere in the USA.[6] There's a coconut palm in front of the house, frangipanis all around it, and sea grapes to one side, and we planted a key lime tree like the one Liliane had given us in Martinique, as well as Scotch bonnet peppers, papayas, *maracudjas*, and other Caribbean plants. We still hear the sounds of fishermen's outboards as they head out in the morning—though they're mostly recreational rather than professional now. But we miss the sound of distant church bells—from Saint-Henri, which reached us in Anse Chaudière from down in the bourg of Anses d'Arlet, or Sainte-Elisabeth on the rue du Temple, a couple of blocks from the rue Volta. And in some strange way, we feel in exile from Martinique.

---

5   (Footnote added in March 2022, while reading page proofs.) This was a somewhat rose-colored first impression. We later learned that our home is built on landfill that destroyed a vast mangrove (that once belonged to the Tocobaga people, later to the Seminoles, and that during Prohibition served as a landing place for rumrunners from Cuba), now transformed into acres of well-tended suburban homes, fronting an increasingly polluted and fish-depleted bay. Nonetheless, like the rest of our degraded planet, we are obliged to call it "home."

6   Looking back, I feel enormously privileged to have lived much of my life next to the sea, with a view of the waves from my bed or hammock, now reminding me daily of deceased poet friends Walcott, Glissant, and Tooy, for all of whom the sea is history.

Looking out at Tampa Bay from our dock.

(As Ishion Hutchinson writes, "Nostalgia is exile's slippery sequence."[7]) But the special smell of the sea remains and the storms kick up similar waves. We still speak to each other in Saamakatongo or French whenever the spirit moves us, and we often reflect on the ways our experiences outside the United States—particularly the enormous privilege of becoming part, for a time, of the communities of Vicos, Los Olivos, Muktahok, Dangogo, Petite Anse, and Paris—have enriched our perspectives on life. And in good weather, we still hang our hammock for a night under the stars.[8]

On balance, we feel glad not to be teaching in today's academy. Just before Covid confinement, Sally and I were invited to give a graduate

---

7 "Habakkuku," *Times Literary Supplement* 6131 (2020): 15. When we wrote to Raphaël Constant to tell him we had sold our home in Anse Chaudière, he replied—on behalf, I would think, of so many of our friends and agemates—"I hope to see you again someday in a Martinique *libérée*. But will we live to see that day?"

8 Once we were settled in Florida, we drove up to New York to deposit our extensive collection of Saamaka textiles at the Schomburg Center for Research in Black Culture—we had earlier donated our calabash and woodcarving collections to that institution. Eventually, everything we collected among the Saamaka (except our field recordings, which are at Indiana—see above), including our fieldnotes and photographs, will go to the Schomburg.

class in a history of anthropology course at a major university. Afterward, we were reprimanded in a formal letter for having used "derogatory language . . . that caused a great deal of harm to students," making it difficult for the instructors "to create a space where they [the students] can feel comfortable in the classroom." We were obligated to write a letter of explanation to the university. Our offense was to closely paraphrase sentences from three of our books (*Travels with Tooy*, *Saamaka Dreaming*, and *The Root of Roots*), one of which was the class assignment that week, but which were now apparently considered unspeakable in a classroom, because they might make students "feel uncomfortable."

Then, in 2021, a colleague at a New England college wrote an email to Sally, describing the same phenomenon: "I taught two chapters from *Primitive Art in Civilized Places* today as a guest lecture I regularly give in a course on Global Studies. I was warned before class not to read the quote from Kenneth Clark about Negro Art (which I normally do). Apparently, a previous prof read a passage from James Baldwin with the word Negro. And the class went into meltdown for 2 weeks with a counseling session from the Chief Diversity Officer. That's where we are at!" It is hard for us to imagine teaching classes in an ambience where words are policed rather than discussed or debated by students.

We feel fortunate to be able to stay in close touch, on a daily basis, with Caribbeanists around the world through our ongoing work as book review editors for the *New West Indian Guide*. And reading scores of recent Caribbean novels, short story or poetry collections, and other new publications, in English, Spanish, French, and sometimes Dutch, for the "Bookshelf" article we write each year. Thirty years ago, when we started this tradition in *NWIG*, we opened each annual contribution with discussion of a Caribbean recipe (callaloo, rundown, *migan*, *sancocho*, coo-coo [coucou], *ti-ponch*) before offering our minireviews of books—fiction, poetry, photo books, cookbooks, and relevant others that didn't get a full review in the journal. Now, we get right to the books themselves, and we're putting the finishing touches on "Bookshelf 2020," which covers more than one hundred books, as I finish this memoir.

I began this book with a U.S. road trip from the East Coast to the West, with Indian country the highlight. In a story that is still ongoing—if paused somewhat by Covid—it seems appropriate to end it with a more recent drive across the country. We had made several lecture trips after moving to Florida in late 2018—to Zurich, Prague, Paris, Rome, Säo Paulo, and Lyon. And then in January 2020, we were invited by Sarah Vaughn, assistant professor of anthropology at UC Berkeley, to fly out for a day to offer comments on a book manuscript she was preparing for publication, an environmentally oriented ethnography of people who lived in the flood zone of coastal Guyana. We decided to return home by road instead of air, first visiting George and Jane in their senior residence in Oakland, then renting a car and heading down the Pacific Coast. Turning east at San Diego, we drove as close as roads allowed along Trump's notorious wall, seeing rows of frightening Border Patrol vehicles strategically pointing into the inhospitable desert in the direction of Mexico, positioned all through the hauntingly beautiful Tohono O'odham Nation Reservation.

And then a wonderful reunion with Brackette and Drex at their home in Tucson with piles of books in the living room and a panorama of cacti out the kitchen window. Brackette filled us in on her still-unpublished multivolume analysis of the judicial categories and classifications that determine the fate of the men she'd been working with for years on death row in Montana and Arizona, and she also shared some of the imaginative art photos of trees and sunsets she'd started exhibiting. Over some Rhum Barbancourt (5 étoiles) that Drex offered us, he stuck more to Haitian and, particularly, U.S. politics, bemoaning growing inequalities and assaults on social justice in the USA.[9] Today's graduate students, we agreed, all too often seem bent on erasing anthropology's past preoccupations, unwilling to read in the discipline's history, and content to squeeze bits from their often-cursory fieldwork into the latest theoretical discourse, rather than delving deeply into the particular visions of the people who hosted them. Brackette and Drex had recently retired from teaching.

I realized I was still learning from Drex (ever since those Mohammed Ali/Howard Cosell days) . . . that he is often attuned to experiences that elude me. He mentioned that while riding the Paris metro with Rolph in the 1990s, they each noticed, independently, that, unlike what they were used to in the United States, where Blackfolks subtly acknowledge

---

9 As Maryse Condé, with whose words I began this account, recently mused, "We were raised with the prospect that the world would gradually improve[,] . . . the consequences of colonialism, racism, and intolerance would disappear. . . . Today, we realize in amazement that nothing of the sort has happened." https://www.scribd.com/book/451321279 /The-Wondrous-and-Tragic-Life-of-Ivan-and-Ivana.

one another's presence in public spaces by a slight nod or other sign, this wasn't done in France. We wondered whether the recent much-politicized importation of U.S. identity politics (including "Woke culture") into French universities might be changing the situation on (and under) the ground in France today. What a terrific ethnographic project, Drex suggested.

Continuing east, through Texas cow towns and on to New Orleans and a gumbo dinner with Kris Lane, discussing his recent book on the magic mountain of Potosí . . . then a detour to view the devastation of Mexico Beach, where Hurricane Michael had left few houses standing, a stop for oysters at Apalachicola, and back to Coquina Key, where the pandemic (as well as the murders of Ahmaud Arbery, Breonna Taylor, and George Floyd) was getting ready to change life as we, and the rest of humanity, had complacently grown accustomed to it.[10]

Near the end of his memoir, *Recapitulations*, anthropologist/psychologist Vincent Crapanzano wonders, "with a certain anxiety—how autobiographers view their past after the autobiography ends. Do they accept themselves as written? Does their inevitable fictionalizing become their past? Are they obsessed with correcting it, elaborating it, or rewriting it?"[11] All very good questions. But I think I choose—rather than worrying about what people, places, and moments I omitted (where is Franklin, Marilou, Ted, Henna, or Rogério? Where are encounters in Puerto Vallarta, Meknes, Lubbock, or Lisboa?)—to turn my face to the future, toward new friendships and experiences, as they come our way.[12]

---

10 I've been heartened that, in addition to the encouraging embrace of the BLM movement in the United States, the international impact, in Europe and the Americas, has been considerable. As I finish this text, Nancy Morejón writes that she is about to publish a book of poems, *Madrigal para un príncipe negro* (Havana: Casa de las Américas, 2020), dedicated to the memory of George Floyd.

11 Vincent Crapanzano, *Recapitulations* (New York: Other Press, 2015), 355.

12 In any case, as Elena Ferrante points out, "Between the book that is published and the book that readers buy, there is always *a third book*, a book where beside the written sentences are those we imagined writing, beside the sentences that readers read are the sentences they have imagined reading. This third book, elusive, changing, is nevertheless a real book. I didn't actually write it, my readers haven't actually read it, but it's there. It's the book that *is created* in the relationship between life, writing and reading" (*Frantumaglia : A Writer's Journey* [New York: Europa Editions, 2016], 193).

THANKS

A few friends kindly read and improved brief passages I shared as I was writing: Lewis Leavitt, Allan Shedlin, Kevin Yelvington, and Eric Werthman. Several others very generously read a full draft of the text (sometimes several times), offering extensive opinions, suggestions, and corrections: Kenneth Bilby, Charles Carnegie, George Collier, John Collins, Antonio Díaz-Royo, Charles Rutheiser, Drexel Woodson, Leah Price, and Niko Price—the book is far richer because of their contributions. My editor at UGA Press, Nate Holly, patiently and expertly shepherded the project through the publication process.

Sally has been there throughout the writing and revisions (and for sixty years and counting). She is also the archivist of many of the documents on which this account is based.

I take sole responsibility for the contents.

Royalties from this book will go to the Southern Poverty Law Center.

PHOTO CREDITS

209	Courtesy of Ruth Price.
209	Photo by Sally Price.
212	Photo by Sally Price.
218	Photo by Sally Price.
223	Courtesy of Anne Kayanakis, the attorney general of Guyane who had helped us free Tooy from prison; she was vacationing in Martinique.
225	Photo by Sally Price.
228	Courtesy of Cruz M. Nazario.
232	Photo by Sally Price.
236	Courtesy of Alexander Zemlianichenko.
237	Photo by Richard Price.
248	Photo by Sally Price.